AMERICA'S FOUR GODS

AMERICA'S
FOUR
GODS

WHAT WE SAY
ABOUT GOD—
& WHAT THAT SAYS
ABOUT US

PAUL FROESE & CHRISTOPHER BADER

OXFORD
UNIVERSITY PRESS

2010

OXFORD

UNIVERSITY PRESS

Oxford University Press, Inc., publishes works that further
Oxford University's objective of excellence
in research, scholarship, and education.

Oxford   New York
Auckland   Cape Town   Dar es Salaam   Hong Kong   Karachi
Kuala Lumpur   Madrid   Melbourne   Mexico City   Nairobi
New Delhi   Shanghai   Taipei   Toronto

With offices in
Argentina   Austria   Brazil   Chile   Czech Republic   France   Greece
Guatemala   Hungary   Italy   Japan   Poland   Portugal   Singapore
South Korea   Switzerland   Thailand   Turkey   Ukraine   Vietnam

Published by Oxford University Press, Inc.
198 Madison Avenue, New York, New York 10016

www.oup.com

Oxford is a registered trademark of Oxford University Press

Library of Congress Cataloging-in-Publication Data
Froese, Paul.
America's four gods : what we say about God—
and what that says about us / Paul Froese and Christopher Bader.
p.   cm.
Includes bibliographical references and index.
ISBN 978-0-19-534147-8
1. United States—Religion. 2. God.
I. Bader, Christopher, 1969– II. Title.
BL2525.F75 2010
200.973'09051—dc22   2010003101

1 3 5 7 9 8 6 4 2

Printed in the United States of America
on acid-free paper

For Milo and Sasha

For Sara

There are not enough pages in the world
to write a book about God.
—Reverend Herbert Lusk

ACKNOWLEDGMENTS

The Baylor Religion Survey and Interview project was supported by a grant from the John Templeton Foundation. The Gallup Organization collected the survey data and offered valuable feedback on the questionnaires. The Baylor Institute for Studies of Religion under the direction of Byron Johnson and Rodney Stark also provided crucial support and guidance.

The development of the Baylor Religion Survey was the result of a collaborative effort with members of the Baylor Sociology Department. F. Carson Mencken played a key role in the successful administration of the survey and assisted with several analyses throughout the book. The wonderful Sharon Sloan helped navigate Baylor's bureaucracy. A team of talented graduate students completed a myriad of tasks essential to the project; we are indebted to Clay Polson, Ashley Palmer, Jared Maier, Jeremy Rhodes, Buster Smith, and Alessandra Gonzalez.

We thank all of the interview and survey participants and the various groups that welcomed us into their communities. Photographers Nigel Euling and Todd Thiele deserve special praise for their professionalism and artistry. We are grateful to Neil Luft and Ruth Christensen for helping to design our related Web site (www.Americasfourgods. com). And we thank Theo Calderara, Christine Dahlin, and Jill Marshal for their roles in the development and production of the book.

Special thanks from Paul:
Love to my parents, Margaret and Menno, and to my in-laws, Danie and Jack. Heartfelt thanks to Jeff, Lexy, Will, and Mark. And my deepest love and gratitude to Jana.

Special thanks from Chris:

I must thank my biggest support system—family. David Bader read several drafts of this work as did my uncle and aunt, Rick and Donna. All provided helpful comments and advice. And of course, I could not have worked on such a large project without the love, support, and patience of my partner, Sara.

CONTENTS

Photos follow page 124

AMERICA'S FOUR GODS

INTRODUCTION

Why God?

In the representation of God, the believer has the whole of the world, even if he lacks all of its countless particulars.

—*Georg Simmel*

Picture yourself in a grocery store checkout line. You drop a few coins into a donation box for some local charity, and the cashier says, "God bless you." What does he mean? Was it nothing more than a simple thank-you? Or maybe he was actually saying that an all-powerful and all-knowing supernatural being should reward you in this life or the next. Perhaps you are thrilled because you are a devout believer and are comforted by a kindred spirit. Or maybe you simply respond as if the phrase "God bless you" is devoid of any deep meaning. Perhaps you think the cashier is some sort of religious nut.

It is not clear what Americans mean when they talk about God. Yet references to God are everywhere. It is the rare presidential speech that doesn't end with "God bless America."[1] The phrase is all over bumper stickers and billboards. The Pledge of Allegiance informs us that we are "one nation under God," and U.S. currency assures us that "in God we trust."[2]

It's been more than one hundred years since Friedrich Nietzsche declared that "God is dead."[3] And many great thinkers have argued that religion would slowly erode in the face of science and modern thought.[4] But despite living in the most modernized and technologically advanced country, Americans report one of the world's highest levels of belief in God. Americans' faith in God appears constant even as we have come

1

to embrace twenty-first-century technology and the benefits of modern science. Yet the philosopher Charles Taylor offers an important caveat. "Belief in God," he writes, "isn't quite the same thing in 1500 and 2000."[5] The main difference is that belief in God used to be assumed. Now, it is consciously chosen.[6]

Yet few Americans opt out—only a small fraction of them are atheists. And large swaths of Americans still believe in the type of God Taylor associates with Western Europe circa 1500. For Taylor, this God was distinct for three reasons:

1. "because the great events of the natural order . . . were seen as acts of God"
2. because "a kingdom could only be conceived as grounded in something higher than mere human action in secular time"
3. because the world was filled with "spirits, demons, and moral forces"[7]

Although the historical context of these ideas has certainly shifted, a look at the beliefs of average Americans indicates that many agree that

1. God can alter the natural world
2. the United States is tied to God's plan
3. spirits, demons, and moral forces exist

On these basic points, Americans aren't much different from Western Europeans of five hundred years ago.

While references to God are certainly not dying, and many Americans report traditional beliefs about God, the significance of God to social and cultural life still may be diminished in the ways that Taylor asserts. Specifically, do different beliefs about God make people think differently, act differently, or live differently? If they don't, then perhaps God is as good as dead, because God seems not to matter in our modern world.

Who Is God?

The word "God" is often heard in conversation both private and public, yet we tend to avoid deep discussions about God. Pragmatically, this allows us to sidestep potential arguments. We may be well advised to never discuss religion or politics in polite company.

The wisdom of this age-old advice was brought home to Jill, a middle-class professional who recently moved across the country for a new job. She casually joined a conversation about God with her new neighbors and was shocked to learn that they thought anyone who was not a Protestant would spend eternity in hell.[8] Jill, a practicing Roman Catholic, asked us, "How do you overcome the fact that your friends think your whole life is a sin?" In Jill's case, a pointed disagreement about God dissolved her blossoming friendship. Perhaps she would have been better off had she never learned about her neighbors' God, and they could have continued their friendship in blissful ignorance.

While ignorance can indeed be blissful, there are important reasons for knowing what others think about God, even if it is sometimes uncomfortable or off-putting. The United States is a land of religious pluralism, populated by countless denominations and generously sprinkled with non-Christian minorities, not to mention nonbelievers. But Americans are losing sight of what it means to live in a diverse society. In their book *The Big Sort*, Bill Bishop and Robert Cushing show that we have segregated ourselves into enclaves of people who look like us, talk like us, and behave like us.[9] The downside of this growing pattern of self-segregation is that we tend not to meet or interact with many people who appear different from ourselves.

Americans also suffer from growing religious illiteracy.[10] While Americans tend to be religiously devout, we paradoxically tend to know very little about religion, our own or others'. Religion scholar Stephen Prothero has shown that America is composed of "Protestants who can't name the four Gospels, Catholics who can't name the seven sacraments, and Jews who can't name the five books of Moses."[11] Religious illiteracy increases the odds of misunderstanding and conflict.

Our confusion about religion is fueled by our own ignorance of each other, but it is made worse by the agendas of political and public figures. They would have us believe that we are in the midst of a struggle between "true believers" and the "godless" or, put another way, "fundamentalists" and "secular humanists." Newt Gingrich, for example, has written that "there is no attack on American culture more destructive and more historically dishonest than the secular

Left's relentless effort to drive God out of America's public square."[12] The idea that there is an army of atheists bent on undermining God in America is a popular one among conservative pundits. Conservative commentator Ann Coulter, as usual, minces no words: "Liberals can believe what they want to believe, but let us not flinch from identifying liberalism as the opposition party to God."[13] But the simple fact that nearly 95 percent of Americans say they believe in God undermines any notion that we are engaged in a holy war over the existence of God.

We might, however, be in a war over who God is. When you consider the sheer number of religious traditions in America, you quickly realize that there is a deafening cacophony of descriptions of God—a stern white man with a long beard, a loving parent, a distant cosmic force, to name just a few. To give some semblance of order to this theological disarray, we set out to collect stories about God from Americans of all religious varieties and dispositions. We talked about God in cities and in towns, on the East Coast and the West, in towns with tourist attractions and in towns with farmland. Our travels led us to a creationism museum and to the halls of academic science departments. We also attended services at various churches and we visited religious communities, closely observing assorted rituals and recording distinct theological messages. Dozens of people from all over the country shared detailed testimonies of their relationships with God. Beyond the personal narratives of faith that fill the following pages, we also draw from a series of national surveys, which reveal distinct trends across the country.[14]

When talking to average Americans, we began by asking about the "look" of God. Clarice, a young nurse from the East Coast, felt that God must be white and male. "I'm not one of those that think God could be black or Chinese or female," she told us. For Clarice, God has clearly human characteristics, so much so that God has a distinct race and a gender. Some believers are shocked to hear others talk about the physical characteristics of God as if they were describing a neighbor or an acquaintance. These believers feel that God is in no way a physical being and sometimes even suggest that God is another name for the big bang—as did Mark, a day laborer from the Midwest, who felt that it was silly to talk about God's appearance.

Already, some clear divisions are evident in how Americans picture God. Overall, just under half (47 percent) of us believe that God is a "he."[15] A third (33 percent) are undecided about God's gender, and a fifth (20 percent) believe that God is sexless. The sex of God is an obvious indicator of whether a person pictures God in human terms. In contrast to those who believe God is male, approximately half (53 percent) of Americans refer to God as a "cosmic force" and tend to dismiss the idea that God has any physical appearance.

While the "look" of God reveals some basic differences in theology, beliefs about how God behaves are even more crucial. Most Americans (81 percent) say that God performs miracles, and half believe that God "rewards the faithful in small ways." The extent to which we believe that God interacts with us and offers us blessings has a profound effect on what we think is right and wrong and what we feel we should be doing with our lives. The most dramatic stories about God came from Americans who felt that they were directly touched by God. In almost all cases, their divine encounters had powerful ramifications.[16]

One such encounter was described by Suzanne, a doting mother of a soldier fighting in Iraq whose faith in God helps her cope with anxiety about her son's fate. Suzanne explained,

> I was waiting in the airport for my son who was returning from the Iraq War and there is a daddy there with a stroller and there was a little girl about six and a baby. Then here came Mommy, who was also away in Iraq. The six-year-old ran up to her and hugged her and the dad gave her a kiss and then she reached down and picked up the baby. And all of a sudden, I don't know what it was, but the baby looked up and her little eyes opened and suddenly—Joy! It's finding out whose child you are, is what belonging to God means. That is what I hope for every person. It's kind of like the prodigal son coming home. And you realize God's been watching, waiting for you the whole time . . . and the world's pains can be resolved in that kind of meeting.

Suzanne describes God as a watchful, caring, and protective parent—much like herself. God provides her with someone to lean on when so many others are leaning on her for strength and compassion. Suzanne said that she struggled with depression and apathy for most of her life and more acutely once her son went off to war, yet in a miraculous encounter with God she felt unburdened of immediate anxieties and ongoing despair. Like the baby of her story, whose cries instantly subside in a happy reunion with her absent mother, Suzanne finally found joy in a God who became present in her life. For her, meeting God was a profound miracle.

Jack, a retiree living on the West Coast, told us another poignant story. He recalled:

> When our first child was born, she was born nine weeks early. I was called by the hospital the next morning and they said, you get here, it doesn't look good. I went in and looked in the bassinet and she was having real difficulty breathing. I was in the room with my wife and we were waiting, really, for the baby to die. There was a Gideon Bible there and I just took it and opened it up to Romans. I looked down to "all things work together for good for those who love the Lord." That was an important passage for people in the hospital; it had been turned to lots of times. But . . . our baby died after twenty-six hours. But I really felt like God was present. That's probably the strongest sense of that I ever had.

Jack doesn't think God performs the kind of miracles that would have saved his daughter's life. For him, death and tragedy were an unavoidable part of life. Still, he drew enormous comfort from God's presence in this time of extreme distress and even feels a greater intimacy with God during horrible times.

Disagreements about the extent to which God rewards the faithful are followed logically by arguments about whether God punishes sinners. Jack in no way felt that the death of his daughter was a punishment from God. And only a fifth of Americans think that God punishes us in this life. But belief in a wrathful God is the key to some of our most basic perceptions of fairness and justice. Coral, a middle-aged Texan who struggles to make ends meet, relayed her concerns about divine retribution:

> We're going to have to pay for what we've done and that is extremely scary to me because I know that even though I'm sitting here telling you I'm a Christian, I don't practice it 24/7. I don't always get a chance

to read my Bible. I don't always get a chance to pray like I should. Some Wednesdays and Sundays I just have to make myself get up and go to church because I really don't want to go. I'd just like to have a "jammie day" and stay home. But God is going to do the judging on who goes where, and that's real scary to me, very scary.

Americans like Coral, who fear God's wrath, brood over the meaning of the setbacks and tragedies that they encounter.

A displaced victim of Hurricane Katrina, Michelle, agonized greatly about why her family suffered their fate. She lamented:

This hurricane has touched me very close. You know all of my family is there. I just came from there last week and the things I saw . . . [*pausing to regain her composure*]. I don't want to believe that God caused all this pain and suffering. I can't believe that He's caused those things because that's not the God I like to think about.

Michelle was extremely distressed by some clergy who said that the hurricane was a warning from God. While she firmly believed in a God who is all-powerful, Michelle strained to reconcile her image of God with the suffering of her family.

Depending on a person's image of God, God's lack of action can be upsetting and confusing. Michelle pictured God as being in control and was consequently shaken by the fact that her life had spun out of control. Others—like Luis, a devoted father and grandfather struggling to hold his family together—take comfort in the idea that God understands his plan even when they do not. When asked how God has blessed his life, Luis, with much difficulty, said, "My son just went to Afghanistan for a year, my oldest son. He left his little baby and his wife at home and they are having a hard time. And I maybe can't even articulate what I want or what I hope for . . . but God knows, and I have great confidence that God knows." For Luis, God lies at the core of his hopes for the future and offers him ballast as his world spins into disorder.

Sociologists and anthropologists have long noted that humans try to make sense of the competing, often contradictory, aspects of the world by embracing or creating a "narrative" to explain them. As sociologist Christian Smith explains:

> We, every bit as much as the most primitive or traditional of our ancestors, are animals who most fundamentally understand what reality is, who we are, and how we ought to live by locating ourselves with the larger narratives and metanarratives that we hear and tell, and that constitute what is for us real and significant.[17]

When Americans tell stories about how and why the world works as it does, God is usually a central character. Most have a "story of God" that can reveal aspects of themselves and their thinking that may not even be immediately evident to us. Indeed, Andrew Greeley, a Roman Catholic priest and respected sociologist, has proposed that religion is, for most of us, the primary narrative of our lives.[18] "The central religious symbol is God. One's 'picture' of God is, in fact, a metaphorical narrative of God's relationship with the world and the self as part of that world."[19]

For Greeley, God is the foundation of our worldview.[20] If so, then the kind of God we believe in is incredibly important.

Does God Matter?

In 1991, James Davison Hunter introduced us to the idea of "culture wars," an evocative description of American social, political, and religious tensions that has entered our popular language.[21] Hunter argued that Americans have fundamentally different understandings of reality. These different philosophical perspectives, in turn, determine our moral, political, and social values.[22] For Hunter, the culture wars are rooted in radically different conceptions of moral authority. "Orthodox" Americans believe in a transcendent moral authority; "progressive" Americans believe that morality is more subjective.[23]

Hunter's culture war thesis met with some scholarly criticism but was embraced by the media as an elegant way to describe messy and confounding political and social divisions.[24] The popular notion of culture wars is premised on mutually held stereotypes—namely, that two distinct moral cultures exist, one composed of urban, latte-drinking, antiwar, gay-loving, God-hating abortionists, and the other made up of blue-collar, truck-driving, gun-toting, flag-waving, Bible-thumping rednecks. These stereotypes are referenced and reinforced by the national media and political elites. But as with all stereotypes, reality is much more complex.

Still, Hunter is quite right that our conceptions of moral authority are most likely the key to understanding our social and cultural attitudes. But determining the extent to which an American is "progressive" or "orthodox" is a difficult project. How do we go about categorizing the moral philosophy of others when many of us cannot concisely express our own deepest moral and philosophical assumptions? This poses a problem for researchers trying to understand moral worldviews; in most cases, questions about transcendental authority, moral relativism, and root philosophical assumptions are met with blank stares.

Luckily, we can ask people about God. Most Americans believe in God and speak plainly about belief. And to them, God personifies moral authority. Consequently, when we talk to others about God, we gain access to their deepest moral and philosophical assumptions. Essentially, God is the supreme voice in our heads.[25]

We constantly have conversations with ourselves. Should I go out tonight? Should I take this new job? The back-and-forth of our ideas, the pros and cons of our decisions are often played in our imaginations as a conversation. Social psychologist George Herbert Mead gave a name to the part of us with which we speak; for him, the "Generalized Other" is our internal conversation partner, through whom we imagine what others will think of us and our behaviors. It is easy to recall a time, most likely within the past few hours, when you have done exactly this. You get up and reach into your closet. Your hand casually lands on a shirt but then recoils. You imagine what a coworker, a spouse, a peer, or a neighbor will think or say about this article of clothing, and it is not good. What has occurred is a projected conversation between you and someone else—not an actual person but a Generalized Other.

Religious believers often speak about God in this way. What would God think? How would God respond to this? Which path does God want me to follow? Some of these conversations play out quite vividly, with believers saying that God spoke to them and told them what to do. For others, the conversation is subtler. They ponder their vision of God and imagine how God feels about their lives and their decisions. Knowing a person's image of God, therefore, provides us with an opportunity to understand the most intimate moral and introspective conversations they have. Simply put, our picture of God is worth a thousand queries into the substance of our moral and philosophical beliefs.

The Two Big Questions

Attend a party or go to a matchmaking Web site, and you probably will ask and be asked dozens of questions aimed at revealing your true self. But what will your answers really reveal? While it is interesting to know that a person enjoys windsurfing, hates *Pretty Woman*, eats Chinese food every Friday, and hopes to one day write a mystery novel, this information ultimately fails to capture important aspects of who that person really is. Surprisingly, it is when a person talks about God, instead of herself, that she reveals the most.

In asking dozens of questions about God, we have uncovered two that pinpoint the most crucial theological disagreements in America. They are:

1. To what extent does God interact with the world?
2. To what extent does God judge the world?

If we know your answers to these broad questions, then we have tremendous insight into your entire worldview. In fact, our responses to these two questions predict the substance of our worldview much better than the color of our skin, the size of our bank account, the political party we belong to, or whether we wear a white Stetson or faded Birkenstocks. They say something essential about us because they reveal the kind of transcendent authority we look to when making decisions and planning our lives. With a knowledge of the diversity of Americans' conceptions of God, we can begin to dissect our culture wars in ways that exceed the artificial categories of Red states and Blue states, black and white, God-fearing and godless.

God is not dead because God continues to be the clearest and most concise reflection of how the average American perceives his world. As the anthropologist Clifford Geertz observed, "The notion that religion tunes human actions to an envisaged cosmic order and projects images of cosmic order onto the plane of existence is hardly novel. But it is hardly investigated either, so that we have very little idea of how, in empirical terms, the particular miracle is accomplished."[26] By analyzing Americans' answers to our two big questions, we hope to explain how this miracle works.

ONE

America's Four Gods

While I claim a right to believe in one God, I yield as freely to others that of believing in three.

—*Thomas Jefferson*

There are almost as many kinds of God in America as there are people. Possibly more—because some Americans offer more than one description of God. Some tell stories in which God offers boundless love, forgiveness, and charity. Others describe a God who rains fire and brimstone down upon sinners and commands followers to destroy the heathens. Others feel that God is wholly removed from human concerns, a distant force lacking a personality. A few find the whole idea of God absurd.

In 1985, Robert Bellah and his colleagues conducted a landmark study of American religious culture, published as *Habits of the Heart: Individualism and Commitment in American Life*. This book introduced a young nurse named Sheila Larson, whose intriguing beliefs represented a kind of faith distinctive to the American religious landscape. Sheila told the authors, "I believe in God. I'm not a religious fanatic. I can't remember the last time I went to church. My faith has carried me a long way. It's Sheilaism. Just my own little voice."[1] Sheila was intriguing because she was apparently unique—no one quite believed the exact same thing as she did. She even named her religion after herself. But Sheila may not actually be so unique after all. While not fully detached from traditional religious faiths, many Americans similarly express a faith that is exclusive to themselves. This is clearest when

Americans tell personal stories of God—each story is distinctive to the person telling it.

So how do we make some sense out of this endless hodgepodge of Gods? Leo Tolstoy described a childhood memory of lying on the floor and gazing up at his mother as she did needlepoint. The back of her fabric, which was facing him, was riddled with knots and frayed ends of thread. When she finally revealed her handiwork, he was amazed to see a beautiful and symmetrical pattern of flowers and birds. Tolstoy likened this experience to our attempts to understand God's handiwork when we often see only the madness and chaos of our surroundings. Only in the afterlife, mused Tolstoy, would we look upon God's completed embroidery.[2] We, too, hope to find a pattern in the chaos.

Thankfully, we are not attempting to uncover the pattern of the cosmos, just identify some key similarities and differences in our various images and stories of God. Some differences are of no real consequence. It doesn't much matter whether you pray for the New England Patriots or the Green Bay Packers (everyone knows the Packers are God's team). But other differences are crucial to understanding political, social, and personal conflicts, such as whether an American believes that God approves of the Iraq War or that God opposes all war. Or whether a person thinks that God has condemned her alcoholic brother to endless suffering or feels that God would never punish even the worst sinner. In this chapter, we try to give some order to the countless stories of God in America and indicate which differences of opinion are of the greatest significance.

God's Love

In *God: A Biography*, Jack Miles examines how God is depicted in the Hebrew Bible.[3] He makes a surprising discovery. Miles finds no evidence that God feels love for humanity in the early books of the Old Testament. It is not until God declares his "everlasting love" for Israel in Isaiah (54:4–8) that God's capacity for such emotion is revealed in the text:

> Until this point in history, the Lord God has never loved. Love has never been predicated of him either as an action or as a motive. It is not that he has had no emotional life of any sort. He has been

wrathful, vengeful, and remorseful. But he has not been loving. It was not for love that he made man. It was not for love that he made his covenant with Abraham. It was not for love that he brought the Israelites out of Egypt or drove out the Canaanites before them.[4]

If we were to extend Miles's analysis to the New Testament, we would quickly discover a God *consumed* by love for humankind. Indeed, the idea of a God without love is almost entirely foreign to the American religious mind. American Christians focus heavily on the biblical passage John 3:16, which states: "For God so loved the world that he gave his one and only Son, that whoever believes in him shall not perish but have eternal life." This verse is one of the most cited in the contemporary United States. Attend any major U.S. sporting event and you are likely to find someone holding up a "John 3:16" sign.[5] In addition to countless books and blogs that discuss the meaning of John 3:16, Christian bookstores and Web sites offer an amazing variety of John 3:16 products, including plaques, crosses, pendants, Thomas Kinkade paintings, coffee mugs, and even neckties emblazoned with the verse.[6]

Nearly all Americans (85 percent) feel that the term "loving" describes God well.[7] In fact, the term "God" is almost synonymous with the idea of a loving deity. Americans overwhelmingly believe that God cares deeply for the safety of humanity, and even individuals with more abstract ideas about God tend to feel that the universe is guided by a loving force that does not seek to cause us pain.

We met with many believers who spoke passionately about God's love. Most expressed sentiments similar to those of Thomas, a social worker we spoke to in Houston, who earnestly told us:

> God *is* love. The word "love" describes God because it encompasses so much: love in the way of a parent, love in the way of a friend, even love in some ways of a spouse. But I think I see God not as like an old man in the sky with a beard and passing judgment, but more like in the Gospels. I see where Christ tells us to love each other and to serve each other, and I think I've based my view of God on that.

Thomas is greatly inspired by his image of a loving God—so much so that he dedicated his career to serving the neediest in urban Houston and playing an active role in assisting people who were injured and displaced by Hurricane Katrina. While not all of us are as dedicated to serving those in dire need as Thomas, most Americans similarly speak of God as a being with whom they share a deep reciprocal love. As a result, Americans tend not to fear God or feel inhibited in God's presence. Instead, most Americans sense that God cares deeply for us and warmly invites us into a nurturing one-on-one friendship.

When we met with Brian, a laid-back day laborer from the West Coast, we were surprised by his abrupt exuberance when turning to the topic of God's love. Smiling widely, Brain explained,

> I know the feelings I have toward my children, towards my pastor, and I have some feedback on how people feel about me. I know that his love, his endearment towards me, is greater than that. I would almost say incomprehensible. Very loving, very tender, and the greatest characteristic about God is that he desires to be with me. That's one of the neatest things that draws me to him. I think his goodness draws the repentance, but more than that his love, desire to be with me. . . . I don't understand it. Why would he want to be with me?

Interestingly, Brian felt no sense of sublime awe in the presence of God but rather described a sensation similar to hugging a devoted parent. As Brian repeated, "God wants to be with me," so why would anyone not want to be with God? As we shall see, the idea that God loves us and wants to be with us is one of the most powerful attractions to religion that we can find. Brian and many other Americans feel this without doubt.

If we stopped with the fact that nearly all Americans view God as a kind and loving parent, we would have little more to say about American theology. After all, if everybody believes the same things about God, then we learn very little about a person by knowing his conception of God. But as is evident from any trip to a local playground, parents differ greatly in how they express their care and love. Some parents stress self-discipline, responsibility, and self-reliance in order to help their children become independent and happy individuals. They believe that the goodness of a child is enhanced by tenaciously reprimanding any behavior that strays from the right path. Other parents stress fairness and equality and seek to guide children without reprimands but rather through enticements. For these parents, punishment instills the wrong message and, in fact, tends to squelch the freedom and independence of a child.

While Americans almost universally view God as a loving parent, they are divided on whether God is best described as a firm or indulgent parent. And whether God is strict or forgiving proves an important distinction.

God's Judgment

On August 18, 2005, confessed serial killer Dennis Rader received ten consecutive life sentences, one for each of the murders he committed in Wichita, Kansas, between 1974 and 1991. During his crime spree, Rader bestowed on himself the moniker "B.T.K. killer," referring to his tendency to bind, torture, and then kill his victims. Rader avoided the death penalty, despite the gruesome nature of his crimes, due to simple chance. Kansas did not reinstate capital punishment until 1994, three years after his final murder. Relatives of Rader's victims angrily confronted the killer at his sentencing. For Beverly Plapp, the sister of victim Nancy Fox, nothing less than a slow and painful death could be sufficient punishment. "This man needs to be thrown in a deep, dark hole and left to rot," she lamented. But even as Rader escaped the execution she felt he deserved, Plapp was comforted by the thought that Rader's true punishment would await him in the afterlife, asserting that "Nancy and all of his victims will be waiting with God and watching him as he burns in hell."[8]

It is difficult to conceive of an appropriate punishment for Dennis Rader, a man who inflicted inestimable pain on so many. Unimaginable horrors, such as the violence of a madman, the devastations of war, or the brutality of natural disasters, can produce powerful feelings of hopelessness, fear, and anger. In the face of horror, many turn to God for answers and explanations. Beverly Plapp looked to God when her sister was murdered. Now, she trusts that God will settle her score with Dennis Rader.

Exactly *how* God will set things right when injustices or senseless tragedies occur is a subject of much dispute. Some believe God keeps close tabs on our daily indiscretions and inflicts suffering on sinners. Beverly is confident of this. Her need for justice can be satisfied only by supernatural means.

Divine justice was a popular topic in many of our discussions with Americans who do not necessarily have the same magnitude of grievance as Beverly Plapp. Nonetheless, we all feel injustices at times. For example, we spoke with Theresa, a middle-aged African American woman, who thought often of what God is doing to remedy evil in the world. Living in a working-class neighborhood and never having had proper access to higher education, Theresa has felt the sting of inequality acutely. And like Beverly, Theresa felt strongly that wrongdoings do not go unpunished. She told us:

> God doesn't like it when people sin, and if they keep doing the same sins over and over he will punish them to let them know that they're sinning. You know, like someone who robs gas stations and goes into jail and then in good faith is let out of jail and goes back to doing the same old thing again. God's going to punish him to let him know it's wrong. Or an alcoholic who gets drunk and wanders up and down the street, that's sin. God's not happy with that and he punishes that sin.

According to Theresa, our troubles are often the result of some previous transgression, be it a crime, a period of wildness, or a lack of charity. God overlooks nothing, and we all can expect punishment for our sins. Like Theresa, around a fifth of Americans are convinced that God regularly punishes sinners in ways big and small. But Theresa's conception of God creates an interesting dilemma—while God may be punishing the sins of others, why does God punish the innocent with tragedy or injustice?

One way to sidestep this issue is to refuse to believe that God is responsible for our sufferings. In fact, we spoke with many believers who were unwilling to attribute any characteristics of wrath or judgment to God. For instance, Sarah, an active church member from Rhode Island, told us of a God who would never dream of inflicting harm on us, no matter what we have done. Sarah explained:

> I don't believe that God is an angry, wrathful God. That's just been a construct of people. . . . As far as zapping people with lightning bolts,

I don't believe that that happens. And I think that a lot of times, you know, people say, oh, well, that's just, something happened to them because they were a sinner, well, that I can't buy because sometimes things happen to people who look like they're the best people in the entire world.

To prove her point, Sarah provided us with numerous examples in which bad things happened to good people she knows. For her, these misfortunes could not be the work of God.

We talked to many Americans with similar perspectives. Trudy, a lifelong Methodist and suburban mother of three, asserted, "My vision is not of a God filled with anger or hatred. I don't know that I would say God feels disappointment, but I believe God wants the best for everyone and tries to make that happen." God, for Sarah and Trudy, is a vision of forgiveness and tolerance who never inflicts pain but tries to alleviate it.

Two separate pictures of God emerge from this discussion of God's judgment—one the endlessly nurturing figure described by Sarah and Trudy and the other the strict and demanding authority depicted by Theresa. For most Americans, God is somewhere between harshly judgmental and absolutely forgiving. As figure 1.1 shows, most of us feel that God can sometimes inflict punishment but more often forgives.[9]

Many Americans conclude that God severely rebukes the most heinous of sinners yet feel certain that God has no anger toward them, their friends, and their families. Beyond this tendency to believe God will smite very bad people, we still disagree on who those bad people might be. Angela, a Mainline Protestant from California, laughed about the passing of Jerry Falwell in 2006, saying, "I hope Jerry's having an interesting interview!" While Falwell enjoyed a healthy following, Angela fully expected God to hold him accountable for his many perceived wrongs. Still, she felt that God would be lenient about her own improprieties, which she supposed were far fewer than Falwell's.

Where someone falls on the continuum between believing in a severely judgmental God or an overwhelmingly forgiving God proves important to her moral and social attitudes, as we shall see in future chapters. The question of God's judgment naturally leads to another

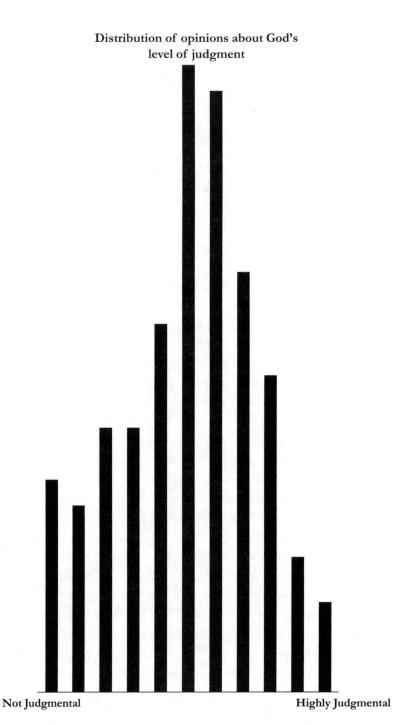

Figure 1.1. Individual scores for God's level of judgment reflect the summary of six response items in which respondents gauge the extent to which God is "angered by human sins" and "angered by my personal sins" in addition to describing God as "critical," "punishing," "severe," and "wrathful."

question: namely, how active is God in our daily lives? Whether strict or nurturing, God can be imagined as eagerly engaged in the world or far removed from it. And as with disagreements concerning God's judgment, the issue of God's engagement is highly significant.

God's Engagement

Philip Yancey, a popular Christian author and editor at large for *Christianity Today*, has written several books on the nature of God.[10] Yancey believes that God is rather shy. He explains, "By that, I do not mean bashful or timid, like a junior high school boy at a party. God may speak in a voice like thunder, and when he shows up in person, humans fall terrified to the ground. Rather, God is shy to intervene. Considering the many things that must displease him on this planet, God exercises incredible—at times maddening—self-restraint."[11] Yancey here taps into a deep concern for many Americans. While a few certainly agree that God is restrained in his activities, most describe God as far from shy. These believers describe God as an extrovert who is happy to intervene in daily activities.

Quite often, Americans told us about "miracles," in which God played an active role in their lives. Fernando, a young man studying to complete his associate degree while working full-time, views his life as guided by God's hand. He credits God with his success in being the first in his immigrant family to get into college. In fact, this gives him the confidence to tread a new path in his quest for advancement. Fernando firmly believes:

> God just sends people into your life and it's almost like they said exactly what you needed and it feels divine. It felt like it wasn't coincidence. It felt like God was going, "Hey, I know where you are." And then there have been times that I felt an audible voice but it's not audible. It's like something that speaks to the inside of me. It doesn't quite feel like a thought I had. It feels like God speaking to the inside man of me and saying something that I needed. It feels like a communication from God. You can't quite explain it. It's not quite audible. It's not like any other sense in your body, but it's just as real.

Fernando describes an intimate and active relationship with God that feels as real as his relationships with others. For Fernando, God is not restrained. Instead, God is a constant and dominant presence who has directly guided him on a path to success.

For individuals like Fernando, the exact nature of God's presence is sometimes difficult to ascertain. This is partially due to the ineffable quality of religious concepts and experience. As Fernando says, God's influence is "like an audible voice but it's not audible." Such paradoxical descriptions are common when individuals attempt to explain their interactions with God. In this instance, Fernando "heard" God's voice in his own thoughts but does not describe an event that could be objectively seen as an act of God. Consequently, any and all events can be interpreted as part of God's handiwork.

In talking about the presence of God, some Americans describe God as even more concretely present in the world—a God with the ability, much like a magician, to manipulate objects and events right before our eyes. Some believers offered fascinating stories of how God presented them with worldly gifts and responded to their prayers with money or some other direct assistance. Peggy, a mother of four who lives in rural Texas, told one of the more memorable stories of God's earthly powers:

> He flushed my toilet one time. I was living overseas and I didn't have a garbage disposal or a sink. My bathroom was where I would wash my dishes and I had left some food, some rice, in a Tupperware container too long in the fridge, and so I had to throw it out. I was going to flush it. Well, it had become hard and kind of compacted in the shape and so it got clogged in the toilet in that shape and I filled the toilet bowl to the rim with water and it just sat there. Nothing happened. I didn't know what I was going to do. I was so embarrassed. I didn't want to call the janitor and have to explain to him that a stupid American had clogged her toilet with rice. And so I just started to pray and as soon as I started to pray it just went . . . flushed.

In this instance, God did not give Peggy an idea of how to solve her problem or miraculously deliver a plumber to her doorstep, but instead decided to actually flush the toilet for her. It was a direct and simple solution to a very real problem. Peggy further maintained that her miracle proves that "God really does care about the infinite tiny little details of our life!" Although many Americans speak of God's daily presence, few go as far as Peggy in attributing mundane physical acts to God's hand. Fernando would never see God's hand in such minutiae and believes that God reserves his miracles for times of need.

Tom, a middle-aged Presbyterian deacon, not only doesn't see God's hand in minutiae but also takes offense at the idea that God determines things like whether he "puts on a yellow shirt instead of a blue shirt." Instead, Tom feels that God's presence and activity are less direct, and any language concerning acts of God should be thought of as a metaphor for the effect of our church and friends on our lives. Tom explained: "Weekly worship is without question an act of God in my life through his means, which would be the community, the church, the revealed word, preaching of the word, sacraments. . . . All of those things are evidences of his activity in my life. As far as any clearly miraculous events? Never." While he is clearly a devoted church member, Tom's belief is more abstract than that of Fernando or Peggy. For him, his church community and the sacraments of his religious tradition are the main manifestations of God on earth. Tom's God certainly does not flush toilets, but God can be felt within the rituals of one's religious life, and in these moments of religious expression, God is real.

Individuals like Tom who believe in a less active God tend to describe God as a "cosmic force." These Americans may be Christians or members of other traditional religious groups but tend to think of biblical and religious stories as metaphorical, expressing something conceptual rather than literal. For them, God is not a "man in the sky" but a more amorphous and mysterious reality. Becca, an elderly schoolteacher from the Midwest who identified herself as "very religious," described such a reality. But unlike Tom, Becca does not see God in a particular religious tradition or ritual; rather, her God might be best described as nature. She explained, "I feel God most vividly when I am close to nature. When I am sitting on the porch and hear the birds singing and see the flowers and feel the wind, that is God's presence to me." While Becca is confident that this cosmic or natural force called "God" pervades the universe, she is also certain that God does not act on the universe as an independent or consciously calculating agent.

The idea that God is part of nature or another word for "nature" is off-putting to most. In general, few Americans agree with Becca. Instead, many Americans think that God is very directly involved in world affairs and their personal lives (see figure 1.2).[12] This stands in contrast to Americans' views about God's judgment. A clear majority of Americans say that God is engaged, but far fewer Americans are willing to call God judgmental. On the question of God's judgment, the outliers are at both extremes—those who completely deny God's judgment and those who stress it. But the outliers with regard to God's engagement are only at one end—those who feel strongly that God is distant and impersonal.

America's Four Gods

So far, we have identified three distinct dimensions of God's character: (1) the extent to which God *loves* the world, (2) the extent to which God *judges* the world, and (3) the extent to which God *engages* in the world. Because nearly all Americans think that God is loving, a person's belief that God is loving tells us next to nothing about her—simply by virtue of the fact that *everyone else* believes that God is loving, too.

Instead, beliefs about God's judgment and engagement are widely disputed and render a rich portrait of American theological differences. Using these two dimensions of belief, we split the American public into four categories:

1. Americans who believe in a God who is both engaged in the world and judgmental—**The Authoritative God**
2. Americans who believe in a God who is engaged, yet nonjudgmental—**The Benevolent God**
3. Americans who believe in a God who is judgmental, but disengaged—**The Critical God**
4. Americans who believe in a nonjudgmental and disengaged God—**The Distant God** (see figure 1.3)

Distribution of opinions about
God's level of engagement

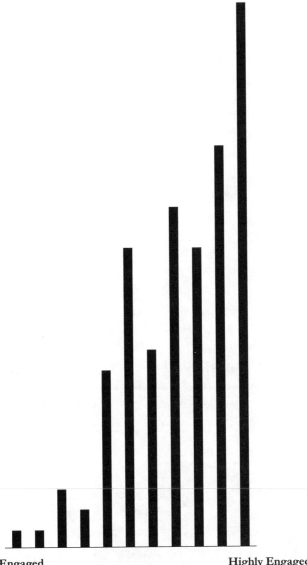

Not Engaged   Highly Engaged

Figure 1.2. Individual scores for God's level of engagement reflect the summary of eight response items in which respondents gauge the extent to which God is "removed from worldly affairs" (reverse coded), "removed from personal affairs" (reverse coded), "concerned with the well-being of the world," "concerned with my personal well-being," "directly involved in worldly affairs," and "directly involved in my affairs" in addition to describing God as "ever-present" and "distant" (reverse coded).

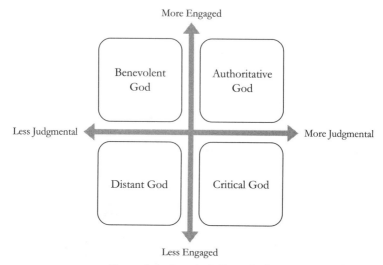

More Engaged

Benevolent
God

Authoritative
God

Less Judgmental

More Judgmental

Distant God

Critical God

Less Engaged

Figure 1.3. America's Four Gods

In general, we find that no single type of God dominates the American religious landscape. The largest group of all, 31 percent, believes in an Authoritative God (see figure 1.4). About a fourth (24 percent) of Americans believe in a Distant God, while another fourth (24 percent) believe in a Benevolent God. The smallest groups are those who believe in a Critical God (16 percent) and atheists (5 percent).

Let's take a closer look at each type of God.

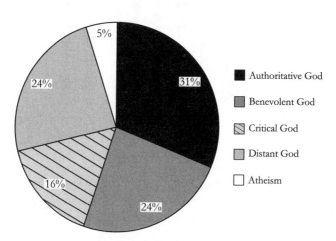

5%
24%
31%
16%
24%

■ Authoritative God

▨ Benevolent God

▨ Critical God

▨ Distant God

☐ Atheism

Figure 1.4. God's Popularity

The Authoritative God

The horrific disaster of Hurricane Katrina will not be soon forgotten. In its wake, many Americans questioned the larger meaning of the suffering and destruction wrought by the storm. In private and public conversations, Americans pondered whether those killed or left homeless by Katrina were simply unlucky, needless victims of a failed emergency system, or part of a larger atonement for the sins of our culture. Believers naturally contemplated the religious meaning of the massive destruction, and in the first days after Katrina hit, some commentators were quick to point out the fact that the city of New Orleans had borne the brunt of the damage. In a column he distributed to local news outlets, Alabama State Senator Hank Erwin wrote, "New Orleans and the Mississippi Gulf Coast have always been known for gambling, sin and wickedness. . . . It is the kind of behavior that ultimately brings the judgment of God."[13] Pat Robertson also described New Orleans as a mecca of partying and other excesses that dramatically—and, in his opinion, appropriately—incurred God's anger.

Pat Robertson has become renowned for attributing large-scale tragedies to God's wrath. After learning that citizens of Dover, Pennsylvania, had voted their school board out of office for supporting the teaching of intelligent design, Robertson warned, "I'd like to say to the good citizens of Dover: If there is a disaster in your area, don't turn to God; you just rejected him from your city."[14] During an interview on the *700 Club* that aired three days after 9/11, Robertson and Jerry Falwell discussed whether the terrible events would lead to religious revival in the United States. Concerned about the potential for future attacks, Falwell warned Americans to stop angering God:

> The ACLU has got to take a lot of blame for this. And I know I'll hear from them for this, but throwing God . . . successfully with the help of the federal court system . . . throwing God out of the public square, out of the schools, the abortionists have got to bear some burden for this because God will not be mocked and when we destroy 40 million little innocent babies, we make God mad. I really believe that the pagans and the abortionists and the feminists and the gays and the lesbians who are actively trying to make that an alternative lifestyle, the ACLU, People for the American Way, all of them try to secularize America. . . . I point the thing in their face and say you helped this happen.[15]

Comments like these depict an extremely severe God. Believers in an Authoritative God similarly think that God is involved in world affairs and can be quite wrathful, although certainly not all believers in an Authoritative God would go as far as to attribute Hurricane Katrina and 9/11 to God's hand. In fact, these believers also describe God as loving and concerned about humankind. Of the four types, believers in an Authoritative God are most likely to imagine God as a literal father—humanlike, male, and commanding in appearance. What distinguishes believers in an Authoritative God is their strong conviction that God judges human behavior *and* sometimes acts on that judgment. Indeed, they feel that God can become very angry and is capable of meting out punishment to those who are unfaithful or ungodly. This judgment may be leveled on a large canvas via natural disasters or on a more personal scale through illness or misfortune. This is the God of the Old Testament, who became incensed with the debaucheries of Sodom and Gomorrah and threatened to destroy both cities as Abraham begged for mercy.

Believers in an Authoritative God tend to feel that God allows bad things to happen to those who displease him. In other words, God can turn his back on the unfaithful and sometimes refuses to rescue them from peril. Peter, a young Pentecostal from Alabama, told us:

> I remember Hurricane Katrina hit New Orleans. . . . I believe God was in control of that. I believe he could have stopped it. I also believe God allowed it. I believe it got the whole country's attention. I believe the whole country prayed. I believe 9/11 . . . was an act of terrorism. God's not a terrorist, but I believe God wants us to be aware of the times we're living in and how much we need him. So, I believe that was very much a wake-up call to America.

According to Peter, the Authoritative God displays his wrath by allowing tragic events to occur in the hope that these occurrences provide us with a "wake-up call." The underlying message is that God's condemnation of sin is visible in the bad things that happen to us.

Lest readers be left with the wrong impression, believers in an Authoritative God do not focus on the judgmental aspect of God's character to the exclusion of more caring or compassionate characteristics.

Believers in an Authoritative God are just as likely to see God as a loving being as those with other conceptions of God. The difference is that these believers, like Peter, show a greater tendency to think that God is *also* willing to judge and punish and that the bad and good things that happen to us are likely of his making. As such, Americans with this perspective view human suffering as the result of divine action.

The Benevolent God

Like believers in the Authoritative God, believers in a Benevolent God see his handiwork everywhere. But they are less likely to think that God judges and punishes human behavior. Instead, the Benevolent God is mainly a force for good in the world and is less willing to condemn individuals. Believers in this God feel that whether sinners or saints, we are all free to call on the Benevolent God to answer our prayers in times of need.

The issue of tragedy clearly reveals an important distinction between the Authoritative and Benevolent Gods. Two people with different images of God may see signs of divine intervention in the midst of the same event, yet interpret God's actions and motivations differently. Someone with an Authoritative view of God is more likely to believe that God either caused a bad event to happen or allowed it to happen to teach someone a lesson. Someone with a Benevolent image of God is unlikely to see God's hand in the tragedy itself. Rather, evidence of God's presence is found in stories of amazing coincidences or apparent miracles that saved people in the midst of the disaster. For example, Rosie, a Mexican American grandmother, explained how she helped the victims of an auto accident because of God's prompting:

> I guess around Easter I was driving back home from a conference and there was an accident that had just happened. No help had arrived yet and cars were just driving by but there was a person out on the road and there were children that were crying and there was a vehicle turned upside down and for some reason God told me, "Stop." And, so I stopped my car. I pulled over and I had no idea why I was doing that and I know that there was a reason why God made me do that.

I went over and I gathered the children and I helped comfort them until help arrived to take care of them. But I know that that is a concrete example of when God was with me, specifically to help me help the family and help the children that were there.

Rosie did not focus on the accident itself per se. She did not speculate as to why God did not prevent the accident in the first place, nor did she assume that the crash was the result of his judgment. Rather, God's intervention was limited to compelling Rosie to pull over and help out. Rosie expresses a very popular conception of God in the United States, since many Americans believe that God is a reliable source of comfort and strength while rarely or never the catalyst for misfortune.

SQuire Rushnell (yes, capital Q) has built a minor industry out of God's benevolence. A former ABC executive, Rushnell created several programs geared toward children, such as *Schoolhouse Rock* and the ABC Afterschool Specials, but left television after 9/11 to focus on writing and speaking about God's little and not-so-little miracles. In *When God Winks at You*, Rushnell recounts a collection of tales that illustrate the often unseen ways in which God assists us, communicates with us, and gives us inspiration. Indeed, Rushnell believes that God had an active hand in his book's success by prominently placing it in Oprah Winfrey's home at the moment she was conducting a televised tour. After she held the book up to the cameras, sales skyrocketed. Rushnell calls such a happy occurrence a *godwink*, a term he has trade-marked. He explains:

Do you remember when, as a child, you would look across the room and someone would wink at you? This is what I am talking about. With that wink the person was telling you, "I'm here and I care about you!" That is what God is doing with godwinks, every day. Think of life's path as being lined with godwinks. Look back and you will see them.[16]

Many Americans do exactly that. They see the handiwork of God all around them and attribute their happy accidents or good fortune to divine intervention. We heard Americans talk about God's good works, ranging from lifesaving events to helping them find an elusive parking space. For these believers, God is an immediate source of assistance and inspiration in all things, from the biggest of life's decisions to the smallest daily choices. As Rushnell said, "When people ask how often God answers prayers I have to say 'Do you mean today?'"

The Benevolent God is seen by many as a kind of all-powerful and ever-present life coach. This God rarely chastises his followers, and in turn, they cannot imagine that he would ever inflict harm on them. In fact, believers tend to view tragedies as merely opportunities for God to express his love. For instance, when Rudolph Giuliani wondered why God had not answered his prayers for healing when he was diagnosed with prostate cancer, forcing him to drop out of his Senate race against Hillary Clinton, Rushnell offered an explanation typical of believers in a Benevolent God. He pointed out that "if Giuliani had not had prostate cancer and had remained in the race for the Senate against Hillary Clinton, win or lose, he wouldn't have been mayor on 9/11. He would not have been a calming voice for a mourning and shocked nation."[17] The overarching message of believers in a Benevolent God is that everything comes up roses if we only care to look and believe. Believers in a Benevolent God can be amazingly upbeat. As Rushnell cheerfully mused:

> Imagine you gave me an assignment where I had to list all of the ways God has shown his benevolence to me and all of the ways he has shown anger. I would have to stop myself on the benevolent list when I reached 100. I would have a hard time coming up with a single item for the "anger" list. I just cannot conceive of anger coming from God.[18]

The Critical God

During a visit to Brazil in 2007, Pope Benedict XVI delivered a speech to 6,000 people at the Fazenda de Esperanca (Farm of Hope), a drug rehabilitation center in rural Guaratingueta. With approximately a fourth of his audience consisting of people suffering from addiction to cocaine or heroin, the Pope focused his speech on the "scourge of illegal narcotics." Special attention was paid to those profiting from the drug trade: "I . . . urge the drug dealers to reflect on the grave harm they are inflicting on countless young people and on adults from every level of society," Benedict warned. If the drug dealers do not change their ways, he continued, "God will call you to account for your deeds. Human dignity cannot be trampled upon in this way." As the crowd cheered, the Pope walked through the crowd smiling and shaking hands.[19]

Many in the crowd took comfort in the Pope's assertion that those who caused their suffering would someday face divine punishment for their crimes, a clear reference to the Critical God. A significant percentage of Americans believe in a God that is highly judgmental but simultaneously disengaged from the world. It is this lack of earthly intervention that distinguishes the Critical God from the Authoritative God. Nevertheless, a Critical God still observes the world with a judicious eye and sometimes views the current state of the world unfavorably. These believers think that God's displeasure will be felt in another life but that divine justice will not be meted out in this world. Pope Benedict attributed such a personality to God in his remarks. He did not call on God to smite drug dealers in the here and now, nor did he focus on God's healing powers to cure those suffering from drug addiction. The heartbreaking social problems of Guaratingueta will not be solved by divine intervention. Nonetheless, the Pope invoked the power of God as a promise to the Brazilian people that justice will ultimately prevail.

For believers in a Critical God, divine justice exists but mainly in the afterlife. Pope Benedict is quite adamant about this issue, insisting that "hell really exists and is eternal, even if nobody talks about it much anymore."[20] And Pope John Paul II also made the reality of the afterlife a central part of his message, often reminding people that hell is "the ultimate consequence of sin itself."[21] By concentrating on judgment in the afterlife, both popes stressed the qualities of a Critical God—a divinity who may be slow to act now but is still all-powerful and all-knowing.

As we shall see, ethnic minorities, the poor, and the exploited often believe in a Critical God. Perhaps because those in need may not see the blessings of God in the here and now, they take comfort in the idea that God's displeasure will be felt in another life. Pope Benedict spoke of a Critical God in his remarks to a poor and oppressed population with resounding success. The Critical God appears to hold a special place in the hearts of those who are the most in need of help yet are denied assistance. As Jerome, a struggling middle-aged service worker and believer in a Critical God, told us, "It's kind of hard to believe that something or someone in particular would have any interest in me. So I just have to assume that it is part of a bigger picture kind of thing that's not just about me but is a driving force called God." Jerome's economic hardships and bleak prospects have done little to diminish his faith in God. But at the same time, Jerome expects nothing from God and, because of this, has little faith that his lot will improve.

The Distant God

Benjamin Franklin reflected on God in ways that would trouble many devout American Christians today—and would make it hard for him to run for office. He posited:

> I imagine it a great Vanity in me to suppose, that the Supremely Perfect does in the least regard such an inconsiderable Nothing as Man. More especially, since it is impossible for me to have any positive clear idea of that which is infinite and incomprehensible, I cannot conceive otherwise than that he the infinite Father expects or requires no Worship or Praise from us, but that he is even infinitely above it.[22]

Franklin's words are potentially shocking for a number of reasons. First, he intimates that God may not be paying much attention to us mere mortals. Second, he indicates that church attendance and prayer might be not only fruitless endeavors but also reflections of our own inflated self-importance. Such sentiments would probably not be welcomed by the millions of Americans who faithfully attend church, pray daily, and believe that God is intimately involved in their daily lives.

That said, approximately a quarter of the American public would find Franklin's theology appealing. These are believers in a Distant God. They view God as a cosmic force that set the laws of nature in motion but does not really "do" things in the world or hold clear opinions about our activities or world events. In fact, believers in a Distant God may not conceive of God as an entity with human characteristics and are loath to refer to God as a "he." When describing God, they are likely to reference objects in the natural world, like a beautiful day, a mountaintop, or a rainbow, rather than a humanlike figure. These believers feel that images of God in human terms are simply inadequate and represent naïve or ignorant attempts to know the unknowable.

In addition, a Distant God does not require offerings or praise and does not respond directly to our personal wants and desires. Nevertheless, believers in a Distant God may still be regular churchgoers and may still draw genuine inspiration and strength from the idea that a greater power exists and is essentially a force for good in the universe. How this good is realized is much more abstract than it is for believers in an Authoritative, Benevolent, or Critical God. Believers in a Distant God rarely speak of miracles or judgments in the afterlife. Instead, the calming effects of meditation, contemplation, and the beauty of nature are ways in which believers in a Distant God tap the positive force guiding the universe. And their beliefs can range from popular New Age mysticism to more academic ruminations about the supernatural.

A popular theologian among religious intellectuals and divinity students is Paul Tillich, a thinker who attempted to depict a highly abstracted and nuanced version of the Christian God. Like Benjamin Franklin, Tillich advanced a religious perspective derived from Christian scripture, yet one that is largely foreign to the average American believer. He argued that God is really the object of our "ultimate concern" and is subject to our personal interpretations and dispositions.[23] This version of God is a far cry from the God described in concrete detail by most Americans. In turn, Christian believers in a Distant God tend to view biblical stories as metaphors that communicate some larger truth but are misunderstood when interpreted literally. In other words, these Christians don't feel that the Red Sea actually parted in the story of Exodus, even though they find spiritual inspiration from this tale of religious freedom from oppression.

Finally, we find that when pressed, individuals who at first describe themselves as "agnostic" are actually believers in a Distant God. For the most part, agnosticism is a reaction to conventional images of God that strike the believer as mistaken. While not firm in their conception of God, many "nonbelievers" and "agnostics" believe in a supernatural realm but are troubled by traditional religion.

Atheism: The Un-God

Although they are not included in our four-God typology, around 5 percent of Americans indicate that they are atheists. Atheists are certain that God does not exist. For them, the concept of God is wholly fictional and is not even useful as a metaphor for some supernatural realm or higher power. Paul, a retired technical consultant, fits the profile of many atheists—highly educated and a self-described freethinker. In a culture where belief in God is virtually assumed in many sectors, Paul bucks the trend when proclaiming:

> God is just something that answers the questions of the unknown in a lot of cultures and a lot of people's minds. The idea that physical life here on earth is a random flash in the pan as far as time is concerned is too difficult for people, so believing in God and things like going to heaven where you are reunited with your family is just a way of maintaining hope for the future.

For Paul and other atheists, the idea of God is false security—something we cling to in the face of death and the unfamiliar.

We include atheists in our study of God because their nonbelief is as important in defining their worldview as another person's belief in God. Our four ideal types of God exhibit very different personalities. To summarize our discussion so far and provide you with a handy reference as you read the rest of the book, we provide the following abbreviated personality profiles for each God (see table 1.1). The next logical question is: Where does one's image of God come from? What leads one American toward an Authoritative God and another to a Distant God? The next chapter addresses that tricky and controversial issue.

Table 1.1. Personality Profiles

	Authoritative God	Benevolent God	Critical God	Distant God
Gender:	Male[1]	Probably Male[2]	Uncertain[3]	Not Applicable[4]
Judgment:	Wrathful	Forgiving	Wrathful	Forgiving
Engagement:	Very Active	Very Active	Inactive	Inactive
Proclivities:	An Authoritative God is a male deity with definite opinions on worldly affairs and a willingness to involve himself in those affairs should he deem fit. God's intervention may take the form of blessings, but he sometimes allows or even causes bad things to happen to get our attention. A strict but loving parent, God's punishments arise from a desire to correct human behavior.	The Benevolent God is most likely a male entity with a very "hands-on" approach to the world. Showing a lesser propensity for judgment than the Authoritative God, this God's interactions with the world tend to be uniformly positive. The Benevolent God will comfort the sick, answer prayers, and sometimes rescue people from certain disaster, but rarely acts to frighten or punish.	The Critical God is more mysterious than the Authoritative God and Benevolent God. Of uncertain gender, this God chooses to avoid direct interaction or intervention in world affairs. However, the Critical God is highly displeased with evil in the world and will harshly assess sinners come Judgment Day. But that final judgment is reserved for the afterlife and sinners go free for the time being.	More cosmic force than entity, the Distant God is mysterious and unknowable. The Distant God set the universe in motion and then retreated to watch its handiwork unfold. Such a force is far removed from human affairs and does not concern itself with the judgment of mankind or direct involvement in world affairs.

[1] When asked their level of agreement with the statement "God is a He," 72.5% of respondents with an Authoritative image of God agreed or strongly agreed.
[2] When asked their level of agreement with the statement "God is a He," a slight majority (55.4%) of respondents with a Benevolent image of God agreed or strongly agreed. The remainder were split between being undecided about the descriptor and disagreement.
[3] Those with a Critical image of God provided very mixed responses to the question of God's gender. The most common response was "Undecided" (42%).
[4] Similar to those with a Critical image of God, those who believe in a Distant God provided mixed responses to the question of God's gender. Unlike those with a Critical God, however, Distant God believers were most likely to disagree that God is a "He."

TWO

God, Self, and Society

God becomes the most reliable and ultimate significant other.
—*Peter Berger, "The Sacred Canopy"*

T he idea that one's God reflects something essential about oneself is a popular notion among believers and nonbelievers alike. The Book of Genesis (1:26) is clear on the matter: "And God said, 'Let us make man in our image after our likeness.'" Social scientists and psychologists tend to reverse this causal order and argue that an individual essentially invents God by imagining a being that reflects his parents, his culture, or even himself. The theologian Herbert Youtz boldly asserted this idea in 1907, stating: "The savage man has a savage God; the cruel man has a cruel God; the effeminate man has an effeminate God; while the good man lifts up holy hands to a God who rewards goodness."[1]

How do we develop our ideas about God? Is our God simply ascribed to us from our culture, is God a reflection of our personal desires, or does God reveal himself to us through divine interactions? Depending on the individual, a wide range of answers is possible. Because most of us heard about God as young children, our initial introduction to God appears to be a logical place to begin investigating how we come to know our God.

James W. Fowler, author of *Stages of Faith*, conducted extensive interviews about God with children age three through seven. At what Fowler calls "Stage 1" of their faith development, "children combine fragments of stories and images given by their cultures into their own

37

clusters of significant associations dealing with God. . . . Children from non- or anti-religious homes show similar tendencies, though their sources of images and symbols may be more limited." At this early age, a distinct image of God is already beginning to take shape.[2]

Our initial introduction to God has a lasting impact on how our brains function. In *How God Changes Your Brain*, neuroscientist Andrew Newberg and therapist Mark Robert Waldman make this powerful claim, citing evidence from Newberg's extensive brain-scan studies of religious believers. They conclude:

> We all begin with a simple neural circuit that captures our earliest impressions of God, and as we associate new meanings and qualities, these circuits interconnect, becoming larger and more complex over time. As brain-scan technology becomes more refined, I suspect we will see that each human being has a unique neural fingerprint that represents his or her image of God.[3]

One of the many interesting aspects of Newberg's research is that it suggests that once the idea of God is introduced, it becomes an important part of the way in which our thinking develops. Our earliest childhood image of God may be crucial in determining who we ultimately become.

Childhood images of God emerge from myriad sources—our parents, our religious tradition or denomination, our peers, and our culture. While there are never absolute predictors of a person's religious belief, there are clear patterns indicating which relationships are most influential in shaping one's image of God.

God and Parents

In seeking to understand where conceptions of God come from, psychologists have tended to focus on parent-child relationships.[4] This is a natural avenue of inquiry since God is so often conceived of as a kind of supernatural parent. Indeed, some psychologists hypothesize that our God is apt to look strikingly like our parents.[5] Conversely, our image of God could compensate for something lacking in our parents.

We found that Americans with more authoritative parents did indeed tend to believe in an Authoritative God. For instance, more than half of Americans who believe in an Authoritative God remember being spanked regularly as a child (see figure 2.1). Only a quarter of those with a Distant God recall being spanked. Again, the connection appears obvious—an Authoritative God is punishing while a Distant God is not. But the relationship between spanking and images of God disappears when we look at belief in Benevolent Gods, Critical Gods, and even atheists. These believers (or nonbelievers) are as likely as not to have been spanked regularly. What this tells us is that while there are some connections between how parents behave and how their child perceives God, this relationship is never perfect. As we delve into individual lives, we find a complex web of past experiences and memories.

Take Maggie, a middle-aged woman with no children who lives alone in her small apartment and draws a direct line between her biological and heavenly fathers. But in Maggie's case, God became a surrogate for her inadequate father. Maggie explained:

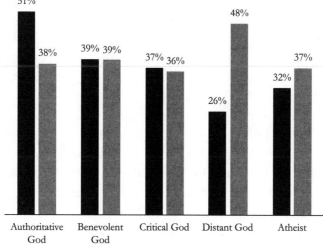

Figure 2.1. God and Parents

I think of God as my father. You know I've missed sitting in a father's lap, but God is always there. . . . I guess my father never praised me or made me feel like I was worthy. I was never good enough for him. I always had faults, and God is not that way with me. You know, he is the only one that I know that accepts me as I am, faults or no faults. I am somebody to him. That's something I always struggle with, low self-esteem, knowing that I don't have to do anything to please him, that he's there for me to love me and take care of me.

For Maggie, God is the father she longed for but never had. She developed a mental picture of a Benevolent God from a very early age and, since then, has learned to rely and reflect on God to gain emotional strength and personal validation. Dispelling the anxieties instilled by her critical father, Maggie now seems content with her life because, as she explained, it was enough for God.

Danie, a professional woman who lives in a devoutly religious community, explained how her image of a Benevolent God allowed her to cope with feelings of anger toward others. Shortly after her mother died, Danie's evangelical friends talked about her mother's sins and implied that she was not going to heaven. Danie was enraged. Her friends described an angry and vengeful God, one whose alleged wrath was hard to square with the intense love Danie felt for her mother. Danie admitted that "for years and years and years, I had to psychologically find my way back. . . . But when I meditate or when I pray, my whole world is different." Looking back to her childhood and her relationship with her mother, Danie rediscovered a caring, loving, and more Benevolent God who embraced her mother as she did, even when her religious community did not. In the end, Danie retained her inner conception of God and rejected the story of God offered by her friends. Although Danie was on the verge of abandoning her church, she came back to it through deep contemplation of her most fundamental ideas about God. Her earliest image of God won out. Interestingly, Maggie developed a very similar image of a loving and forgiving God under very different circumstances. Her father was not loving at all; in fact, he was cold and distant. That sent Maggie looking elsewhere for support, which she found in a Benevolent God.

Maggie's disillusionment with her father might have led to complete disillusionment with God. This happened to Sandra, a committed atheist, who explained that her hatred of church stemmed from the religious hypocrisy she witnessed as a child. Sandra found that Christians in her midst talked about love but stabbed each other in the back. This powerful experience of betrayal and dishonesty led her to question the very idea of God. Her childhood doubt grew into full-scale atheism. Now a successful banker and new mother, Sandra is convinced that church attendance has a negative impact on children, and she is committed to raising her child outside a religious environment. While Sandra's attitude is easy to understand, one could just as easily imagine a very different outcome—one like Maggie's and Danie's—in which a deeper attachment to God was forged in the face of disillusionment.

What about parents' direct efforts to influence their children's ideas about God? Relatively few Americans, about 13 percent, were raised by families who attended church on a weekly basis. Even fewer (7 percent) were raised in families who skipped church altogether. The vast majority of Americans attended at a rate somewhere between those two extremes. When looking at the relationship between childhood church attendance and images of God, we find that children who spent the most time in church are the ones most likely to believe in an Authoritative God as adults (see figure 2.2). Unsurprisingly, many atheists (33 percent) never attended church as children.

There are some clear and obvious trends here. Yet what do they tell us about how belief in God develops? Most likely, children who are taken to church all the time had parents who felt strongly about their religion and sought to instill it in their kids at an early age. It is also likely that these parents felt that God demanded religious participation—a characteristic of an Authoritative God. By contrast, children with parents who were more lax in their church attendance were introduced to Gods who were less severe and less engaged. This relationship seems intuitive and simple, yet there are clear exceptions. Sandra, the atheist, attended church often as a child, and the religiously devoted Maggie was rarely taken to church by her father. These cases remind us that a single factor can never fully explain belief—even when strong patterns exist.

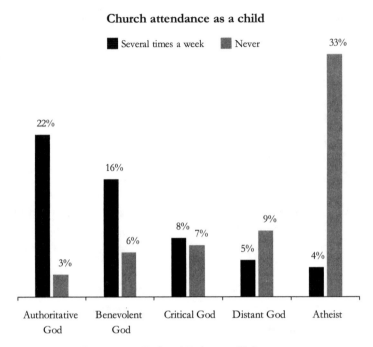

Figure 2.2. God and Religious Upbringing

In general, it is rare for a person to adopt a story of God that is radically at odds with that of her family and community.[6] The same can be said of those without religious faith. Nonbelievers are just as strongly influenced by their families and friends and, for the most part, will follow in a family tradition of secularism. The God we ultimately imagine reflects something about our early childhood and how we first became familiar with religious concepts, even though God cannot be shown to be a direct product of a particular personality trait, parenting style, or religious upbringing. The process is complex. Once an image of God is introduced to our minds (usually by a parent), it takes on a life of its own.[7] And as we age, our image of God develops more fully and continues to be influenced by new experiences, which are reconciled with—or completely undermine—our earliest image of God.

One of the most important aspects of our religious life is our continued interaction with a religious or spiritual community, which will influence, and be influenced by, the kind of God we imagine. To better understand this relationship, we can look at the social institution of religion and how it connects to our image of God.

God and Religion

As we have seen, the God of our childhood is a critical factor in who we will become and the kind of religious life we will lead. Similarly, our continued adherence to specific religious traditions, our personal religious experiences, and our ongoing interest in religious teachings are closely related to how we view God. Clergy will be encouraged to hear that we don't think their sermons fall on deaf ears (at least, much of the time). A person's image of God can change as she encounters new environments and hears more sermons, yet a person's image of God can also lead her to reject those sermons and question the attitudes of her friends. Our image of God is never simply a reflection of the beliefs of our religious community. The traditional method of classifying people as Catholics or Baptists or Jews tells us little of consequence about what they believe.

The intensity of a person's overall level of religiosity or spirituality is difficult to gauge. Often, researchers look at participation in religious rituals, feelings about religious texts, and religious experiences to get a sense of a person's religious devotion. While these things are all related to one another (and to images of God), they are not always perfectly aligned. For instance, Mori, a housewife in Texas and recent immigrant from Japan, attends a Christian church every week but does not believe in God. She goes at the request of her husband. Partially due to her upbringing in a nonreligious family, Mori feels no real connection to Christian spirituality or the sermons she hears every week. So is Mori religious? Based on her stellar attendance record, she would strike us as very devout; her pastor probably thinks of her as a true and committed believer. But as she confided to us, away from the ears of her friends and family, she is in fact a committed atheist. How many Americans share a similar story of outward devotion and inward doubt?

We also met Herbert, a man who talks to God regularly but does not belong to any church. In fact, he openly derides organized religion. He feels that churches create obstacles between us and God. So how religious is Herbert? He is certainly exceptional in certain ways. For example, Herbert says he hears God's voice daily, which is something few Americans profess. But judged by the traditional measure of church attendance, Herbert is not religious at all. Both Mori and Herbert demonstrate that our traditional measures of religiosity are superficial. Appearances can mask the truth.

Like Herbert, many Americans describe themselves as "spiritual" but not "religious." When people say this, they tend to mean that they do not affiliate with a specific church but still believe in God and the supernatural. But unlike Herbert, who describes a very active and engaged God, Americans who say they are "not religious" tend to believe in a Distant God (see figure 2.3). By contrast, nearly all those who believe in an Authoritative God or a Benevolent God think of themselves as "very religious." What does this imply? Essentially, two things. First, many believers in a Distant God and even a small number of believers in a Critical God feel outside what is traditionally thought to be "religion." Second, believers in an Authoritative God or a Benevolent God tend to be strongly attached to a specific denomination or religious tradition.

The relationship between images of God and outward signs of religiosity is complex. How is our reading of religious texts related to how

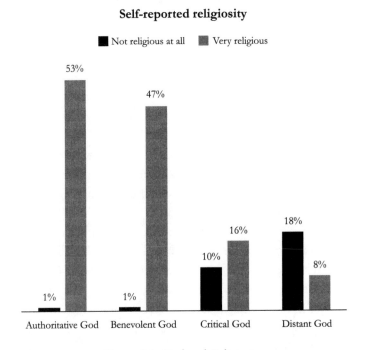

Figure 2.3. God and Religiosity

we perceive God? How does our church influence our image of God? What about our religious experiences? These three aspects of our religious life are all related to our image of God in important but not always straightforward ways.

Sacred Texts

When we asked Americans (most of whom are Christians) about God, many directly referenced a biblical story. In fact, American Christians spend a lot of time reading the Bible. Nearly a third report that they read the Bible, outside religious services, weekly if not more often. As many as 38 percent of American Christians attend monthly Bible study meetings.[8] Stand outside a Christian church on Sunday, and you will more than likely see a host of congregants carrying Bibles. Look more closely, and you might see multiple bookmarks that provide easy access to favorite passages. American Christians place enormous importance on the Bible as the most accessible route to understanding God.

Of course, Christians can understand the Bible in radically different ways. One basic way to capture these differences is the extent to which someone feels that the Bible should be taken literally. Did it actually rain for forty days once Noah completed his ark? Or does that just mean it rained for a really long time? Or is the whole story of the flood to be understood metaphorically? Did God actually form Adam and Eve, or is the story of creation meant to communicate, in a more general sense, that all life originates from a creator, who may have instigated the process of evolution? We tend to separate American Christian believers into "biblical literalists" and everyone else. For Americans who maintain that the Bible should be taken literally, the person of God must be found in the pages of the good book. Nonliteralists are open to various interpretations of the Bible and are also more likely to rely on sources outside the Bible for spiritual insight. But even for biblical literalists, we cannot always be sure what they think about God, because the Bible has many different (and contradictory) things to say on the topic.

Overall, self-proclaimed biblical literalists tend to believe in an Authoritative God—a God who smites his enemies and rewards the faithful (see figure 2.4). But around a quarter of biblical literalists feel that God is Benevolent, and a few literalists even believe in a Critical

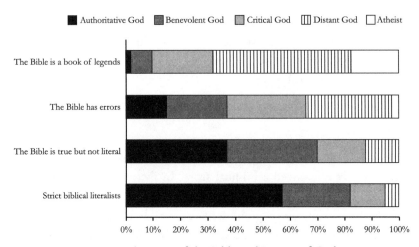

Figure 2.4. Views of the Bible and Images of God

Note: The American population is divided as follows regarding their view of the Bible: 21 percent are strict biblical literalists, 35 percent believe the Bible is true but not literal, 13 percent believe the Bible has human error, 25 percent believe the Bible is a book of legends, and 6 percent have no opinion. Source: Baylor Religion Survey, Wave 1 (2005).

God or a Distant God. While Christian literalists may claim to be opposed to the idea of "interpreting" the Bible, speaking with literalists reveals a vast array of disagreements about what the text says and means.

Sam, a professed biblical literalist, talked to us about a God who brought down the walls of Jericho to smite his enemies. He was adamant about closely following biblical truth and described a God who was decidedly Authoritative. Yet when we spoke to Stella, another fervent biblical literalist, a very different picture of God emerged. She spoke of a God who allowed his son to be sacrificed to demonstrate the power of love and humility. Stella is averse to thinking of God's wrath and explained that a close reading of the Bible reveals a Benevolent God. Two biblical literalists offered two very different images of God. And neither felt that there was any personal interpretation involved.

The fact that many Americans claim to be biblical literalists says something important about the religious identities they wish to project and their desire to remain loyal to their sacred text. But biblical literalism is not the same as a person's image of God. We still find fundamental disagreements among biblical literalists about who God is and what God wants.

As one might expect, Americans who think that the Bible contains "some errors" are even more varied in their ideas about God. They tend not to draw a direct line between their image of God and a particular biblical passage. And Americans who describe the Bible as a "book of legends" are mainly either believers in a Distant God or nonbelievers.

A person's relationship to her sacred text is different from her relationship with God. We cannot simply read religious texts to understand what is in the minds of believers. Regardless of what biblical literalists assert, the Bible is necessarily subject to the interpretations of individuals; the fact that self-proclaimed literalists have disagreements about the Bible is undeniable. Consequently, we place less importance on whether a person describes herself as a literalist and more importance on how a person views God. This ultimately tells us much more about how believers see the world.

Religious Experience

While Americans often reference biblical stories to describe God, many Americans also tell stories about their personal interactions with the divine. In fact, encounters with God are surprisingly common for average Americans. Nearly half of all Americans (45 percent) indicate that they have "felt called by God to do something."[9] Despite their frequency, the substance of these religious experiences is largely unknown. Talking about God across America, we heard an amazing array of testimonies about vastly different religious experiences. Many Americans described seeing miracles, hearing the voice of God, and experiencing extraordinary coincidences that they attributed to God's hand. In turn, they offer these instances of divine communication as evidence of God's character and desires.

Andrew Newberg hypothesizes that certain religious conceptions tend to be in place prior to religious experience and provide the interpretive framework through which a person understands her miraculous encounter. He argues: "Spiritual experiences appear to emerge spontaneously in human brains, but as far as we can tell, they rarely occur in early childhood. Instead, your children are introduced to the idea of

God by their parents. . . . This becomes our neurological basis for future religious beliefs, and they will color our spiritual experiences for the rest of our lives."[10] This argument makes logical sense. Hearing a voice, seeing an unexpected apparition, or witnessing a miracle requires some type of explanation. Nonbelievers are likely to say they are having a delusion; believers in God are likely to attribute their experience to the divine. Consequently, religious experiences tend to fit with preestablished images of God. This was certainly the case with the many stories of religious experience we heard.

The most memorable stories are not brief flashes of magical wonder but rather heartfelt testimonies of how God took hold of a person's life. Janet, a native New Yorker, struggled with alcohol and drugs for most of her life—a struggle so severe and debilitating that she twice attempted suicide. Janet was always a believer in a Benevolent God, and she often looked to God to aid in her recovery. One night her prayers were answered.

After her second suicide attempt, Janet awoke in her hospital room and immediately felt a presence she knew was God. Having been rushed to the emergency room and barely revived, Janet was struck by an epiphany that God was finally "with me that night." For her, the fact that her suicide attempt failed and she was rescued at the last minute was clear evidence of divine intervention. At this moment of realization, Janet felt God's hand touch her. After her powerful religious encounter, Janet entered recovery and eventually went back to school and became a nurse who now provides the same care she received when her life was in peril.

From an outside perspective, we can unequivocally state that Janet was saved by the routine work of emergency technicians. Nonetheless, Janet felt God working through her rescuers and interpreted her escape from death as a miracle. Janet's perception of this miracle was premised on her prior belief in a Benevolent God; without this belief, she might have attributed her rescue to dumb luck. But her belief in a Benevolent God and her experience of God in that single moment continue to shape her years later.

Jeremy, a man who had just gotten out of prison, described a similar experience. Like Janet, Jeremy had a prior belief in God—in his case, an Authoritative God. Jeremy suffered a long and arduous prison sentence, which he came to view as proper punishment for his crimes. Jeremy realized that God demanded that he suffer. But after years in prison, Jeremy had a life-altering experience. One day in his cell, he began "singing a song that I've sung for years, the one about where God took my feet out of miry clay and put them on a rock. The miry clay was my life before prison. The rock was when He started to build something while I was in prison, and he has continued to establish since I have been out." Jeremy felt that God accepted his remorse and reached out his hand in forgiveness. This moment of divine grace reflected a turning point in his process of redemption. Again, it seems that Jeremy's prior belief in an Authoritative God, along with his acceptance of God's punishment, was crucial in setting the stage for this redemptive encounter.

Jeremy now feels that God watches him closely, and God's vigilance inspires him to walk the straight and narrow. For him, God is a savior and a taskmaster, an Authoritative God who influences his daily decisions and, for one miraculous moment, visited Jeremy in his prison cell to tell him his punishment was over and his new life was to begin.

While many Americans talk about dramatic encounters with God, other believers speak of a different kind of religious experience—the experience of viewing the world through "religious eyes." For these Americans, ordinary encounters and objects take on religious significance. For them, God exists within all things—specifically things that are not miraculous in any sense. Leslie, a suburban homemaker and believer in a Distant God, explained that God would never literally speak to a person or lay his hand on someone. Her belief in a Distant God precludes these kinds of religious experiences. Still, Leslie explains that her life is rife with religious encounters of a much different sort. She explains: "If I'm moving with God, then my eyes are open to [God's handiwork]. And if not, I miss it. You blink and you miss it. I mean, look around, flowers are clear evidence of God's perfection and a platypus is clear evidence of his sense of humor. If you can't see it, you've missed it. It's all a miracle, every bit of it."

Leslie's image of God is more abstract than those of Janet and Jeremy. In turn, Leslie's understanding of and familiarity with religious experience is also more abstract. She does not attribute unexplained or unusual feelings to God's presence but rather sees God's miracles in the natural world. For Leslie, God is less like a human and more of an abstract essence that exists within all things. This image of God does not preclude religious experiences but alters the quality and content of them.

If we look at how believers in the four types of God describe their religious experiences, we find clear patterns. Believers in an Authoritative or a Benevolent God are very likely to have "felt called by God," and nearly a third of them report actually "hearing the voice of God speak" to them personally. Around a fifth of believers in a Critical or Distant God felt called by God, and almost none of them have heard God speak. Interestingly, atheists and believers in a Distant God are the most likely to have "felt one with the universe," a type of religious experience with New Age overtones, similar to Leslie's description of her spirituality. The fact that nearly a third of atheists report this otherworldly sensation indicates that while atheists explicitly deny the existence of God, some of them still hold beliefs about the existence of a spiritual or supernatural realm.

In sum, believers in a more engaged God (Authoritative and Benevolent) tend to experience what they call "miracles"—clear detours from the normal course of events. Believers in a less engaged God (Critical and Distant) tend not to experience miracles but still view the world through "religious eyes." They see God in creation but do not feel that God is changing the natural flow of events.

For some, like Jeremy and Janet, dramatic and unusual events powerfully reaffirm their images of God. For others, like Leslie, miracles are common events and objects that exude religious significance for those willing to see it. While Jeremy, Janet, and Leslie all talk about miracles, their different Gods indicate that their definitions are vastly different. And in these differences lie deep disagreements about how the natural world functions and God's role in it.

Religious Communities

When asked about their religion, Americans often answer that they are Christian, Jewish, Muslim, Buddhist, or a member of one of the numerous other traditions flourishing in the American religious landscape. Because most Americans are Christian, they often go further to identify themselves as Roman Catholic, Evangelical, Pentecostal, Orthodox, and a seemingly endless list of Protestant denominations, whose teachings vary from very liberal to fundamentalist.

An individual's religious community presents him with a distinct image of God in the doctrines it offers. For instance, evangelicalism is a popular cross-denominational movement in the United States that stresses a personal relationship with God. Like many large-scale movements or groups, evangelicalism is difficult to define and concretely identify; some researchers even advocate breaking evangelicalism down into a series of smaller conceptual categories. But in general, evangelicalism is popularly known for its conservative ethic, and as sociologist Christian Smith notes, "Evangelicals see themselves as embracing traditional, common-sense values in a broader culture that has abandoned them in pursuit of narcissistic, licentious, and self-destructive values and lifestyles."[11] With moral concerns at the forefront of their theology, evangelicals tend to advocate a God who is present in their daily lives, guiding their choices and judging their missteps. As such, we would expect evangelicals to believe in an Authoritative God, a God who is intimately engaged with us and our moral decisions.

Comparing American images of God across different religious traditions reveals several patterns.[12] As expected, evangelicals tend toward belief in an Authoritative God (see figure 2.5). African American evangelicals are the most likely group to believe in an Authoritative God. By contrast, Americans who report no religious affiliation favor either Critical or Distant Gods. But within several religious traditions, there are high levels of disagreement about God. For example, a Roman Catholic is as likely to believe in an Authoritative God as a Distant God. Consequently, saying someone is a Roman Catholic tells you virtually nothing about his image of God. The same is true of Americans in Mainline Protestant denominations; their beliefs are spread equally across all God types.

National religious organizations and identities that link thousands of individual churches under a single umbrella—such as Baptist, Methodist, or Presbyterian—have been losing their significance.[13] Individual churches and individual congregants feel less of a need to adhere to the doctrines and dogma of their denominations. This partially explains why we can find such disagreement about the character of God within

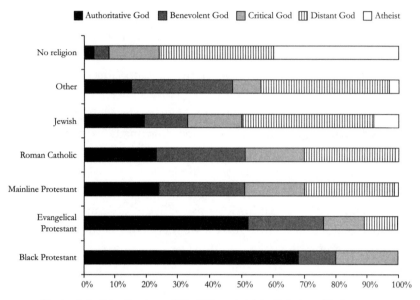

Figure 2.5. Distribution of God Types within Religious Traditions

American religious traditions and communities. As Nancy Ammerman explains in her extensive research on American congregations, church communities represent "arenas for everyday practice, rather than ideologically-defined camps."[14]

While different images of God certainly persist within large groups of Christians, Muslims (who are included in the "other" category), and Jews, perhaps within smaller groups—at the level of the church, synagogue, or mosque—this wouldn't be the case. Perhaps all members have nearly identical ideas about God because they listen to the same sermons, attend the same religious study groups, and pray together. We investigated this issue in a tiny rural Southern Baptist church in central Texas. We picked this church because unlike urban churches or megachurches, which have the potential to attract a wide variety of people, the location and size of this particular church ensured that not many walk-ins would enter its doors. Not that the congregation was unwelcoming, but the church is hidden down a long dirt driveway that snakes off a long and deserted country road, making it hard to find even with meticulous directions.

The small sanctuary was built in the late nineteenth century and is surrounded by a cemetery. An initial look at the congregants supported our assumption of demographic homogeneity. Rugged men in cowboy shirts and boots escorted their modestly dressed wives from their American-made trucks to the church steps. Boys with freshly combed hair and girls in floral dresses followed obediently. Overall, this looked like the quintessential southern Protestant church. Stereotypes of rural, hard-working, gun-toting, God-fearing Americans were appeased.

Surveying the congregants, we confirmed that they are all white and almost all affiliated with the Republican Party. Almost all members call themselves biblical literalists and believe that the government should allow prayer in schools. There is little question that members of this congregation share a common history. When we asked members how often they attend church or about their faith in the Bible, the divinity of Jesus, or many other basic questions about their religiosity, we received nearly unanimous agreement.

Yet when our discussions turned to God, something interesting happened. They disagreed. Or at least talking about God led them to ask some questions, voice some confusion, and offer some divergent views about God and what God wants from them. For instance, not all members of the congregation agreed that God is a "he." Nearly a fifth of them believed that God was definitely *not* male. This finding approximates the national evangelical average and indicates that variation can appear within individual churches, even one as small and isolated as this one.

Daniel, the longtime minister of this little church, was actually surprised to hear that so many of his parishioners did not share his beliefs about God's gender. Daniel is a charismatic preacher who dazzled his congregation this Sunday with a fervent sermon about God's rewards in the afterlife and his distaste for sinners. Daniel clearly believed in an Authoritative God and repeatedly described God as a powerful and intimidating male figure. He felt confident that his flock shared the "proper" faith for getting into heaven. Yet he was disappointed that all his congregants did not answer the question about God's gender "correctly" and vowed to deliver a future sermon on the topic.[15]

Daniel was also saddened to hear that nearly a third of congregants referred to God as a "cosmic force." While this is less than the national average for evangelical Protestants, it still demonstrates that members of this small, conservative church talk and think about God differently.

Daniel argued that God should be properly understood as a being and that the image of a cosmic force could lead some to underestimate God's authority. As we left this small church, we realized that we had instigated a series of discussions about God that we did not expect. The people, who were intimately acquainted with one another and shared similar opinions on a host of national and local controversies, were surprised to hear what their friends and minister had to say about God. And we expect that we provided Daniel with sermon fodder for the next few weeks.

One of the reasons that God can look different to two people sitting in the same pew is that religious language is sometimes used metaphorically and other times literally. Even the most literal-minded preacher will admit that God is a topic and concept too big to properly communicate in simple language. As one preacher warned us, "There are not enough pages in the world to write a book about God!" Similarly, there do not seem to be enough words to properly talk about God. Consequently, all stories and sermons about God fall short of their object of study. All of the congregants in the small Baptist church we visited professed faith in their preacher, but interestingly enough, they heard different things from his sermons. Some concluded that God was a "he" because that is what Daniel, not to mention the Bible, said. Others tacitly assumed that Daniel was simply applying a male pronoun to God for rhetorical purposes and that God's gender was not something concrete. This simple example can be expanded to the countless conversations and interactions we have about God.

Clearly, the religious group we belong to is a major influence on the kind of God we imagine. The sermons we hear, the religious experiences we have, and the sacred texts we look to for inspiration all shape our image of God. But the relationship is not a one-way street. Texts, sermons, and experiences all require interpretation, and in making sense of them, we often rely on basic concepts and images that have been instilled in us since childhood. In this way, our image of God guides us in how we read sacred texts, respond to conversations and sermons, and comprehend unusual events and daily routines.

The complex bundle of beliefs, behaviors, and experiences that we call our religious or spiritual life has no central origin. That said, our image of God is one of the first religious concepts to develop in childhood and remains intimately connected to how we live our religious lives.

God and Society

Social scientists have long noted clear patterns in the relationships between social class, race, gender, and religion. Rich people tend to go to church with other rich people, whites tend to sit in pews with other whites, and women tend to worship more frequently than men. In other words, our social and demographic differences predict religious differences. H. Richard Niebuhr made this argument in *The Social Sources of Denominationalism* in 1929, and not much has changed since. Sociologists Michael Emerson and Christian Smith argue that part of the reason is that we have the freedom to pick where and what we want to worship; they explain that "to the extent that people can choose [their churches], they choose to be with people like themselves."[16]

Because social and demographic differences predict religious variation, it comes as no surprise that they are also closely related to one's image of God (see figure 2.6). Women tend to picture a more Benevolent God than men, and African Americans are more likely than whites to believe that God is angry. More educated and wealthier Americans favor distant images of God. All of these patterns indicate that our image of God does not emerge at random.

In particular, regions of the country favor different Gods. One of the longest-standing misunderstandings about religion in the United States is that certain parts of the country are religious and other parts of the country are not. Terms such as "Bible Belt" suggest that the South is a hotbed of religion. Conversely, the coasts are assumed to be safe havens for atheists. If we just look at church attendance, it appears that this popular conception might be correct. More than a third of those who live in the Midwest or South attend religious services at least once a week, compared with only about a fifth of those on the coasts. If we map the four Gods across America, it becomes clear that the country is not divided into the religious and the irreligious but rather by specific images of God (see figure 2.7).

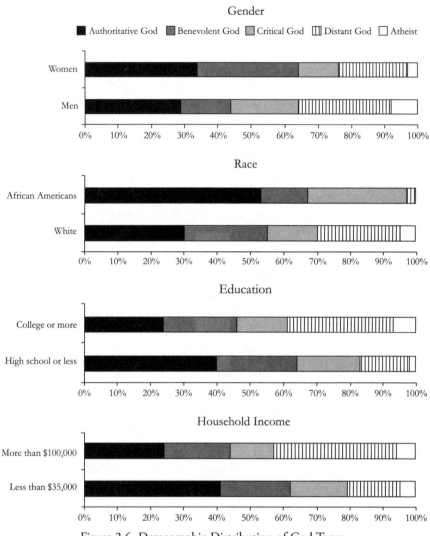

Figure 2.6. Demographic Distribution of God Types

In no part of the United States do atheists make up even 10 percent of the population. Certainly, the West Coast is slightly more amenable to atheism than the South, but not much. Rather, regions of the country are distinguished by different conceptions of God. More than a third of southerners believe in an Authoritative God. Midwesterners look similar to southerners, but with a bit less of a tendency toward an Authoritative God. Most prefer a Benevolent God. The propensity toward a Distant God on the West Coast fits with its perceived laissez-faire attitude. And

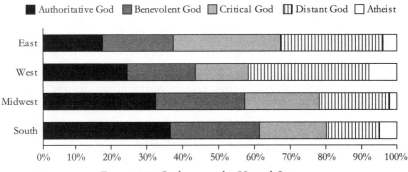

Figure 2.7. God across the United States

the best chance of meeting the Critical God is on the East Coast, where God reserves ultimate judgment for the afterlife.

By knowing where you live, what you look like, and how much money you make, we can begin to guess your image of God. For instance, a white man with a professional degree who lives on the West Coast will most likely believe in a Distant God, whereas an African American woman with a minimum-wage job who lives in the South will probably believe in an Authoritative God.

Still, these predictions will never be 100 percent accurate, and the trends, while statistically powerful, reflect only national tendencies; local patterns may vary dramatically. For instance, it is possible to find fervent enclaves of believers in an Authoritative God in wealthy, highly educated, and predominantly white areas. We can also find groups of poor southerners who believe in a Distant God. And in the final analysis, we hope to show that a person's image of God proves more important to their worldview than all of these demographic characteristics combined.

God and Political Identity

During one of our nation's darkest hours, Abraham Lincoln expressed sincere bewilderment about God's designs for our country. Reflecting on the two sides in the Civil War, Lincoln said:

> Both read the same Bible, and pray to the same God; and each invokes His aid against the other. It may seem strange that any men should dare to ask a just God's assistance in wringing their bread from the sweat of other men's faces; but let us judge not, that we be not judged.

The prayers of both could not be answered; that of neither has been answered fully. The Almighty has His own purposes.[17]

For Lincoln, the mysterious purposes of God are hidden from us and appear all the more baffling when one considers that wars and political battles are often waged between two sides who both firmly believe that God wishes them victory.[18] Lincoln further recognized the irony that the American Civil War was a war between devout Christians.

Today, Americans who profess to believe in the same Christian God still remain in conflict over key political issues. In particular, whether we identify as "liberals" or "conservatives" is closely linked to the type of God we believe in. Among registered voters in the United States, around 38 percent of Americans say they are "conservative," 20 percent say they are "liberal," and the rest identify as "moderates." These identities are important to the extent that they predict political party affiliation, voting behavior, and attitudes on a host of moral and policy issues.[19]

It is popularly believed that conservative people are more religious. You would be hard-pressed to find a more common sentiment about the relationship between religion and politics in America.[20] Consequently, our own understanding of what it means to be religious or conservative may be altered by the fact that so many people think that these two identities perfectly overlap. As we indicated before, calling oneself "religious" does not mean that you necessarily believe more strongly in God, but rather suggests that you probably are attached to more traditional forms of religion and you tend to believe in types of God depicted in traditional sacred texts.

But when a person calls himself "conservative," what does this mean? Does he cherish traditional family values, such as wanting mothers to stay home to care for their children? Or does he advocate laissez-faire capitalism with fewer regulations on business? Perhaps he is supportive of an aggressive foreign policy. Being "conservative" can mean all of these or none. For instance, an American who forcefully opposes gay marriage can be very distrustful of big business, and a person who supports a muscular foreign policy can be indifferent to the legality of abortion. In rare cases, self-identified conservatives may express few, if any, traditionally conservative opinions. The same can be said for self-identified liberals.

If defining what it means to be conservative or liberal is difficult, adding religion into the mix complicates things further. Currently, religious advocates on both left and right are intent on illustrating their political party's compatibility with American Christianity. Amy Sullivan, an evangelical, and E. J. Dionne, a Roman Catholic, have both written books arguing that religious faith fits firmly within the Democratic Party platform.[21] And some conservative Christian leaders are beginning to question the political agenda of pundits who claim an exclusive attachment to God. In May 2007, a group of evangelical leaders claiming to represent more than 42,000 congregations across the United States released an "Evangelical Manifesto," which stated that when politicians use faith to gain support for policy, "Christians become 'useful idiots' for one political party or another, and the Christian faith becomes an ideology."[22]

But the 2004 presidential campaign of George W. Bush provides a reminder that the link between evangelicalism and conservatism is a powerful one. In the months prior to the election, President Bush was often touted as nothing less than "God's candidate" by key figures in the conservative evangelical movement. Pat Robertson famously proclaimed, "I think George Bush has the favor of heaven. . . . He's a godly man. He prays on a daily basis. He wants to do what's right before the Lord, and I think God has honored him." A few evangelicals we spoke with agreed with Robertson's assertion and fully believed that God had a hand in George W. Bush winning the presidency. Carson, a resident of Tampa, went so far as to claim that God had tampered with ballots in Florida during the 2000 election to ensure that Bush came out the victor—a supernatural spin on electoral corruption.[23]

In response to the popular perception that religious people must be conservative, many American liberals have become less likely to think of themselves as "religious." In fact, some sociologists argue that liberal Americans who have traditional religious beliefs are beginning to identify themselves as "nonreligious" simply because they fear being improperly identified as conservatives.[24] In recent decades, religious and conservative identities have had a gravitational draw on each other; in turn, these identities have a strong relationship with how a person views God. Conservatives tend toward an Authoritative God, and liberals favor a Distant God (see figure 2.8). While most atheists are liberals, most liberals are not atheists—there are not nearly enough atheists in America for that to be possible.

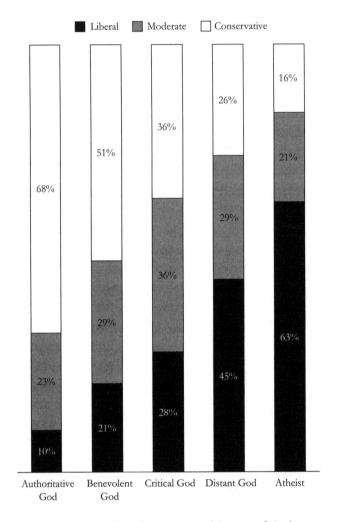

Figure 2.8. Political Leanings and Images of God
Source: Baylor Religion Survey, Wave 2. An item on the Baylor Religion Survey asks respondents to rate themselves from "extremely liberal" (1) to "extremely conservative" (7). This categorizes those from 1 to 3 as liberal, those from 5 to 7 as conservative and those in the middle (4) as moderate.

The complexity of defining what it means to be "religious" appears to be lost on pundits who discuss "godless" liberals and/or "devout" conservatives. Still, their insistence on the connection between conservatism and religiosity has so seeped into the public consciousness that it seems impossible to counter. This appears to have led some conservatives to inflate their own religiosity and some liberals to downplay their faith. A far better way to think about the connection between religion and politics is to forgo any discussion of who is more religious and focus on the type of religion a believer advocates. Again, a person's image of God gives us a concrete means to distinguish the religiosity of individuals without assuming anything about their devotion or lack thereof.

God's Independence

Simply knowing that a person's beliefs are strongly influenced by her upbringing, her religion, and her social circumstances does nothing to undermine the importance of her image of God once it has been instilled.[25] As William James asserts:

> [Gods] determine our vital attitude as decisively as the vital attitudes of lovers is determined by the habitual sense, by which each is haunted, of the other being in the world. A lover has notoriously this sense of the continuous being of his idol. . . . He cannot forget her; she uninterruptedly affects him through and through.[26]

James's analogy of a lover's absorption with his love interest nicely illustrates the fascination believers have with their Gods. Lovers do not ask themselves about the "real" source of their affection, and even if they could attribute it to something biological, to changing cultural attitudes about what is beautiful or desirable, or to some other mundane root cause, it would not change for a moment the emotional connection and commitment they feel for one another. Would a lovesick youth care for a moment that her longings are predictable? The true importance of our love is not in its origins but in its effect on our happiness and behavior.

Similarly, a believer's connection to God follows certain social and psychological patterns but also grows into a complex and unique relationship. Lovers develop an attachment that is unique to their partnership. Couples create private jokes, pet names, and a shared sensibility about the world. A similar dynamic occurs in a person's relationship with God.

In the first pages of this book, we introduced the idea that God acts as a person's Generalized Other—the voice in our heads with which we have an ongoing conversation. Because God interacts with believers, the effect that God has on a believer cannot be reduced to any static social or demographic factor. To demonstrate this, throughout this book, we control for a host of these factors. This means that we look for the relationship between God type and Americans' attitudes and behaviors that cannot be explained by things like their race, their gender, their income, their education, their age, their political identity, their church attendance, their religious tradition, or their view of the Bible.[27] In this way, we can think more deeply about the logical connections individuals make between their God and the numerous attitudes and beliefs that make up their worldview. We also test this against what Americans tell us directly about their interactions with God.

For example, we spoke with Matthew and Jessica about global warming. Both are conservatives from the Midwest, both college-educated with professional jobs, and both devoted to their evangelical tradition. In a traditional survey, they'd look exactly the same. But Matthew and Jessica have different conceptions of God: Matthew believes in a Distant God, and Jessica believes in a Benevolent God. This makes a big difference in how they understand the science of global warming and how they view their responsibility to the planet. For Matthew, global warming is a real threat to the future of Earth and humanity because he feels that "man is responsible for his own fate." He told us that his attitude stems directly from his belief that God is distant. God set creation in motion, he said, but it is up to us to care for the planet. His personal perspective fits neatly with the trends we found among believers in a Distant God.

Jessica, on the other hand, rejects the possibility of global warming because she feels that "God controls the universe." Her belief in an active and loving God leads her to think that God simply would never allow global warming to occur, and to question any scientific claim that purports to explain the climate without reference to God's influence. Again, her perspective fits with general trends.

Matthew's and Jessica's divergent opinions about global warming cannot be explained by their church memberships, their Midwest upbringings, their conservative identities, or their educations. They appear identical on these counts. It is their different beliefs about God that are important. Images of God matter greatly and have the power to explain differences over and above those that can be traced directly back to our social divisions and differences.

The remainder of this book demonstrates how images of God influence our beliefs and behaviors regardless of our upbringing, our religion, our political identity, and an array of other factors.

THREE

God and Morals

Noting the decay of our morals is a popular pastime. This is one concern that unites all American generations—each grumbles that the next is a sorry reflection of the last. By these accounts, it appears that we are in a constant downward moral spiral heading toward a state of universal decadence.

But what complicates the common perception that America is in moral decline is the fact that Americans portray this decline in contradictory ways. For instance, some feel that the decision of *Roe v. Wade* was a critical lapse in our nation's morality. For others, our American principles are upheld by giving women the right to choose abortion. These Americans fear that religious dogmatism might blind the moral vision of a progressive and tolerant nation. In the end, we all tend to identify people and actions that we feel are morally corrupting and nervously look for signs of their ascendancy. The battle lines in our culture wars are drawn around those we think are without morals.

Instead of trying to separate Americans into those with morals and those without, a good way to think about our moral differences is to consider each individual's level of moral absolutism. A moral absolutist feels that certain activities are wrong no matter what the circumstances. A moral relativist wants to know the circumstances before making such a decision. For instance, Martin Luther King Jr. was a moral absolutist with regard to violence—he felt that there was no circumstance in which it was justified. But most Americans are relativists—we feel that there are times when violence is necessary.

Deciding whom to tolerate and which sins to condemn can trouble even the strictest moral absolutists. Alaska Governor Sarah Palin emerged on the national scene as a staunch antiabortionist and advocate of abstinence-only sex education. Consequently, it was unclear how the news of her teenage daughter's pregnancy would be received by her supporters. Would Americans who shared Palin's moral absolutism view this as a monumental failure of parenting? In the end, Palin's fans rallied around the fact that her pregnant daughter kept the baby. The fact that Palin had taught her daughter to despise abortion came to be seen as good parenting.

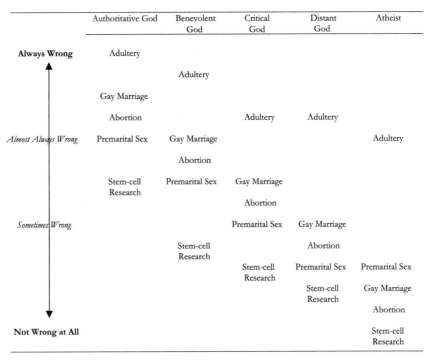

Relative morality of hot-button issues

	Authoritative God	Benevolent God	Critical God	Distant God	Atheist
Always Wrong	Adultery				
		Adultery			
	Gay Marriage				
	Abortion		Adultery	Adultery	
Almost Always Wrong	Premarital Sex	Gay Marriage			Adultery
		Abortion			
	Stem-cell Research	Premarital Sex	Gay Marriage		
			Abortion		
Sometimes Wrong			Premarital Sex	Gay Marriage	
		Stem-cell Research		Abortion	
			Stem-cell Research	Premarital Sex	Premarital Sex
				Stem-cell Research	Gay Marriage
					Abortion
Not Wrong at All					Stem-cell Research

Figure 3.1. God and Sin (Average Response from Each Group of Believers)
Note: Responses were averaged from maximum scores of 4 = "always wrong" to minimum scores 1 = "not wrong at all."

When reflecting on which moral values are absolute and evaluating the moral lives of others, most Americans look to God for answers. And whether his God is loving, forgiving, or wrathful indicates the extent to which a believer is a moral absolutist. In figure 3.1, we show that the tendency to rate behaviors as "always wrong" versus "never wrong" is directly related to our image of God and follows a very clear pattern. On all of these topics, believers in an Authoritative God are the most absolutist. Believers in a Benevolent God or a Critical God occupy the middle ground between moral absolutism and relativism. And believers in a Distant God and atheists are moral relativists who shift their opinion about the morality of a behavior based on circumstances.

Of course, there are exceptions. Moral attitudes toward war and environmentalism tend to upend the close association between moral relativism and belief in a Distant God. In fact, nonbelievers and believers in a Distant God tend to be *more* absolutist in their disapproval of war and environmental depletion. These important exceptions indicate that the logical connection between an Authoritative God and moral absolutism depends on the issue under consideration. It comes down to how a believer thinks God feels about the issue. (We will return to discussions of war and environmentalism in subsequent chapters.) That said, there remains a strong logical link between belief in an Authoritative God and belief that certain acts are always and unforgivably wrong. Quite simply, a judgmental and engaged God will not permit certain acts.

But note the relative ranking of moral issues for all believers—they are exactly the same. Specifically, no matter what kind of God a person believes in, he ranks the comparative immorality of behaviors in exactly the same order. Adultery is always considered the most unforgivable, while stem-cell research always ranks last in terms of its perceived immorality. Of course, certain individuals will drastically reverse and reorder the immorality of these acts, but overall, there is an amazing agreement among the American public.

Before investigating our often-forgotten moral agreements, let's first look at how God affects our most divisive moral disagreements. The issues of gay marriage and abortion can sway elections. They run the complete range of moral responses from "always wrong" to "not wrong at all." By knowing a person's God, we gain deep insights into how he justifies and navigates his stance on these core issues in our culture wars.

God and Homosexuality

There is solid evidence that American attitudes toward homosexuality are becoming more tolerant over time. The percentage of Americans who believe homosexuality to be "not wrong at all" has steadily increased, from 11 percent in 1973 to 30 percent in 2004.[1] Such changing attitudes are reflected in public policy. To date, five states have legalized gay marriage while four other states have legalized "civil unions," which extend the legal rights afforded by marriage to gay couples.[2] And in pop culture, there's an unmistakable trend toward increasing acceptance of gays and lesbians.

But there are also many who fear that America is becoming *too* accepting of homosexuality. In 2007, after a judge in Iowa ruled that same-sex couples could legally marry, a host of Iowans contacted their representatives. Twenty-four hours and one gay wedding later, the judge stayed his ruling. The political traction of this issue gained prominence at the federal level in 2004 and again in 2006, when Congress voted on a constitutional amendment to ban marriage between same-sex couples. The amendment did not pass, but it garnered much publicity and enlivened a public debate about the effects of homosexuality on American culture. While the vast majority of Americans (around 70 percent) say that homosexuality is "wrong," they also tend to see civil rights for homosexuals as a question of tolerance rather than morality. In other words, most Americans still view homosexuality as immoral, but whether they are willing to condemn homosexuals for their "sins" is open to question. Many who feel that homosexuality is wrong are quite willing to keep the law out of it.

We were struck by the length to which conservative Americans went to indicate that they were not homophobic, even when declaring the immorality of homosexuality. This suggests that outward expressions of hatred toward gays are becoming socially unacceptable. Many believers are careful to express a genuine compassion for homosexuals, albeit compassion leavened with pity and sorrow. In short, even the most vigorous opponents of gay marriage feel that homosexuality is just one in a litany of sins, none of which are acceptable in the eyes of God. Bill, a forty-nine-year-old construction worker who attends a Pentecostal church in Texas and believes in an Authoritative God, summarizes this common sentiment: Homosexuality is "probably one of the most grievous sins written about over and over and over in the Old Testament and the New Testament. But it's no different than . . . drugs and alcohol and premarital sex. God has no more judgment passed on homosexuality. It's all wrong in God's eyes." Clearly, Bill feels that the Bible unequivocally states that homosexuality is a sin, but at the same time, he does not revel in the thought of homosexuals going to hell. Bill even admitted to engaging in behaviors, such as drug use, that he believes to be as sinful as homosexuality. Nonetheless, Bill strongly supports legislation that reflects what he feels is God's moral law.

Believers in Critical or Benevolent Gods tend to be less morally absolutist than Bill. Eighty-five percent of those with an Authoritative God, like Bill, believe that homosexuality is always or almost always wrong, but only around two-thirds of those with a Benevolent God (67 percent) and 58 percent of those with a Critical view of God are certain that it is a sin. Make no mistake, all three types of believers have a strong tendency to believe that God disapproves of gays and lesbians, but the disapproval of the Benevolent and Critical Gods is not complete and often depends on circumstances.

Indeed, in discussions with believers in a Benevolent God, we found some open disagreement on what God thinks about gays. John, a forty-seven-year-old Roman Catholic man from Providence, Rhode Island, and believer in a Benevolent God, argued:

> Homosexual acts go against the nature of God. Basically, God didn't make us that way. The body wasn't made for that. And what about the people involved? Can they be saved or are they all going straight to hell? That's entirely in God's hands, that's not up to me. If they are trying to live a moral life and abstaining from illicit relations, then, obviously, they can be saved, just like you and me, you know. Because if we're trying to live a moral life and abstain from illicit relations, then we can find salvation also.

In Seattle we spoke to another believer in a Benevolent God, Marilyn, a seventy-year-old retiree who used to work as a bookkeeper at a welding supply store. A self-described Republican, Marilyn considers herself conservative on most social issues. And she believes in a particularly engaged God—one who inspires her to write daily religious affirmations in lipstick on her bathroom mirror and who "touches her life" in ways big and small. In fact, talking about God brought her to tears. Marilyn told us:

> God thinks it bad. . . . It was happening in the Bible days. There were orgies, men with men, women with women. And that was something God looked down on. Now today, you see some guys that are gay and they are so different. It must be that God made them that way. And that makes me think, we're supposed to be open and loving to everyone. I am going to be open and loving to those people, you know. I . . . and it's hard when there's a gay teacher. You think, "What if he's looking at the young boys and wanting stuff," and I don't like that. But if he isn't, I think he should be their teacher. I think if he's a good teacher, he should be left alone. And unless there's any evidence of the contrary, I don't know. I want them to be active in churches and everything, and I do. I just can't hate them. I can't.

While John's attitude reflects the majority sentiment among Benevolent God believers, Marilyn embodies a more inclusive, welcoming attitude toward gays and lesbians. John thinks gays must change to make things right with God, while Marilyn wonders how we can expect them to change.

The source of this disagreement lies in differing opinions on the nature of homosexuality. For John, homosexuality is a choice. God has control of the world, and if he did not make homosexuals, then they were not meant to be. Marilyn finds herself faced with a conundrum. She says that she heard in the news that homosexuality is biological. So she ponders why God would allow homosexuals to exist, only to punish them. Thus, her beliefs about the nature of homosexuality and her strong beliefs about God coalesce into a more welcoming attitude toward gays.

Indeed, the nuances in John's and Marilyn's attitudes reflect the complicated ways religious conservatives grapple with the issue of homosexuality. Both these individuals describe themselves as strong

Republicans, and both support bans on gay marriage. Yet Marilyn's belief that homosexuality is biological leads her to conclude that we should be more tolerant of homosexuality.

Believers in a Distant God have just as many inner conflicts on this issue. But unlike believers in an Authoritative God, believers in a Distant God tend to view homosexuality as a part of the natural order of things. Even when someone with a Distant God disapproves of homosexuality personally, they seem willing to view homosexuality as a minor immorality, one that is really not a big concern to others and will not have an overarching effect on American culture. As such, homosexuals do not require special attention and tend to be regarded as good people who are trying their best to be moral. Furthermore, believers in a Distant God commonly expressed a sentiment articulated by Carl, a fifty-six-year-old singer who attends a Disciples of Christ congregation in San Fernando: "How somebody can quote Jesus chapter and verse and then turn around and smear paint on somebody's car, you know, it's not . . . God doesn't have anything to do with that. For heaven's sake! [Laughs] He doesn't have time for that. I don't think God is concerned at all about homosexuals." Carl makes two important points. First, he wonders why others pick on homosexuals, especially those who "quote Jesus" only to condemn others. They are all hypocrites, in his view. Moreover, his opinion about gays and lesbians reflects his idea that God is distant from earthly matters, and the issue of homosexuality would be far beneath the concern of the almighty creator. Carl continues, "I don't attribute anything that we do here as God's fault or God's responsibility. . . . You know, he's not playing with toys here. He set us in motion and what we do here is our own damn fault. So I don't see him moving in the world today as far as, you know . . . tornadoes or cyclones, or, you know, world wars or any of that stuff." In Carl's view, God has bigger things on his mind than our petty moral quandaries.

Similarly, atheists tend to think that homosexuality is a nonissue. However, they differ from the religious public in that they also tend to think that homosexuality is not at all immoral, and in fact, atheists balk at labeling anything "sin." But atheists closely resemble believers in a Distant God in their attitudes and again show that they do not so much inhabit a different moral sphere as occupy a more tolerant end of the American moral continuum.

As we found in our discussions with Marilyn and John, much of what determines whether Americans are willing to tolerate homosexuality, even when they disapprove of it, is the complex issue of whether homosexuality is a choice or an innate characteristic.[3] Quite simply, Americans who view homosexuality as a choice are more likely to want to deny gays and lesbians their civil liberties and limit their freedom to live openly. Americans who view homosexuality as a biological predisposition tend to think that society should accommodate gays and lesbians.

Conceptions of God are directly related to whether individuals feel that homosexuality is a choice or a predisposition (see figure 3.2). Atheists are the most likely to believe that homosexuality is biological, and believers in an Authoritative God tend to think of homosexuality as a choice. The reasons for this relationship are not immediately evident. For instance, one would expect that someone who believes in an all-powerful God would also think that God has predetermined our individual dispositions, sexual or otherwise. Nevertheless, most religious believers feel that God has given humans free will to choose their own life paths. Because most American Christians tend to view homosexuality as a sin, it follows that God must have given individuals the freedom to reject it. Consequently, for these believers homosexuality must be a choice.

Still, around a quarter of believers in an Authoritative God think that homosexuality is an inborn trait. But for this small group, the belief that homosexuality is innate does nothing to mitigate their conservative attitudes about gay marriage and the immorality of homosexuality. Interestingly, individuals expressing these two attitudes feel that God can manipulate the natural world so that if homosexuals ask God for help in overcoming their sexual predisposition, God will grant them the strength to overcome their natural urges. Consequently, whether homosexuality is a choice is irrelevant because God's moral order supersedes biology.

In the end, most Americans are careful to point out that they do not "hate" homosexuals. Even the most conservative Christians tend to express compassion and forgiveness toward homosexuals and state that they have as good a chance at salvation as anyone else. And even some of the most liberal religious believers view homosexuality as immoral or,

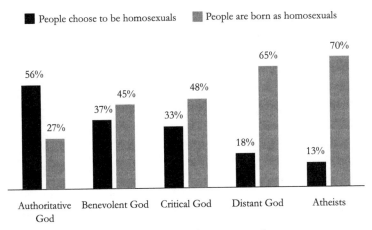

Figure 3.2. God and Homosexuality

at least, something that should not be celebrated or encouraged. The phrase "hate the sin, love the sinner" perfectly reflects most Americans' views of homosexuality.

Abortion

Abortion has become something of a litmus test within both political parties. But Americans' views on this issue are far from absolutist. Most Americans believe that abortion is definitely wrong in certain instances and should be avoided if at all possible. Only 16 percent of Americans feel that abortion is "never wrong."[4] Conversely, only 14 percent of Americans feel that abortion is "always wrong." The vast American middle takes into account mitigating circumstances, such as rape or a threat to the woman's health.[5] And responses to questions about abortion have been relatively stable since *Roe v. Wade* in 1973.[6] This undermines the conventional view of militant prochoice and prolife camps.

In addition, we tend to think that prolifers are religious while prochoice advocates are secular.[7] Yet an examination of how images of God relate to abortion reveals a much more nuanced and complicated story. The wide range of opinions on abortion becomes clear when individuals are asked about the situations under which abortion would be appropriate.[8] Believers in an Authoritative God, on average, think that abortion is acceptable only when a woman's health is in danger or the pregnancy is the result of a rape (see figure 3.3).

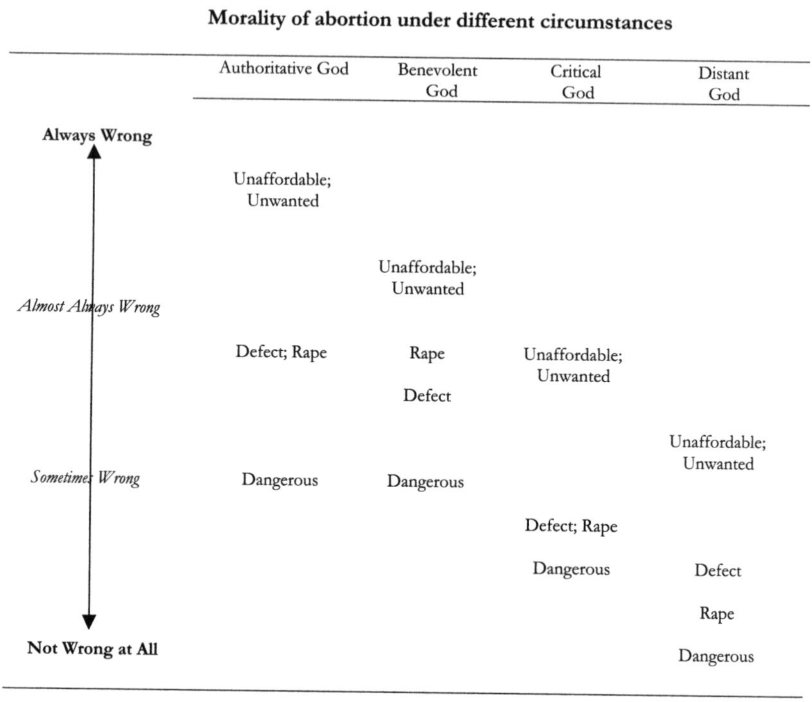

Morality of abortion under different circumstances

	Authoritative God	Benevolent God	Critical God	Distant God
Always Wrong	Unaffordable; Unwanted			
		Unaffordable; Unwanted		
Almost Always Wrong				
	Defect; Rape	Rape	Unaffordable; Unwanted	
		Defect		
				Unaffordable; Unwanted
Sometimes Wrong	Dangerous	Dangerous		
			Defect; Rape	
			Dangerous	Defect
				Rape
Not Wrong at All				Dangerous

Figure 3.3. Abortion under Different Circumstances
Note: Responses were averaged from maximum scores of 4 = "always wrong" to minimum scores of 1 = "not wrong at all." Defect = when the baby may have a serious defect; Dangerous = when the woman's health is in danger; Rape = when the pregnancy is the result of a rape; Unwanted = when the woman does not want the child; Unaffordable = when the family cannot afford the child.

Clearly, the relationship between the images of God and abortion attitudes is complex.[9] When a woman might die in the act of giving life, the concept of saving a life becomes rather complicated. It is a conundrum felt by the prochoice and the prolife alike. Accordingly, there are only small differences between Authoritative, Benevolent, Critical, and Distant believers on whether abortion is wrong when the woman's health is in danger; most agree that it should be allowed. However, with regard to pregnancies that are the result of rape, people with Authoritative and Benevolent Gods are significantly more restrictive on abortion than are those with Critical or Distant Gods. Perhaps those who imagine a very engaged God, a characteristic shared by the Authoritative and Benevolent Gods, believe that everything is part of God's larger plan.

Believers in an Authoritative God stand apart when asked whether abortion is wrong when the family cannot afford, or the woman does not want, a child. In these circumstances, an Authoritative God has the least patience for abortion. Perhaps the most interesting circumstance is when the family simply cannot afford the child. Here the Authoritative God is the strictest, followed by the Benevolent God, while those with Critical and Distant Gods are significantly more forgiving. Why?

Consider the nature of the Authoritative God—a God who judges but also intervenes. First, these believers tend to think that God condemns abortion. Second, these believers tend to think that if a pregnancy is the result of a sin, like sex out of wedlock, then a woman needs to bear the consequences of her sin. Third, these believers insist that an expectant mother trust in God to provide for the child. Fourth, and perhaps most important, believers in an Authoritative God fear that the sin of abortion may result in punishments that outweigh the troubles of having an unwanted child. As Clay, a young Pentecostal and devoted follower of an Authoritative God, warned, "Abortion is something that will bring harsh judgment on us as a whole nation." Although Clay's opinion is not widespread, it can powerfully motivate those who share it; picketing abortion clinics is not only preventing women from getting abortions but also saving the rest of us from God's wrath. For Clay and others like him, outlawing abortion is nonnegotiable because we have no better way of showing God that we are a faithful and moral nation.

But not all prolifers fear the wrath of God. Believers in a Benevolent God tend to agree that God opposes abortion but still feel that God will be tolerant of young women who make the decision to terminate a pregnancy. Frances, a young woman who has personally pondered undergoing an abortion and is a believer in a Benevolent God, expressed this common perspective:

I think that God grieves with families that have to have abortions. It is a horrible decision for everyone involved. The women I know who've had them are not proud of it and are mostly devastated. . . . I think that there are situations in which it is the right choice and God honors that. [Abortion] should not be legislated because I think it's an incredibly personal decision between a woman and her doctor and there's no way a law can know all the stuff involved, but God can know.

Frances argues a very interesting point—she rejects the idea that a law can reflect the true nature of God's plan. For her, God understands the mind of a pregnant woman; consequently, she hopes that all women should consult with God and "walk with God" in making their final decisions. Her Benevolent God is forgiving. Rather than punishing a woman who has an abortion, a Benevolent God will grieve with her, offering comfort and understanding. And Frances is skeptical that we can legislate abortion in a way that is always consistent with God's wishes.

Believers in a Critical God are also unsure about how the law might reflect God's true opinions. Like believers in a Benevolent God, these believers feel that a Critical God will not always condemn a young woman facing an unwanted pregnancy. Still, they believe that when pondering an abortion, women must give some thought to how their decision will displease God, even if God's wrath is not immediately felt. Chuck, a middle-aged science teacher and believer in a Critical God, explained:

> It's about the choice that the individual is making. And they have to square that with [God]. . . . If you're going to assume that the unborn child is alive and it is [sinful] to kill, then it seems like it's another array of sins, why are we so adamant about those? We can settle all those up with God. . . . It's between that individual and God, I guess is what I am trying to say.

For Chuck and other believers in a Critical God, people are left to their own devices. They cannot simply call on God to solve their problems. Still, they feel that pregnant women must ponder the morality of abortion because, ultimately, God will judge them based on their decision. Chuck cannot say for others whether abortion is absolutely wrong, but he still believes no moral decision should be made lightly.

Americans who believe in a Distant God are uncomfortable talking about God when discussing abortion. Although many are troubled by abortion, they often stressed to us that they did not know God's opinion on the issue, or that God simply may not have one. This does not necessarily mean that these believers are automatically prochoice, just that they don't pretend to know the mind of God.[10] When we asked Laura, a successful professional, a prolife advocate, and a believer in a Distant God, whether God has an opinion on abortion, she told us directly: "No . . . but I certainly do!"

Overall, believers in a Distant God are the most likely to argue that the decision to have an abortion should be left to the woman. This perspective is related directly to the fact that they posit a God who is not involved in daily decision making. Consequently, individuals must decide for themselves the morality of their choices and actions. In the end, believers in a Distant God are apt to take into consideration intervening circumstances and to see moral decisions not as a joint venture with God but rather a struggle within themselves to find the good in an ambiguous world. While they view God as part of that good, God remains enigmatic and is rarely considered a source of direct assistance.

When we talk about the relationship between abortion and God type, note that we are reporting tendencies, not absolutes. Nevertheless, the relationship between a person's image of God and her thoughts on abortion is powerful. We typically think of America as being divided into prolife and prochoice camps. But this is far from accurate. Most Americans are not happy about abortion. Few individuals advocate a complete ban on all abortion; similarly, few Americans want abortion to become stigma-free.

When God Hates

While the issues of homosexuality and abortion are quite divisive, we also see that there is more agreement on these moral issues than cable news would have you believe. Namely, when we scratch the surface of the polemics, we find that most Americans are moral relativists and, more important, behave civilly toward one another even when moral disputes arise. But this cannot be said of everyone. There are moral extremists, and in these atypical cases, God can often play a dominant role. Individuals who foster hatred tend to also have a hateful God.

The Southern Poverty Law Center classifies Westboro Baptist Church as a hate group. Church members regularly harass individuals at the funerals of their loved ones. For instance, the church famously picketed the funeral of hate-crime victim Matthew Shepard, shouting that Matthew was in hell because he was gay—or, as church members say, living a "Satanic lifestyle." Westboro Baptists have staged similar rallies at the funerals of dozens of soldiers killed in Iraq, carrying signs reading "Thank God for IEDs" and "God hates America." During the funeral of Supreme Court Justice William Rehnquist, church members stood with signs reading "Judge in Hell." The church even distributed a flyer following the death of beloved television personality Fred Rogers ("Mr. Rogers"), calling him a "diabolical propaganda expert" and tool "of the devil."[11]

Westboro Pastor Fred Phelps moved to Topeka in 1955 and launched the church out of his home. As Phelps began to develop a more and more peculiar religious mission, his neighbors became increasingly frightened, and one by one, they gradually put their homes up for sale. Church members purchased these homes and united their backyards with a shared fence. A de facto church compound developed on their block. The growing physical isolation of Westboro Baptists' homes mimics their mounting isolation within the American moral landscape.

The Westboro Baptists, not surprisingly, have an unusual conception of God. Their God is a nastier version of the Authoritative God.[12] He is quite opinionated and does not hesitate to respond to our failings in terrifying ways. But unlike most believers in an Authoritative God, Westboro members believe that God's grace is extremely limited. A handful of people on earth, Phelps argues, are the elect, those whom God has selected for admission into heaven. All others are damned to an eternity of torment in hell. In the first camp are the seventy-eight members of the Westboro Baptist Church (WBC). The latter?—everyone else. And for these unfortunate souls, there is no hope of avoiding the fire.

The Westboro Baptists' image of a God filled with hatred makes the group a conspicuous anomaly in an American theological landscape dominated by believers in a loving God. Edward, a forty-two-year-old financial adviser who has been with the group for seven years, explained:

We preach God's hatred. Hatred is an attribute of God that is completely glossed over and overlooked. . . . If preachers told people what the Bible really says about your manner of life and your eternal prospects and all that kind of stuff, there wouldn't be anybody in the seats when the plate got passed. . . . I say hatred . . . it's simply [God's] fixed determination to punish the wicked in hell for their sins.

Sharon, a thirty-year-old registered nurse and lifelong church member, seconded this assessment, saying that God is "wrath, vengeance, hatred, and words that are stronger than hatred. And jealous. One of the names of God. Capital J, jealous, man of war." But do the Westboro Baptists also think that God can love? The response from one member was clear: "It is simple: God loves us and hates you."

Armed with this image of a hateful God, Westboro Baptists are actively engaged in fighting what they perceive as sources of God's disgust. Most of their picket signs include disparaging references to homosexuals: "God Hates Fags" and "Fags Doom Nations." In fact, the WBC attributes America's problems almost exclusively to the existence and acceptance of homosexuality:

Without any doubt, homosexuality and the enabling of homosexuality is the greatest national sin in America. Same-sex marriage is the ultimate smash-mouth, in-your-face insult to God Almighty, as it blasphemously desecrates the holiest of Bible metaphors: Christ and His Bride the Church. Eph. 5:32. Same-sex marriage defies the law of nature and nature's God, with deadlier—though sometimes delayed, but even more certain—repercussions than defying the law of gravity at 30,000 feet.[13]

Westboro Baptists rally around their opposition to same-sex marriage and even go so far as celebrating disasters, diseases, and misfortunes, which they feel are God's response to homosexuality. Here is a representative press release:

Thank God for the Utah Mine Disaster! WBC to picket the memories services for the six dead miners in the central Utah coal mine—assuming they are dead, after so long a time missing without a word or a sound; in religious protest and warning; to wit; God Hates Fags!

& Fag-Enablers—Ergo, God hates Utah and America for surrendering to the fag agenda, and because of which God is now punishing this evil, sodomite nation with disaster after disaster, including 9/11, Iraq, Katrina, West Virginia Mine Disaster, Virginia Tech Massacre, [and] The Shuttle Disaster.[14]

Thankfully, very few Americans imagine a God with such hateful qualities. The Westboro Baptists resemble some other Americans in their belief that God has laid out clear moral guidelines that we must follow lest we suffer his wrath. But nearly all Americans still think of God as predominantly a force of love. And the love of God prevents most believers from going to such extremes.

Our Moral Enemies

One of the founders of sociology, Émile Durkheim, imagined a hypothetical "society of saints" composed of flawless individuals who never lie, cheat, steal, or murder.[15] Would a place where everyone followed the dictates of a loving God still argue over morality? Durkheim says, unequivocally, "Yes." But why? Durkheim argues that behaviors that seem benign or inconsequential to us would become the basis of bitter disputes in a society of saints. For instance, one saint might be notorious for his bad breath or irritating voice. Another might be pilloried for her unkempt hair or poor manners. For Durkheim, the process of identifying sinners serves a vital societal function, because sharing moral standards enhances our collective strength.

Kai Erikson provides an interesting example of this dynamic in his examination of the Salem witch trials.[16] In many ways, seventeenth-century Massachusetts was as close as one could get to a society of saints where almost everyone followed strict codes of conduct and there was little fear of violence or crime from within the community. But according to Erikson, this bucolic life fostered the birth of a wholly fictitious moral enemy—the dreaded witch. Consumed with the possibility that witches were in their midst, Salem residents famously accused their neighbors and friends of witchcraft—even killing some of them. But far from tearing the community apart, Erikson argues, these acts of betrayal and murder strengthened the unity and resolve of the "good" colonists.

Indeed, finding an enemy of sufficient evil helps us feel better about our own more petty sins. Consider the popularity of the "To Catch a Predator" series of television specials produced by NBC's *Dateline*. For the show, *Dateline* would conduct "investigations" in Internet chat rooms where volunteers pose as underage kids and wait for men to contact them. When the online conversation becomes sexually explicit, the decoy claims he or she will soon be home alone and suggests meeting in person. As the decoys lure potential sexual predators, the *Dateline* crew lies in wait with hidden cameras. In a typical case, the predator is prompted to enter the home by a young actor, who then quickly exits the scene with some excuse, asking the target to wait. The show's host then emerges to chastise the man and inform him that all of his nefarious activities will soon be televised.

Considering the role that the "bad" people play in making the rest of us look good, the popularity of "To Catch a Predator" is easy to comprehend. Viewers are invited to delight in the public humiliation of this common enemy as the show's host reads embarrassing transcripts from chat sessions. Later episodes involve local police, providing the additional satisfaction of watching the potential pedophile thrown to the ground and handcuffed. Suddenly, taking supplies from the office or cheating on your taxes doesn't seem so bad.

The culture wars provide us with clearly defined moral enemies. For some, the enemies are religious fanatics like the Westboro Baptists, who threaten our freedoms and civility by insisting that their fringe views be imposed on the rest of us. For others, the enemies are godless degenerates who threaten our moral communities with the temptations of secular hedonism.[17] These two feared enemies, one bursting with fanaticism and the other consumed by depravity, have long existed in our country and are often connected to religious concerns. In 1822, Thomas Jefferson warned that "the atmosphere of our country is unquestionably charged with a threatening cloud of religious fanaticism, lighter in some parts, denser in others, but too heavy in all."[18] Twenty years earlier, President John Adams proclaimed, "I have never read of an irreligious character in Greek or Roman history, not in any history, nor have I known one in life, who was not a rascal. Name one if you can living or dead."[19]

Yet the religious nut and the depraved atheist are harder to find than we are led to believe. It is tragic when the Westboro Baptists, or similar extreme fundamentalist groups, come to represent religious conservatism in America, because they do not espouse the beliefs of any substantial portion of the population. While we are wise to carefully scrutinize extremists in our midst, too often we create misinformed exaggerations or deliberate misrepresentations of the vast majority of our moral opponents.

The threat of atheism is especially exaggerated. Atheists are among the most despised minority groups in America.[20] But why? Perhaps they are easy targets because their numbers are so limited. Their demonization by conservative pundits fuels the misperception that atheists are bent on the obliteration of religion. While specific atheist groups and antireligious intellectuals can be quite vocal in their disdain for religion, most atheists in the United States just want the freedom to hold their own beliefs without derision. For instance, we spoke with Bill, a civic-minded man who has never proselytized his atheism yet feels attacked for his beliefs. Bill asked, "Why do I have to believe in God to raise my children to respect other people, respect lives, respect the rules of society in general, and to be good productive human beings?" Like Bill, law-abiding Americans without faith in God feel unjustly obliged to defend their goodness, as if it is presumed to be lacking.

As Durkheim noted, we will never be rid of our tendencies to exaggerate our moral enemies, but when it comes to morality, we are actually more alike than we are different. Americans share a general moral culture in which we behave civilly, respect the rights of others, and feel outrage at similar injustices, cruelties, and depravities. We tend to agree on the relative importance of immoral behaviors. And most significantly, a vast majority of Americans agree that God is loving. These countless believers feel compelled to take into consideration, when pondering the sins of others, their belief that God loves all humanity. In the end, a belief in God's love is extremely influential in keeping believers well mannered and compassionate. For this reason, we all benefit from the idea of God's love, whether we are sinners or saints, believers or atheists.

FOUR

God and Science

The human mind evolved to believe in the gods. It did not evolve to believe in biology. . . . The uncomfortable truth is that the two beliefs are not factually compatible. As a result those who hunger for both intellectual and religious truth will never acquire both in full measure.

—*E. O. Wilson, biologist*

I believe God did intend, in giving us intelligence, to give us the opportunity to investigate and appreciate the wonders of His creation. He is not threatened by our scientific adventures.
—*Francis Collins, head of the Human Genome Project*

On June 26, 2000, as "Hail to the Chief" played in the background, President Bill Clinton entered the East Room of the White House, flanked by Francis Collins and J. Craig Venter. Collins, director of the Human Genome Project, had led an international group of scientists in an effort to decode the human DNA sequence. Venter's private company, Celera Genomics, had engaged in a parallel endeavor using different techniques. Their efforts had resulted in the "most important, most wondrous map ever produced," the president announced. "More than a thousand researchers across six nations have revealed nearly all three billion letters of our miraculous genetic code."[1]

But as President Clinton continued speaking, he veered into a seemingly unrelated topic—God: "Today, we are learning the language in which God created life. We are gaining ever more awe for the complexity, the beauty, the wonder of God's most divine and sacred gift. With this profound new knowledge, humankind is on the verge of gaining immense, new power to heal."[2] What place does God have in understanding the Human Genome Project? The mapping of the genome was the result of years of hard work that drew on the skills of geneticists, physicians, statisticians, computer scientists, and a host of other specialists, as well as countless earlier breakthroughs in genetics. Francis Collins skillfully managed an endeavor some described as bigger than the Apollo space program, arguably the greatest scientific accomplishment in the history of mankind.[3] Was Collins appalled by Clinton's injection of religion into an event to celebrate the work of scientists? Not at all, actually.

A former atheist, Collins began to consider the existence of God during medical school, when he was struck by the faith of seriously ill patients. He studied world religions, spoke with a Methodist minister, and read *Mere Christianity* by C. S. Lewis. As Collins explains in his meditation on science and religion, *The Language of God*:

> I had started on this journey of intellectual exploration to confirm my atheism. That now lay in ruins as [C. S. Lewis's arguments and others] forced me to admit the plausibility of the God hypothesis. Agnosticism, which had seemed like a safe second-place haven, now loomed like the great cop-out it often is. Faith in God now seemed more rational than disbelief.[4]

Collins sees no conflict between his scientific research and his belief in God. And no one would claim that his work in sequencing the human genome is fundamentally flawed because of his faith. In fact, Collins's faith provides some of the motivation for his work and influences his interpretation of its significance. When given his turn at the podium, Collins echoed President Clinton's comments: "It's a happy day for the world. It is humbling for me, and awe-inspiring, to realize that we have caught the first glimpse of our own instruction book, previously known only to God."[5]

But we also wonder what J. Craig Venter, the *other* scientist seated behind the president on this historic day, was thinking as Clinton and

Collins spoke about God. We imagine that he was not so pleased. An atheist himself, Venter provided an effusive back-cover blurb for *The God Delusion*, an argument against the plausibility of religious belief by Oxford professor Richard Dawkins. "Richard Dawkins is the leading soothsayer of our times," Venter wrote.[6]

So who is correct—the believer or the atheist? We cannot provide the answer to this question, but we can at least tell you what most Americans think.

Science and Atheism

In their fight against religious dogmatism, some academics and scientists argue that the world of ideas is hopelessly divided, with faith on one side and science on the other. While the back-and-forth between religious scientists, such as Francis Collins and John Polkinghorne, and antireligious intellectuals, such as Richard Dawkins and Victor Stenger, makes for fascinating reading, we expect it has little real impact on either science or religion. Although discussions about the truth or falsity of atheism may engage academic scientists, many of whom struggle with the idea of belief in God, the concept of atheism has never appealed to the American public.[7] Consequently, attitudes about the compatibility of science and religion don't pit atheists against believers.

In fact, there has never really been any question *whether* average Americans reconcile faith and science. They do so every day, even if they do not realize it. Most Americans utilize the latest technologies and medicines with full confidence that science will continue to improve our knowledge, comfort, and health. It is rare for even the most devout Americans to eschew medicine or technology for religious reasons. With this in mind, it makes more sense to ponder *when* and *how* Americans seek scientific or religious answers to their questions. For most, choosing between science and religion is not an either-or proposition but rather an ongoing collaboration and negotiation between two commitments— one to science and the other to God.[8]

The late biologist and historian of science Stephen Jay Gould attempted to reconcile science and religion by claiming that they were "non-overlapping magisterial" (often called NOMA). According to Gould, the domains of science and religion have different areas of expertise.

Science excels at investigating the "empirical construction of the universe," while religion focuses on "the search for proper ethical values and the spiritual meaning of our lives."[9] Neither sphere is properly equipped to comment on the other. Science lacks the ability to explain morality and the human conscience; religion provides guidance on moral issues but lacks the tools to effectively test truth claims. A proper understanding of the world, Gould concludes, requires input from both spheres.

Gould argued that science and religion are complementary as long as they are mutually respectful partners. But herein lies the problem—what questions and problems should be "respectfully" the sole domain of religion or science? Certain secular intellectuals balk at the idea that religion can assert the true answer to moral or existential questions. As Dawkins argues, the NOMA argument is reckless "to allow religion to make claims and then place those claims outside scientific scrutiny."[10] On the other side, some believers staunchly oppose widely accepted scientific theories, such as the theory of evolution, on the grounds that it contradicts biblical descriptions of creation. As a college-educated woman told us, "The earth was created in seven literal days! And any true science goes along with that." Consequently, it would be difficult, if not impossible, to get believers, nonbelievers, and scientists to agree on the proper domains of religious and scientific expertise.

A key predictor of where Americans draw the dividing line between science and religion is the type of God they worship. In the end, some Gods tread boldly into the realm of working scientists while other Gods happily leave science to its own devices.

Einstein's God

When asked about his religious faith, Albert Einstein replied, "I believe in Spinoza's God who reveals himself in the orderly harmony of what exists, not in a God who concerns himself with fates and actions of human beings."[11] With this simple statement, Einstein provides us with a deep insight into how his belief in God was compatible with his commitment to scientific discovery and rigor.

Baruch Spinoza, a Dutch philosopher, is often associated with the modern concept of *pantheism*—the view that God and the universe are one and the same. Because God is indistinguishable from the laws of nature, Spinoza argued, the universe unfolds according to observable mechanisms of cause and effect. Indeed, Spinoza felt that the idea that God would subject nature to his momentary whims was "absurd." He complained bitterly that "some assert that God, like a man, consists of body and mind, and is susceptible of passions. How far such persons have strayed from the truth is . . . evident."[12]

Because Spinoza believed God was infinite and ever-present, he felt that God could not logically be distinct from his creation. Thus, the best way to understand God is through his creation, and the way to understand creation is through science. Spinoza made it clear that faith in God needs to be informed by science and not vice versa. Spinoza's God—the God of nature—fit ideally with the intellectual, philosophical, and scientific culture of the Enlightenment.

Philosophical attempts to break with tradition often come into conflict with established religion, and Spinoza's God is no exception.[13] As philosopher Matthew Stewart notes in *The Courtier and the Heretic*, the character of God formed the basis of a heated debate between religious traditionalists and religious progressives for centuries to come, and that debate can be summarized by the exchange between Spinoza (the "heretic" of Stewart's story) and Gottfried Leibniz (the "courtier"). Leibniz, a brilliant German mathematician, was deeply offended by Spinoza's thought and advocated a more biblical conception of God—one who thinks, feels, judges, and exists independently of the laws of nature.[14] God could have made any of an infinite variety of worlds, Leibniz argued, each operating under slightly different rules and laws. Yet he chose to make this one, which happens to be perfect for human habitation and shows evidence that we are to play an important role in the religious purpose of the universe. For Leibniz, subsuming God within the fabric of nature was tantamount to killing him.

The Gods of Spinoza and Leibniz are still with us today and inform discussions of science in modern America. A true estimation of how many Americans believe in Spinoza's God would be admittedly meager. Nearly all American believers report affiliation with some traditional religion, mainly Protestant Christianity, which advocates a personified version of God. In other words, most Americans have some sense that God is a being separate from nature who has opinions about the world and acts outside the usual restrictions of cause and effect.

That said, there is great variation in the extent to which Americans feel that God manipulates nature. We asked Americans a question that addresses this very issue: "Does God often perform miracles which defy the laws of nature?" Those who believe in a God who brings people back from cardiac arrest, who holds up falling buildings for a few extra seconds to allow the innocent to escape, or who produces storms as warning signs to sinners express faith in a kind of God who is the antithesis of Spinoza's. Believers who doubt the existence of such miracles tend to feel that nature is God's miracle and that he does not suspend the laws of physics for any reason.

Overall, we find that Americans who believe in Authoritative and Benevolent Gods are much more likely to think that God is manipulating the world in both big and small ways (see figure 4.1). A vast majority of them (92 percent of believers in an Authoritative God and 88 percent of believers in a Benevolent God) think that God very often disrupts nature with divine intervention. Consequently, we can think of Authoritative and Benevolent Gods as irreconcilable with Spinoza's conception of a God of nature, while the Critical and Distant Gods display, at the very least, a tendency to stay out of the way of the natural order. In this way, the Critical and Distant Gods avoid Spinoza's main criticism of traditional conceptions of God—that God cannot, under any circumstances, override the laws of science.

With these new categories in mind, we can begin to test some possible connections between images of God and one's view of science. Namely, are Americans with a more Spinoza-like God also more likely to approve of and accept current scientific thinking on a number of topics? Or put another way, to what extent do believers in an Authoritative or Benevolent God feel that modern science is stepping on the toes of the almighty?

Skeptics: Part I

We often think of skeptics as individuals who disparage faith and persistently question the beliefs of their peers. The scientist ideally approaches her work as a true skeptic and rigorously challenges her own beliefs in hopes of exposing false knowledge. Following this practice, many Americans question claims made by professional scientists. But their skepticism is based on preexisting beliefs about the world. In fact, the

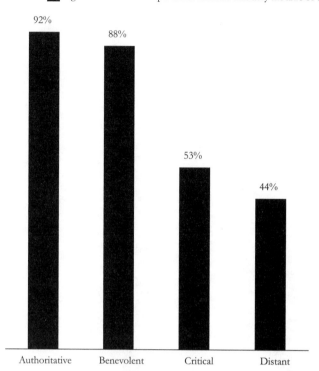

Figure 4.1. God's Intervention

Americans most skeptical of the claims of scientists are the ones who believe most firmly that God closely guides their daily actions and the world around them. Given their strong faith in God's plan, these believers express a deep suspicion of the ultimate promise and importance of science.

Americans who believe in a highly engaged God (both Authoritative and Benevolent Gods) are most likely to think that science will *not* provide solutions to most of our problems (see figure 4.2). They also fear that we rely too heavily on science to solve our problems and fail to properly consider the importance of faith in creating a better world. Believers in a Spinoza-like God (both Critical and Distant Gods) reverse this trend and express more confidence in the long-term potential of science. Not surprisingly, atheists rely most heavily on science to resolve the current and future problems of humanity.

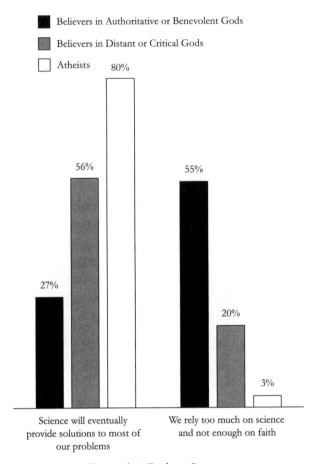

■ Believers in Authoritative or Benevolent Gods

▨ Believers in Distant or Critical Gods

□ Atheists

Figure 4.2. Faith in Science

This general skepticism of science among believers in Authoritative and Benevolent Gods carries over into attitudes about specific scientific claims. Most manifestly, the vast majority of these believers are skeptical of the theory of evolution, with less than a fifth reporting to think that "humans evolved from primates" (see figure 4.3). The number of Americans who keenly doubt evolution is striking, given that, as the late biologist Stephen Jay Gould passionately argued, the academic community is firmly convinced that evolution has occurred. Gould asserted that debates between professional scientists are not about *if* evolution occurred, but instead about *how* it occurred.[15] In no other instance do we find such a considerable incongruity

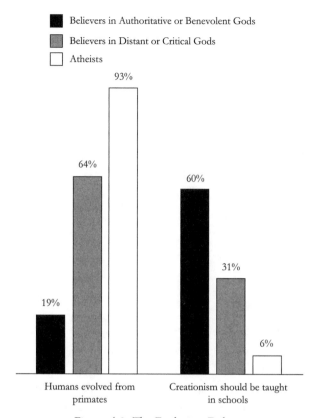

Figure 4.3. The Evolution Debate

between the attitudes of the religious public and those of the scientific community.

A clear majority of believers in Authoritative and Benevolent Gods feel that "creationism should be taught in schools." For these believers, the theory of evolution is an attack on religious thought, not an established scientific principle. As Elaine, a secretary from a small firm in the Midwest, told us, "You have to have a lot more faith to believe in evolution than to believe that God created everything. Evolution seems like a totally crazy theory." When confronted with scientific statements that appear to contradict biblical accounts of creation, Elaine chose to side with her religious faith.

This is not the case for believers in Distant and Critical Gods, a vast majority of whom think that creationism has no legitimate scientific merits and cannot be justifiably taught in science classes.

Consequently, the evolution-creationism debate is premised not on religious faith but on differences of opinion about the role of God in the world. It comes down to which domain of knowledge is given priority when a conflict arises; some prioritize their preestablished religious beliefs, and others prioritize the claims of professional scientists. Simply put, believers in Authoritative or Benevolent Gods want to temper scientific claims with the wisdom of their religious texts. This is partly because they tend to view God as hands-on. Authoritative and Benevolent Gods have agency and decide how the world will unfold. Believers in Distant or Critical Gods more often temper their interpretation of religious texts with the wisdom of scientists. Distant and Critical Gods are removed from the world. It follows that the world operates via a natural order that was put in place by God.

Playing God

A pervading skepticism of scientific research within certain religious enclaves has ramifications beyond the school curriculum. Conflicts between science and religion make for good stories. Western culture is full of anecdotes in which scientists arrogantly play God by using scientific research in ways that are immoral or unnatural and, ultimately, suffer disastrous consequences. *Frankenstein* is the prototype of this morality tale. In it, a man of science audaciously creates a new life-form. His creation becomes a monster that ultimately kills him. Believers who stress God's earthly authority often think that modern scientists are as brash as Dr. Frankenstein and similarly feel that "most scientists are hostile to religion."[16] As such, these believers imagine that some scientists cunningly hope to disprove religious doctrines and challenge the authority of God. Therefore, scientific claims about the world are to be mistrusted, especially when they address issues of creation, life, and cosmic order. Like the morality tale in *Frankenstein*, these believers warn us that if we place too much faith in science, we will suffer grave consequences.

A good example of where some believers feel that science has overstepped its moral boundaries is stem-cell research. The best predictor of whether an American thinks that embryonic stem-cell use is "always wrong" is the person's image of God. In fact, within Mainline, Catholic, and even evangelical religious traditions, we find that believers in Spinoza's

God are likely to support the use of stem cells in research (see figure 4.4). It tends to be believers in Authoritative and Benevolent Gods, regardless of their church affiliation, who oppose using stem cells under any circumstances. Again, this issue is driven by a perception that stem-cell research is undermining God's authority, and in the end, any benefit we reap from this endeavor will ultimately be outweighed by the costs of usurping God.

Scientists who follow biotechnology policies around the world have found that variations in research laws directly correspond to the dominant religion of the country. Namely, countries with Christian traditions are far more likely to ban the cloning of human embryos for scientific research than countries with Hindu or Buddhist traditions.[17] Molecular biologist Lee Silver speculates on why this is the case:

> Most people in Hindu and Buddhist countries have a root tradition in which there is no single creator God. Instead, there may be no gods or many gods, and there is no master plan for the universe. Instead, spirits are eternal and individual virtue—karma—determines what happens to your spirit in your next life. With some exceptions, this view generally allows the acceptance of both embryo research to support life and genetically modify crops.[18]

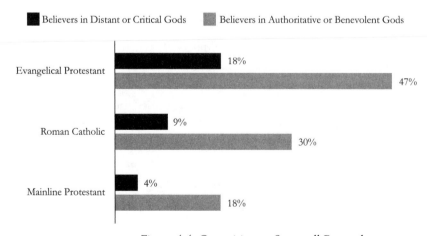

Figure 4.4. Opposition to Stem-cell Research

Similarly, American Christians who believe in Spinoza's God find nothing morally provocative about stem-cell research, mainly because they do not view this scientific activity as infringing on their understanding of God's authority.

Overall, American skepticism about research tends not to be the product of an exhaustive commitment to the scientific method but rather a commitment to the idea that God is in control of nature. From this perspective, scientific research runs the risk of infringing on God's authority. By contrast, those who believe in a God who is one with nature view science not as a potential threat to their faith, but as the very means to better understand their spirituality.

The Cult of Science

While American believers are divided in how they feel about the motives of the scientific establishment, its legitimacy, and its supposed overconfidence, they are united by a commitment to the idea of science. In other words, a vast majority of Americans want to appear "scientific." The alternative is being irrational or crazy. American culture is pervaded by a deep respect for and deference to anything scientific.

When directly asked about the importance of science, most believers attempt to reconcile science and their faith at a very basic level. We often heard Americans talk about scientific advances as evidence of divine power. As a middle-aged Roman Catholic man told us:

> I think science is a great thing. I think what we have accomplished in the last twenty-five years in medicine is phenomenal. I believe that is something that is unexplainable for all the diseases that we have been able to look at and taken care of. I think God had something to do with those findings. I think the minds of very intelligent people had a lot to do with that and I think they would love to believe in their minds. I think that they were guided by God. . . . I would say knowledge is from God, because he gave us the ability to learn and to perform our jobs as we see it. . . . He is trying to help us to live better. And it might be just through science and that the Lord is all working [it] out.

Because most Americans recognize and are surrounded by the concrete advances of science, they mostly treat the idea of science with profound respect, often attaching to it a divine mission. As an elderly woman told us, "I think that, basically, science gives us a sense of a wonder of God." Within our shared respect and awe of science, debates about evolution or stem-cell research tend not to be about the falsity of science but rather the accuracy and legitimacy of particular scientific claims and methods.

Not surprisingly, we find that when believers feel that God's authority is threatened by science, they try to reroute conventional science rather than completely disregard it. The effort to bring scientific authenticity to the biblical story of creation is a perfect example of how even biblical literalists fear being labeled "unscientific." Demanding that the story of creation be taught in science classes represents, perhaps ironically, a deference to the importance of science.

The Science of Genesis

The quiet town of Glen Rose, Texas (population 2,000), sits at the confluence of the Paluxy and Brazos rivers and the junction of two highways, about an hour from Dallas. Over the years, the town has struggled to survive through changes in industry and identity. A small college opened in 1879, passed through several administrations, and had ceased operations by 1910. An assortment of doctors and healers flocked to Glen Rose during the health and wellness crazes of the late 1800s, taking advantage of abundant "medicinal" mineral springs. Entrepreneurs built sanatoriums, and local businesses advertised the healing powers of the local water. It proved a passing fad. The Depression, declining agriculture, and the flight of many residents in search of jobs consigned Glen Rose to quaint, small-town status. Today, the historic downtown consists of a magnificent county courthouse, ringed by a haphazard assortment of antique, gift, and coffee shops. Locals do most of their business along highway 67, which is lined with fast-food restaurants, gas stations, a grocery store, and a few hotels. It is safe to say that Glen Rose might be entirely forgotten, were it not for something that occurred more than a hundred million years ago.

During the Cretaceous period, a brontosaurus (or apatosaurus) ambled through the Paluxy riverbed.[19] The thirty- to fifty-foot-long beast left behind clawed back footprints and elephant-like front prints. A predator stalked the riverbed nearby. At twenty to thirty feet long, the meat-eating, bipedal acrocanthosaurus was a formidable hunter. It left behind clawed footprints measuring more than two feet in length. For some, the coincidence of the two trackways merely demonstrates that the area was a fertile feeding and hunting ground for multiple dinosaur species. The Texas Natural Science Center provides a more exciting alternative—the tracks are evidence of an ancient battle between hunter and hunted.[20] Whatever their meaning, a series of fortuitous circumstances preserved the tracks, which were discovered in 1930. Glen Rose had finally found its identity. Dinosaur Valley State Park provides views of the riverbed and its tracks. Two enormous fiberglass models of a *Tyrannosaurus rex* and the apatosaurus stand guard outside the park's gift shop. Inside, one is confronted with a bewildering variety of dinosaur trinkets. Lodging is available at the nearby Dinosaur Valley Inn and Suites.

Still more dinosaur-related tourism is available in Glen Rose. It seems that a set of humanlike tracks have also been preserved in the Paluxy riverbed, at times even overlapping those of the dinosaurs. For most scientists, these are simply the distorted tracks of a smaller dinosaur, outright hoaxes, or the result of erosion. But for Carl Baugh, the tracks are rock-solid proof that "man and dinosaurs lived contemporaneously." Baugh belongs to a small subculture of conservative Christians, often called Young Earth Creationists, who believe that the world was created in six days and is only a few thousand years old at most.[21] Proving that man coexisted with dinosaurs would demonstrate that the time line of Earth is too short to support theories of evolution. Still better would be to prove that dinosaurs *still* exist, which has prompted Baugh to lead three expeditions in Papua New Guinea in search of living pterodactyls. A controversial figure even among creationists, Baugh opened the Creation Evidence Museum in Glen Rose in July 1984 to present "academic evidence" for God's creation.[22]

The museum houses reproductions of key pieces of creationist evidence, including a purported fossilized human track, an ancient human finger, and a hammer embedded in stone.[23] Several exhibits depict humans' coexistence with dinosaurs, and a large mural shows children frolicking in a lake next to a friendly brontosaurus. Quite clearly, these images are meant to appeal to youthful fantasies. A distinct focus on children becomes more evident in the museum's bookstore, which is dominated by texts, such as *In the Days of Noah*, *Animals of the Bible*, and *Dinosaurs by Design*, targeted specifically to young adults. *What Was It Like at the Beginning?* concludes with the promise that "the earth will be restored or changed back to what it was like in the beginning. Once again dinosaurs will roam the earth."[24] What child wouldn't want to ride a dinosaur to school? The museum leaves young visitors with the sense that this is a very real possibility.

When asked why so much of their literature is geared toward bringing Young Earth Creationism to a young audience rather than meaningfully addressing the scientific evidence of evolution, the gift shop's manager answered that the ultimate purpose of the museum was to show children the continued authority of God. He mused that "young people today want a God that lets them do what they want. They've moved God out of their lives. They don't want to think that God judges. They don't want to think that God might flood the world, like he did with Noah."

So while the pretense of engaging the scientific record of prehistoric times pervades the museum, its primary message is about the ultimate authority of God. Scientific language merely provides a rhetorical veneer for its true purpose—bringing a particular image of God to the masses. The commitment to demonstrate the earthly authority of God with pseudoscience bluntly demonstrates the museum's inability to shake off science entirely. Put more simply, to understand why someone would use the tools of science to promote seemingly unscientific claims, we must appreciate their conception of God.

Skeptics: Part II

The Creation Evidence Museum and other shrines to the young Earth clearly illustrate the extent to which believers want their religion to be consistent with science. Survey research consistently finds that between 40 percent and 50 percent of Americans accept a biblical creation narrative, but to say that half of the public rejects evolution entirely would be incorrect.[25] A 2007 *USA Today*/Gallup Poll found that more than half of

Americans believe that evolution is "definitely true" or "probably true." And yet nearly two-thirds of respondents to the same poll also believe that creationism is "definitely" or "probably true."[26] Many believers feel that it is by no means illogical to believe in both, stating that God presided over the whole process of evolution.[27] Karl, an elderly man who is retired from the ministry, pointed out that "the creation story in scripture does not say how God created it. It says in the beginning God created. And so, I have no problem at all with the theory of evolution. God can work however God chooses to work. I don't see any conflict between religion and science that we don't manufacture." Like Karl, most religious believers, regardless of whether they are Young Earth Creationists or proponents of evolution, come together in a shared conviction that religion and science can exist in perfect harmony.

Only a small minority of believers in Authoritative and Benevolent Gods (11 percent) and believers in Distant and Critical Gods (18 percent) think that "science and religion are incompatible" (see figure 4.5). In other words, nearly all believers think that science is not a true threat to their faith, even though they often bitterly dispute the legitimacy of specific scientific claims and the political motivations of professional scientists.

Instead, skepticism about the ultimate compatibility of religion and science comes overwhelmingly from the nonreligious community. More than half of atheists feel that science and religion cannot productively coexist—that one will naturally try to diminish the other. When one considers some of the more outrageous attempts by believers to turn their religious beliefs into "science," the skepticism of nonbelievers is understandable. Creation science museums certainly do not help the cause of reconciliation. Howard, an ardent atheist, explained that he fears religion because it could undermine our scientific progress. Howard worries:

> A lot of organized religion is contradictory to science; very openly in some respects. They believe that the earth is only six thousand years old, and we were created in seven days by God. In most cases they think biblical time lines are correct and science is wrong. . . . You say you're rational, but there is a conflict in a lot of cases where religion based on their beliefs of evolution or whatever contradicts science.

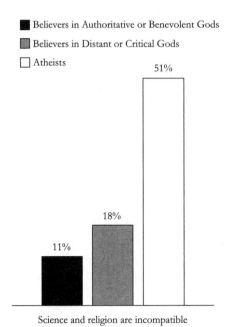

Figure 4.5. Science and Religion

Howard's concerns are shared by many nonbelievers, who simply do not trust religious people to be rational. They worry that believers will always allow the Bible to trump scientific findings. Just like some believers are skeptical of the scientific community, we find that nonbelievers are dubious of any believer who claims to understand and support science.

Nonbelievers are also wary of attempts to adapt religion to fit science. For instance, attempts to reconcile evolution with the Bible have led to ongoing reinterpretations of the story of creation. Day-age theories of creation equate the "days" of Genesis to millennia. Gap theorists prefer to call a day a day but hypothesize that those days occurred millions of years apart. Progressive creationists accept mainstream scientific research on the geological history of Earth but believe that major changes in species require God's direct intervention. Evolution can happen, according to progressive creationists, but only after God provides the template. These various versions of the story of creation appear silly to nonbelievers, many of whom feel that these constant revisions are missing an obvious point—that religious accounts of creation are just stories made up by people who knew nothing about modern-day science.

The concept of intelligent design (ID), championed by the mathematician William A. Dembski and others, has received considerable attention in recent years.[28] Though similar to progressive creationism, advocates of ID champion it as a scientific alternative to disinterested agnosticism. Proponents argue that the natural world is too "irreducibly complex" to have arisen without a designer guiding its development. Mainstream evolutionary scientists have rebutted such claims with contradictory evidence.[29] But no matter how sophisticated or intricate the ID argument gets, most nonbelievers simply are uninterested in hearing about God or an "ultimate designer" when discussing physics and biology. As with creation science, the ID movement has done little to quell the ire of nonbelievers who feel that activists are inappropriately attempting to insert their personal religious beliefs into investigations that should remain strictly scientific. But the question of what is "strictly scientific" is the very crux of the debate. Proponents of ID argue passionately that the question of a creator is one that can and should be addressed by science.

The extent to which an American is sympathetic to the ID perspective is determined by her image of God. While believers in Authoritative and Benevolent Gods find it crucial to combine religious and scientific wisdom, most believers in Spinoza's God are happy to leave science alone while still allowing their personal religious interpretation of science to flourish. Believers who work in science-related fields tend to be examples of this phenomenon. For instance, Cynthia, a believer in a Distant God and a lab technician, explained to us:

> I think that a lot of times, some of the scientific discoveries actually support God in ways that we never anticipated. It doesn't matter what you call God. . . . I find that the more I know about science, the more nascent I think God is. And this is a discussion we have in our household very often, because I have a son who is a biology major who's planning to go on to medical school. And so we have these discussions, and he was so concerned about how his faith would stand with the science. If anything, it's strengthened it. . . . I think that people need to be open to scientific discoveries and things.

For believers like Cynthia, scientific discoveries produce reverence for the natural world, which they view as God's creation. As such, they tend to be unconcerned with debates over intelligent design or creation science because their faith needs no scientific justification. An Episcopalian who studies biology and physics, and is especially interested in the science of the brain, argued that "the stuff people are doing with the brain and consciousness just takes us deeper into the heart of God." The comments of believers like these, who understand academic science and believe in a Distant God, mirror closely the spirituality of Albert Einstein.

Many nonbelievers and skeptics of the compatibility of science and religion tend to discount the manner in which scientifically minded people reconcile their faith and their respect for scientific knowledge. In their view, science will benefit from the disappearance of religion. While this is strictly theoretical, we can look more specifically at how differing religious beliefs affect public opinion concerning the funding of science. Because science is dependent upon public support, this seems to be the place where we can see the extent to which our collective commitment to science is merely rhetorical and whether religion really impairs the daily workings of scientists.

Does Religion Hurt Science?

Given the unquestionable success of the American scientific enterprise, it is striking that the primary predictor of whether an American feels that the government should provide more or less financial support for science is her image of God. In a certain sense, the future of America as a scientific leader depends on our conceptions of the unseen and unprovable.

Evangelical Protestants are often painted as inherently unscientific and unsupportive of science. A simplistic analysis might seem to support such a contention (see figure 4.6). Only 24 percent of evangelical Protestants believe we are spending too little as a nation to support scientific research. Mainline Protestants and Catholics are significantly more supportive of the scientific enterprise.

But this hides an important division within the ranks of evangelical Protestants. Namely, evangelical Protestants who believe in Distant or

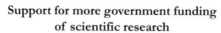

Support for more government funding of scientific research

Figure 4.6

Source: Baylor Religion Survey, Wave 2 (2007). Respondents were asked, "How do you feel about current government spending" about several programs, including "supporting scientific research." Possible responses included "too little," "just about right," "too much," and "don't know." In the above figure we examine those who say that current government funding for supporting scientific research is "too little."

Critical Gods are much more likely to support science funding than evangelicals who believe in Authoritative or Benevolent Gods (see figure 4.7). An evangelical who believes in a Distant or Critical God is nearly twice as likely (41.4 percent) to call for increased funding for scientific research than a fellow evangelical who prefers an Authoritative or Benevolent God (24.1 percent). The same is true for Roman Catholics. The effect is less pronounced for Mainline Protestants but still significant—Mainline believers in Distant or Critical Gods are the most supportive of science.

The potential for both accord and conflict between God and science is further revealed by responses to the statement "Science helps to reveal God's glory" (see figure 4.8). More than two-thirds of those with Authoritative or Benevolent Gods agree that science is a window into God's plan, compared with only a third of those with Critical or Distant Gods and, strangely, a handful of atheists. In a certain sense, we should expect the belief that science reveals God's handiwork to be beneficial to the development of science, for it reveals a belief that science is "good." On the other hand, Christian believers in Authoritative and Benevolent Gods stress God's authority over the natural world so much that they are skeptical of any scientific claims that appear to contradict

**Support for more government funding
of scientific research**

■ Believers in Distant or Critical Gods ▨ Believers in Authoritative or Benevolent Gods

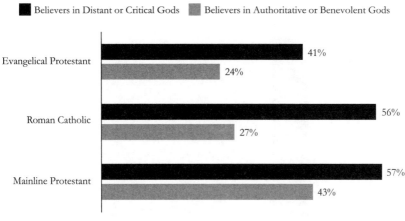

Figure 4.7

the Bible. After all, if science is to reveal God's glory, then perhaps it must defer to his book.

Because many Authoritative and Benevolent God believers remain committed to the idea of science, they tend to seek scientific explanations that support their beliefs, like creation science and intelligent design. These believers feel that government funding of academic research is questionable, mainly because they believe there is an antireligious bias in the scientific community.

Believers in Distant or Critical Gods express the opposite view. They retain their faith in God but don't believe scientists have an antireligious agenda. Instead, they see academic science as an important source of human knowledge that partially fulfills their striving to understand God's creation. In turn, they are much more likely to want science generously funded by their tax dollars.

Therefore, in simple dollars and cents, it is evident that religion is not inexorably bad for scientific research. Clearly, a proportion of the American public wants to reduce spending on science for religious reasons, yet at the same time, another segment of the religious population values science not only for what it produces but also for its exploration of the unknown. For these Americans, the great unknown goes by the name of God. And their devotion to science is almost religious.

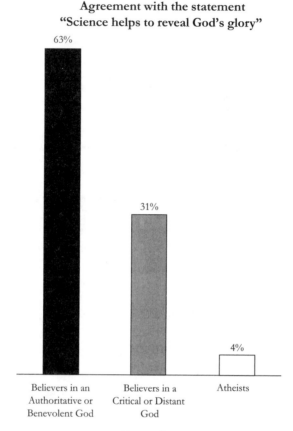

**Agreement with the statement
"Science helps to reveal God's glory"**

Figure 4.8

Accounting for God

Most Americans think that belief in God is fully compatible with modern science. The world's major religious traditions have demonstrated an amazing ability to incorporate scientific thinking. The fact that many of our leading scientists still express a faith in God is also solid evidence that scientific understanding need not erase religious belief. The perspective of Francis Collins is shared by a vast majority of Americans. While other examinations of the interplay between science and religion tend to contrast the scientific import of atheism versus belief, this line of inquiry is relatively meaningless in a culture where belief in God is ubiquitous. Current books about the intellectual deficiencies of believers have sold very well to a specific segment of the

American public, but overall these arguments fall on deaf ears. There is no doubt that most Americans are believers and still revere science.

This is not where the story ends. Many American religious believers also feel that scientists overstep the boundaries of science and begin to tread on religion's turf. This fact stems from a persistent belief in the supreme authority of God over nature. If history is any guide, steadfast believers in Authoritative and Benevolent Gods will routinely cede more ground to the advances in science but will remain the staunchest skeptics of professional scientists, whom they view as a continued threat to God's authority.

FIVE

God and Mammon

Let no man seek his own, but every man another's wealth.

—*1 Corinthians 10:24*

"American culture encourages us to view economic problems essentially in moral terms," argues sociologist Robert Wuthnow, explaining that "whether a person attributes these problems to greed or to men shirking their God-given male roles, the logic is still that morality is at fault, rather than something endemic in the economic system itself." Economist Charles North views this tendency as counterproductive, especially for a religious public that values fairness and equal opportunity; he laments, "Too often, Christians ask only one question when choosing a course of action—'Is it righteous?'—and forget to ask whether a thing is likewise prudent or possible."[1] As we have seen, what Americans think is righteous is dependent on their God. In turn, our Gods have very different things to say about what we can do to cure our economic woes.

In our discussions with all kinds of believers, we encountered confusion about how God feels about secular solutions to poverty and economic inequality. Gary, a middle-class evangelical from California and believer in an Authoritative God, expressed a common concern:

> I don't know if God views social welfare as a way of caring for those
> around us, or does it just feed a broken system. Does it help people,
> or does it give a Band-Aid to a system where alcoholics are on welfare
> to feed their addiction . . . but, then again, there are moms on welfare

107

who eventually get off of it, and this is a good result. I think God can find good in that. But my question always comes up, is social welfare being faithful to the gospel and faithful to our calling?

Like Gary, many Americans who believe in an Authoritative God struggle with how God wants them to address poverty and inequality. A big problem for these believers is the extent to which secular intervention fails to tackle the core problems of poverty, which, in Gary's opinion, tend to be moral weaknesses in the form of drug use, laziness, or sexual misconduct (like having children out of wedlock). For these believers, poverty is best addressed by changing the behaviors that, they believe, lead to poverty.

The White House Office of Faith-Based and Community Initiatives, initially created by the Bush administration, provides a potential solution to this dilemma. Federal funding is channeled through religious organizations to provide a holistic approach to fighting poverty and other social problems—one that addresses both the social and spiritual circumstances of the individual. Faith-based funding is palatable to many believers but still creates an additional question of how exactly the government should partner with religion.

While the overwhelming majority of Americans think we should take care of the needy, we feel very differently about whether this care should come from public, private, or religious sources. Atheists and believers in a Distant God are the least likely to support faith-based social welfare (see figure 5.1). Those with a more judgmental and more engaged God (Authoritative) are far more likely to argue that public funding should be funneled through religious organizations.

In an effort to further investigate how God calls believers to deal with economic inequality, we made a trip to Philadelphia to visit Pastor Herb Lusk and his congregation at the Greater Exodus Baptist Church, which is on the front lines of the fight against poverty. What we discovered was a surprising mix of political and religious allegiances.

God and Charity

The Greater Exodus Baptist Church lies in the heart of Philadelphia and presents a weathered and worn façade to a neighborhood populated

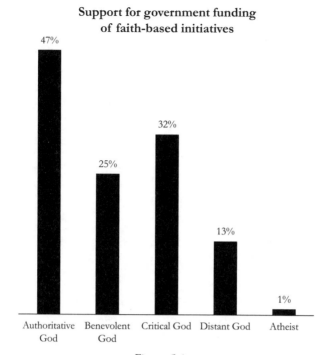

Figure 5.1

mainly by working- and lower-class African Americans. But the traditional exterior of the sanctuary belies the vibrant and joyous community within. For years, the church has steadily expanded its social outreach by supplying an endless stream of services to those in need. The lead pastor, Reverend Herbert Lusk, is a local celebrity, partially because he played professional football for the Philadelphia Eagles, but also for his twenty-five-year crusade to lift the Greater Exodus Baptist Church from near collapse to local and national prominence.

African American evangelical churches are renowned for their energetic and emotive services, and the Greater Exodus Baptist Church is no exception. Our visit proved an intensely emotional experience. Seated next to us was a recovering drug addict who had begun attending Greater Exodus five months earlier, and during the three-hour service, he repeatedly thanked Jesus for his deliverance from addiction in whispers, sobs, and shouts. His enthusiasm and heart-felt devotion was hardly unique. Parishioners leaped, cried, howled, and collapsed from exhaustion—all in a state of religious ecstasy brought on by the infectious verve of the Greater Exodus gospel choir and the passionate words of Pastor Lusk.

After the service, many congregants told us about their close and cherished connection with God. The religious intensity of their worship was evidence enough—God clearly seemed to be an active participant in the life of this congregation. Moments before our interviews, congregants were visibly in the throes of genuine religious enthusiasm, and when we asked them about God's presence, we received looks of disbelief as if we had somehow failed to witness what had just occurred. How could they explain something that just had been illustrated in the most vivid and immediate way? They believed in an Authoritative God who reigned supreme, guided every movement of their lives, and revealed himself through the Bible and the sermons of their pastor. In the end, our interviews proved a confirmation of something that was obvious.

In addition to their enthusiastic worship, the members of the Greater Exodus congregation with whom we spoke resemble other African American Christians in another important way—their tendency to support the Democratic Party. While reporting very conservative attitudes on social issues—such as the need to ban gay marriage and abortion—devout African Americans continue to vote for the Democratic Party in overwhelming numbers.[2] They tend to view economic inequality and social welfare in a much different light than their theologically similar white counterparts. Put simply, African Americans tend to emphasize the need for community and societal interventions to help struggling individuals and advocate more liberal approaches to social welfare and economic equality. By contrast, as sociologists Michael Emerson and Christian Smith put it, "Contemporary white American evangelicalism is perhaps the strongest carrier of the freewill-individualist tradition,"[3] which holds that individuals are personally responsible for their own fate and, therefore, that economic success or failure is mainly in their hands. Consequently, white evangelicals tend to oppose social welfare programs and feel that government assistance promotes dependence over self-sufficiency.[4]

The Greater Exodus Baptist Church is home to some fascinating cross-partisanship, which has led to attacks from some African American leaders and advocates. Reverend Herb Lusk is a backer of former

President George W. Bush. The fact that an inner-city African American leader, who consistently ministers to some of the most helpless and disenfranchised people in America, strongly supported a conservative Republican president cuts to the heart of how complex the intersection of religious and economic ideals has become. When we look at the Greater Exodus experience, it becomes clear that Reverend Lusk has not turned his back on his community by aligning with the Republican Party—far from it. Greater Exodus has successfully utilized the White House Office of Faith-Based and Community Initiatives to help fund a number of impressive social services in Philadelphia. The church runs a charter school with more than three hundred students and a nonprofit organization that provides social services, economic development, education, and housing to the surrounding community, including the Employment Advancement Retention Network Center, with job training and skills certifications.

The ability of the Greater Exodus Baptist Church to embrace a controversial conservative social and economic policy and turn it to the advantage of a historically liberal and Democratic community indicates how theological links can sometimes cut across partisan divides. A shared image of God is the key.

This shared faith is evident in the philosophy of compassionate conservatism, a political perspective that marries conservative economic policy with the theology of an engaged God. This perspective is best described by Marvin Olasky, whom George W. Bush called "compassionate conservatism's leading thinker." Olasky, decrying wastefulness in government social welfare services, argues that religious groups are often more efficient and effective in curing social ills. A key component of religion's success, says Olasky, is that it offers individuals a complete solution to their problems. He asks, "Why is it terrible for a welfare caseworker to tell a person who considers himself worthless, 'Listen, there's a way out. There really is love out there that will never stop loving you. There's a real God, and I want to be able to talk to you about him'?" For Olasky and other compassionate conservatives, the answer is clear—we need God to effectively counter poverty, hopelessness, and apathy.[5] This vision of social change is rooted in the idea that God will assist those in need. In other words, if an individual honestly calls on God for help, God will be there to uplift, strengthen, and guide him. And this is a version of God that can only be described as directly and concretely engaged in the lives of followers—an Authoritative or Benevolent God.

Several people from Greater Exodus offer real-life testimonials of how religious conversion can transform individual lives. We spoke to a number of congregants who told stories of salvation through the church. Lucas told us how he had been homeless and addicted to drugs when he came through the doors of Greater Exodus ten years earlier. Embraced by the church community and given employment by Reverend Lusk, Lucas found friendship, security, and faith. Lucas went on to say how his relationship with God allowed him to reconcile with his family and eventually be forgiven by his children for past abuses. Although his face revealed the scars and lines of a hard and troubled life, his eyes shone with hope, thankfulness, and happiness.

Assistant Minister Sydney Flores told us how he and his fellow ministers draw on God to counsel individuals who are going through some of the toughest times imaginable. Reverend Flores said, "What do you say to someone who has just lost a child? I have them focus on God and pour all of their grief, anger, and fatigue into him. And then think about all that he has done for you." Flores emphasized that by focusing on God, you can lead people to shift their thoughts from the negative to the positive, and in the end, this can turn their lives around. Judging from the many stories of redemption and salvation we heard that day, this method of counseling was extremely effective.[6]

Stories like these excite Jay Hein, the former White House director of the Office of Faith-Based and Community Initiatives. He told us that he feels that the faith-based initiative is largely misunderstood, and few are aware of the good that has come out of it. Hein also suspects that more African American churches than white evangelical groups are taking advantage of federal grants—another aspect of the initiative that is not widely known.

African American churches may be more likely to be in contact with individuals in financial need, which may explain their success in getting federal grants. But they also may be less squeamish about accepting government funds to support their religious and social missions.[7] President Obama appears keenly aware of this dynamic, and his support of faith-based initiatives emerges not from a shared philosophy of compassionate conservatism but rather from his knowledge that many of the greatest needs in our society are met by churches who target their ministry to the poor.[8]

For those who hope to fulfill God's will by fighting poverty, federal funding is like additional mammon from God. And the distinction between how Americans feel about fighting poverty and how they think God feels about our economic inequalities is strongly related to their economic and social class.

God and Social Class

During the 2008 Democratic presidential primaries, Barack Obama provoked outrage by stating that rural voters "cling to guns or religion or antipathy to people who aren't like them . . . as a way to explain their frustrations."[9] Although the phrase "cling to religion" has a negative connotation, Obama's sentiment is correct insofar as Americans look to God for help and guidance in times of financial trouble. We spoke to many people who were frustrated with their economic situations and the greed they perceived around them. Terry, a young believer in an Authoritative God, explained how our "culture of greed" stems directly from ignoring God:

> God should be in the schools instead of being taken out. And also TV and the media, Jesus should be more prominent, and we wouldn't be so focused on the negative, drugs and killings, and that sort of thing. . . . We reference God a lot, but we are not studying him wholeheartedly. We have let go of our Christian values for money, for power, for whatever the issue may be.

Patrick, a middle-class Roman Catholic born and raised on the East Coast and believer in a Benevolent God, also lamented that "the nation is greedy . . . and I don't think it makes any difference whether it's Republican or Democrat, because for the last forty years we've been running millionaires for the presidency, so how concerned can they be about people who make less money?" For Terry, Patrick, and other frustrated Americans, the profane world of politics and economics is too far removed from God and his plan.

Other believers feel that God is quite happy with the current state of affairs. Indeed, one's personal economic situation is closely connected to ideas about God and how he perceives the world. For instance, believers in all four types of God differ significantly in their household incomes (see figure 5.2). Believers in a Critical God, on average, make less than any other believer. Believers in an Authoritative God are in the next lowest income group. Interestingly, Americans with the lowest incomes have the angriest and most judgmental Gods. Americans with a Distant God tend to make the most money.

It is not immediately clear *why* income should be related to a God type. What is it about having more or less money that makes one imagine God in different ways? Do people believe they have less money than others *because* God is punishing them in some way? Or do they assume that God is angry with the world because of their suffering and the suffering of others?

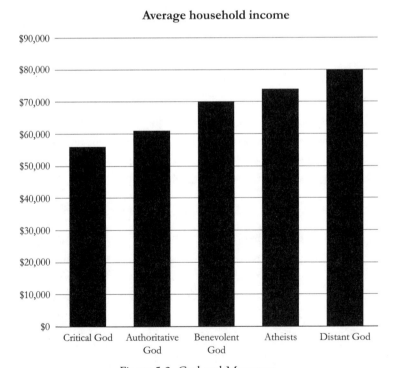

Figure 5.2. God and Mammon

Overall, wealthier Americans are as likely as lower-class Americans to believe that "God is concerned with my personal well-being." In sum, a person's income is unrelated to whether he or she thinks of God as a loving, personal source of strength and meaning. While both rich and poor feel equally close to God, we find some distinct disparities when it comes to what God thinks of them and the world. Specifically, those with lower incomes are much likelier to believe that God is angered by their personal sins and will punish sinners (see figure 5.3).[10]

An angry and wrathful God appears to be a logical choice for the most disadvantaged among us, when we consider the injustices, insults, and injuries they have experienced. Why wouldn't a loving God be angered by what he sees? For individuals who most directly face the cruelties and deficiencies of life in poverty and isolation, the thought that God approves of what happens to them, their families, and their friends is absurd. God must be upset. But what angers God becomes an important point of their theology. Interestingly, while they believe that God is troubled by the state of the world in general, individuals in poverty also tend to think that God is very angry with them personally. But this image of an angry God reflects less a sense of self-loathing than a rational attempt to reconcile the idea of a caring and all-powerful God with the plight of those in need. If God isn't helping them, it is not because he can't, but because they don't deserve it.

To better understand the intimate link between our economic situation and our understanding of God, we visited two small and active churches nestled in the mountains of Colorado. While these two

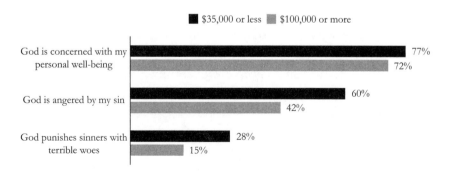

Figure 5.3. God's Personality by Income

churches are within easy driving distance from each other, when it comes to money—and God—they couldn't be farther apart.

Rich God, Poor God

In March 2008, we attended services at Christ Episcopal Church in Aspen, Colorado, and at the Open Door Church in nearby Rifle. Aspen is one of the wealthiest towns in the United States, with many stylish and sophisticated residents who maintain seasonal homes in this ski paradise. Christ Episcopal Church sits on a small downtown lot in Aspen worth around $12 million. The sanctuary is small and quaint but will soon be remodeled by an internationally known architecture firm. Rifle, down the road from Aspen, is a working-class town where employment opportunities are growing because of a recent discovery of natural gas deposits. The Rifle Open Door Church, backed by a trailer park and overlooking a stone quarry, is visible from the freeway. Forty years ago, its sanctuary was built by the current pastor, who is a retired construction worker. He laid the foundation himself and is proud that the solid and attractive church has weathered the years well.

The pastors of both churches were similarly friendly and welcoming. Princeton-educated and trained as a historian, the Reverend Bruce McNab is an ideal fit for a congregation of cosmopolitan Aspenites. Reverend Del Whittington of Rifle, who worked most of his life as a bricklayer, immediately asked us about our faith and intimated that a conversion experience may be in our immediate future. Both pastors introduced us to their congregations, with Rev. McNab joking that we had really come to Aspen to ski and Rev. Whittington carefully identifying us as potential converts.

Karl Marx famously called religion the opium of the masses, arguing that religious faith is an attempt to either cope with or understand the hardships of life.[11] As such, people who are suffering economically are expected to seek out religion to offset their lives of quiet desperation, while those with money and power don't require the feeble and naïve comforts of otherworldly optimism. But this oft-quoted assumption does not fit with some basic facts. Namely, within the United States, wealth is unrelated to religious devotion, and the rich and the poor are equally likely to believe in God.

Contrary to Marx's expectations, religion speaks to members of all social classes. Beyond the material comforts of their lives, wealthy individuals face some of the same concerns as the poor—problems with relationships, the deaths of loved ones, depression, and feelings of meaninglessness. Of course, people of means can better acquire therapy and medication, can afford the consolations of leisure activities (like skiing), and tend to have a wider exposure to the world of ideas—in particular, secular philosophical alternatives to religious belief. Nonetheless, wealthy Americans are as religious as their less-advantaged compatriots, indicating that their financial security has done little to offset their religious and spiritual longings.

As if to illustrate this point, Reverend McNab and Reverend Whittington coincidentally both sermonized on the same topic—suffering. Reverend McNab assured his congregation that "no matter how many times we've felt beaten down by misfortune, disease, prejudice, or any other circumstances, the Life-giver is still among us." At first, the topic of misfortune in a town composed of some of the most fortunate people in the country seemed incongruous, but Rev. McNab pointed out that fortune was not the same as material wealth. He reminded his flock that feeling alive is more than "a great day of skiing or hiking in the mountains, or doing something in the great outdoors." Instead, he argued that to "truly live" is to be fulfilled in a relationship with God and accept the reality of suffering. Nothing less than a close connection with God will allow you to get the most out of life. Reverend McNab admonished his congregation to "come out of the tomb of your self-sufficiency, where you can't admit you need God."

But for those who struggle to make ends meet, self-sufficiency is not a tomb but rather an ideal. In Rifle, Reverend Whittington spoke specifically about the day-to-day reality of his congregants, many of whom yearn for the security of self-sufficiency. As such, he never addressed the question of whether we truly need God. His congregants did not need to be reminded of that. The Rifle service was composed of personal testimonies about painful hardships and the promise of better things in the afterlife. An African American mother, displaced by Hurricane Katrina, spoke of the difficulties of relocating to Rifle and how her children were sometimes called "niggers" at their new school. Several congregants referred to their battles with alcoholism, drug abuse, and illness. A Hispanic woman described the anguish of her agoraphobia that had imprisoned her in a small apartment for years on end. And the pastor spoke about the troubles people face at work, negotiating with difficult bosses in the never-ending struggle to earn a living. It became clear during this lengthy service that suffering was a regular and central topic of discussion in this tight-knit church, and the service provided members with perhaps their only outlet to share their personal plights with others.

After hearing an array of testimonies about adversity and isolation, Reverend Whittington reminded us, in a tone more comforting than threatening, that "the wrath of God will soon be revealed!" He pinpointed the source of our collective troubles in the "secular culture that doesn't want God," assuring his flock that everyone, rich and poor, will receive their just deserts in the end. Then he told a story about the death of the richest man in Rifle and how his wealth and power were of no consequence when he went to meet his maker. "He left the world with nothing but his relationship with God."

By focusing so intensely on the afterlife, the congregants in Rifle appeared somewhat resigned to their earthly troubles. Interestingly, the pastor repeatedly mentioned during his sermon that their church did not advocate prosperity gospel—a theological tradition that asserts that God will provide material wealth to those he favors. The Open Door of Rifle flourishes not because of false promises of riches but rather by focusing on the importance of God for achieving rewards in the afterlife. In fact, Reverend Whittington admonished individuals who concentrate on their bank accounts, arguing that they should be "investing in eternity, not in retirement." He preached that "it shouldn't be about health, wealth, and prosperity *here*, but in the next place" and that living a godly life is the only way to "make deposits for the other side."[12] For him, the "throes of fire" are awaiting those mired in the luxuries of the secular world. From this promise of otherworldly retribution, the congregants drew strength and solace, even though it promised no hope that their troubles at work, school, or home would soon be resolved.

While this congregation—and many other believers at the bottom of the economic ladder—takes comfort in the idea that God will reverse their fortunes after death, there is also a price to pay for their belief in an Authoritative God; namely, if God can punish others for their sins, God can also punish you. Consequently, members of the Rifle Open Door Church are aware that God is watching them and expecting devotion and obedience. By concentrating on pleasing an angry God, many of these believers exhibit a kind of passive resignation to their lot in life, a stance that harks back to Marx's idea that religion acts as a type of opiate to numb the pain of poverty and encourage believers to accept their fate without bitterness or indignation. To that end, Reverend Whittington reminded his congregants that "suffering is a part of life, but you will reign in the next life" and cautioned that they should not respond to their circumstances with hatred, violence, rebellion, or sullenness. Instead, godly behavior requires deference and respect for God, one's neighbors, and secular authorities. The pastor advised that "as an employee, you are a servant" and called on those experiencing troubles at work or at school, as in the case of the family encountering racial bigotry, to draw on the "strength of Jesus" so they could weather these insults and abuses in silence.

Without much sense that economic and social disadvantages can be overcome, many underprivileged believers embrace a theology that eschews economic justice and denounces the decadence and immorality of American culture. In many ways, this is a rational response to insurmountable personal circumstances. It provides a religious framework to understand why life in the wealthiest country on Earth is so hard. Surrounded by riches, the poor are sensible to ask, "What have we done to deserve our lot?" The answer that a godless society bent on material gratification has angered God seems like a plausible response—especially if those who are celebrating now will be crying later.

Even so, there were instances when congregants celebrated the blessings of God in this world. One woman spoke of how her son fell off a galloping horse and sustained only minor injuries; she concluded that God had saved his life. The pastor told a story about how God had led one of his parishioners to give up alcohol, become a better father, and provide for his family. In another story, the pastor explained how God helped a woman—who throughout the church service banged a tambourine at the front of the church—leave the Jehovah's Witnesses and embrace the true faith of Christianity. These few instances of God's grace seemed to contradict the overarching message that God's mercy awaits us in the afterlife, but these earthly mercies were still meager in comparison with what could be found in heaven. Agnes, a ninety-year-old parishioner, explained that she could hardly wait to be called home and finally see the heavenly treasure that she had been investing in all these years.

Members of the Rifle Open Door, like Agnes, walk the tightrope between expressing frustration with their worldly lot and celebrating their otherworldly rewards. The question of how to respond to economic hardship and perceived injustices is closely informed by how we think God wants us to respond. For this congregation and many others like it, God wants our personal loyalty but tends to have little to say about the economic system as a whole.

Members of Christ Episcopal Church and the Open Door Church share a strong belief in God and the desire to develop a closer relationship with him. They also share a concern with answering troubling questions about God, such as why he allows people to suffer. Yet they reach very different conclusions. For Christ Episcopal Church, suffering is part of God's great mystery. For the Rifle church, suffering is a reality that its members must endure to demonstrate their focus on the next world. Still, the result of these beliefs is remarkably similar; both churches ultimately ask their congregants to accept things *as they are*, which would not surprise Marx.

God and Economic Policy

Overall, Americans who believe in a more judgmental God tend to think that most social problems require religious solutions, whereas Americans who believe in a less judgmental God tend to think that most social problems can be adequately addressed with secular solutions. Yet in both cases, God can be world-sustaining or world-shaking. If we believe that God supports the economic and political status quo, we will support it, too. If we feel that God is upset with the world, we might be called to change it. Poorer Americans who believe in an angry God should be the most likely activists; their God may demand major changes in order to avoid his wrath. While many believers in an Authoritative God feel that stricter regulation of homosexual behavior and abortion are necessary to appease their God, there is no similar agreement on how we should address poverty, inequality, or corporate corruption.

Phillip, a retired religion teacher, told us why he thought many of his students didn't understand "that God is on the side of the poor and the oppressed": "All of a sudden one day it dawned on me that these kids were never going to be active about peace, justice, and compassion in the world; these kids were never going to be affected unless they understood the social construction of reality. And at that point it came together for me." Phillip argued that the belief that God hates poverty does not actually inspire social reform. We also need a strong indication that God wants us to transform the system. For believers who are in desperate financial circumstances, their preoccupation with questions of godliness and morality, even at the expense of concerns for economic advancement or reform, is understandable, because they are worried about the hereafter and not the here and now. Their focus on individual salvation overwhelms their sense of social justice.

Some observers of American politics are dumbfounded that working-class Americans tend to vote against their economic interests in favor of candidates and political platforms that advocate "family values" and decry the elitism of secular authorities in the media, schools, and government. In his book *What's the Matter with Kansas?* Thomas Frank asked why working-class Americans support conservative economic policies that favor the rich. He laments, "All they have to show for the Republican loyalty are lower wages, more dangerous jobs, dirtier air, a new overlord class that comports itself like King Farouk—and, of course, a crap culture."[13] Frank concludes that many Americans are duped into voting Republican for "values" reasons.

Frank is correct that Republicans have made inroads with many Americans for cultural rather than economic reasons. The coalition between Republican and evangelical leaders that developed in the 1980s centered on social, sexual, and cultural issues. The alliance paid off, and many absolutist religious believers came to view the Republican Party as a champion of their most treasured causes. But our economic and class differences are a deciding factor when we consider American attitudes about the distribution of wealth.[14]

Overall, Americans tend to agree on two basic points: capitalism is good, and poverty is bad. How we reconcile a system that fosters inequality with an ethic to alleviate poverty is a function of what we think God wants from us. Social status plays a primary role in how we view God and his attitude about our economic system.[15] Consider the difference between those with Authoritative and Benevolent Gods. People with an Authoritative God and people with a Benevolent God share a belief that God is highly involved in the world. This is related to the belief that it is our duty to care for the sick and needy. People with Authoritative and Benevolent Gods are significantly more likely to place great importance on helping the sick and needy than those with Critical and Distant Gods. But how is that help to be provided?

As we learned earlier, believers in Authoritative and Critical Gods tend to strongly prioritize religious solutions to social ills. Indeed, people who believe in an Authoritative God are the most supportive of government funding of faith-based initiatives (see figure 5.1). People who believe in a Benevolent God, on the other hand, are significantly more likely to believe that *government* should make attempts to redistribute wealth more evenly (see figure 5.4). In other words, those with a Benevolent God feel the need to fix the problems they see but are less likely to believe those fixes must come from religious sources. For those

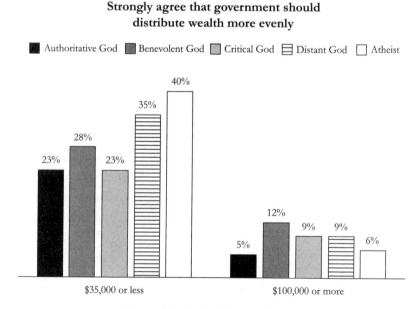

Figure 5.4. God and Inequality

who believe in a judgmental God, faith-based solutions are the answer to our problems.

With regard to economic issues, those with a Distant God are more of a mystery. They are the least likely to favor funding faith-based initiatives to fix social problems. Depending on which other factors are considered, the effect of having a Distant God on the belief in the redistribution of wealth appears and disappears capriciously—a nightmare to statisticians. What is clear is that for those with a Distant God, economic considerations are often largely separate from theological ones.

God and Party

The Gods of the urban Greater Exodus Church, the rural working-class Rifle Open Door, and the upper-class Aspen Christ Episcopal Church mirror the religious and economic divisions of our nation as a whole. Each of these churches views the sources of poverty and the responses to it differently. Greater Exodus Church of Philadelphia draws heavily on federal funds to provide education and job training in its community. Rifle Open Door Church is focused exclusively on proselytizing to anyone willing to listen. The Aspen church seeks to share the pain of those less fortunate—from afar. But in all cases, Americans' religious regrets about earthly greed and corruption have not inspired economic radicalism.

Still, liberal and conservative perspectives are strongly premised on both religious and class differences. Wealthy Americans are more likely to be Republicans (see figure 5.5). But how your image of God affects your party affiliation is similar whether you are wealthy or poor. Believers in an Authoritative God are always more likely to be Republican than all other believers within a particular income bracket. Their attitudes about social and economic policy are a perfect fit with a conservative policy agenda. Believers in a Benevolent God are attracted to the GOP not for economic reasons but for their stance on social and cultural issues; believers in a Critical God tend to favor conservative economic policy, provided they are not in the lower class. Atheists and believers in a Distant God are the most likely to be Democrats. Again, their aversion to a conservative moral agenda can often mitigate their class allegiances.

Identify as Republicans

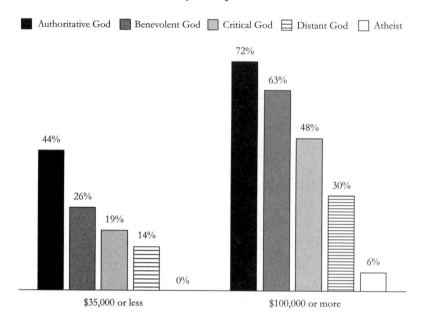

Figure 5.5. God and Party

At the end of the day, we are all "values" *and* "pocketbook" voters. In general, your values reflect your God, and your God reflects your pocketbook. Lower economic status is strongly related to the belief that God harshly judges and is angry with the world. In turn, belief in a judgmental God (both Authoritative and Critical Gods) is related to the belief that the solution to poverty is personal faith or faith-based solutions and not government intervention. The presidency of Barack Obama may shake up this dynamic. Obama's liberal Christian rhetoric seeks to rekindle the religious motivation to fight poverty through governmental assistance. He is attempting to balance conservative Christians leery of government and liberal activists leery of Christian proselytizing. The question that remains is which type of God he will lean on for stability.

Pastor Fred Phelps preaches at the Westboro Baptist Church in Topeka, Kansas. This small religious group, legally classified as a hate group, spreads the unusual message that God hates you. *Photo by Nigel Euling*

Two young women from the Westboro Baptist Church casually chat amid a vast collection of posters. These posters, which contain the most inflammatory messages imaginable, are carried when church members protest at the funerals of homosexuals, military personnel, and respected public figures. *Photo by Nigel Euling*

Reverend Herbert Lusk inspires congregants at the Greater Exodus Church in Philadelphia, which contains members who have overcome some of life's most difficult setbacks. The Greater Exodus Church has effectively utilized funds from the federal Office of Faith-Based and Community Initiatives to provide the needy with education, shelter, and counseling. *Photo by Nigel Euling*

Religious groups with a very engaged God tend to hold rituals high in emotional energy. This woman is experiencing "collective effervescence," or religious ecstasy, because she feels God is actively present in the worship service. African American churches known for their emotive services tend toward belief in an Authoritative God. *Photo by Nigel Euling*

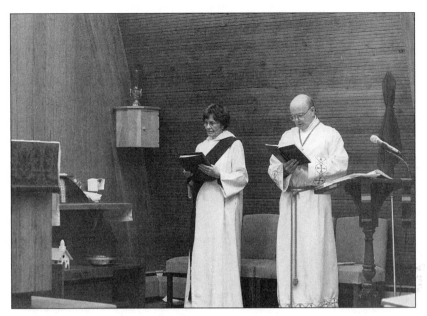

Compare the service style of a church in downtown Aspen (top) with that of a church in nearby Rifle, Colorado (bottom). The clergy in the Aspen church minister to a more educated and affluent congregation and follow a clearly scripted set of procedures. Reverend Del Whittington in Rifle freely and unpredictably interacts with his congregants, who tend to be working class. Class differences are related to both different conceptions of God and different ritual styles. *Photos by M. Todd Thiele*

Worshippers respond to different Gods. Believers in a Distant God appear to favor more moderate expressions of worship; at top, members of the Aspen Christ Episcopal Church stoically sing a familiar hymn. Below, a woman at Open Door Church in Rifle exuberantly dances and sings with the church band, even bringing her own tambourine to more actively join the service's many spontaneous musical interludes. Her God is similarly energetic and impulsive. *Photos by M. Todd Thiele*

SIX

God and Evil

The battle this nation is in is a spiritual battle, it is a battle for our soul. And the enemy is a guy called Satan. . . . Satan wants to destroy us as a nation and he wants to destroy us as a Christian army.

—General William Boykin, deputy undersecretary for defense intelligence, from a series of public lectures in 2003

In the past decade, the United States has faced its share of tragedies and disasters, both natural and man-made. The devastating attacks of 9/11 stunned the American public and left us hunting desperately for ways to comprehend the ruthlessness and scope of this monumental act of terrorism. We were shocked by the power of Hurricane Katrina and the misery left in its wake. Was God trying to tell us something?

The question of evil often arises after appalling disasters, which are sometimes interpreted as God's response to evil in the world, and after horrible acts of violence, which are often described as the result of evil in the hearts of the perpetrators. If God does not prevent a disaster like Hurricane Katrina or a tragedy like 9/11, many believe, there must be a reason. By providing reasons for evil, believers reveal some of their deepest theological differences. In turn, they also reveal how they believe God wants us to respond to evil—sometimes through moral self-evaluation and other times through violence against evildoers.

God and Disaster

There are three possible roles for God in a disaster: (1) God can cause the disaster, (2) God can allow the disaster to occur, or (3) God can have no role in the disaster. Depending on the disaster in question, a believer may hold any of these perspectives. But they tend to choose one of the three, and which one they choose is related to their type of God (see figure 6.1).

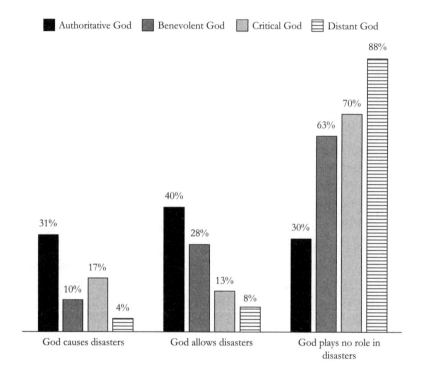

Figure 6.1. God and Disaster

Source: Baylor Religion Survey, Wave II (2007). Valid N = 1,330. Two questions were used to create categories: "God sometimes allows tragedies to occur as a warning to sinners" and "God sometimes causes tragedies to occur as a warning to sinners." Those who disagreed with both statements or were undecided about both statements were classified as believing that God plays no role in disaster. Those who agreed or strongly agreed that God allows tragedies to occur but did not agree that God causes tragedies were placed in the second category. Those who agree or strongly agree that God causes tragedy constitute the third category. Note that the vast majority of those who believe that God causes tragedy (97.1%) *also* agreed that God allows tragedy.

God the Architect

Many Americans believe that when something good happens to us, God was involved. Consequently, if something bad occurs, wouldn't God have to be involved as well?[1] As we saw earlier, some fringe groups, such as Westboro Baptist Church, wholeheartedly profess that God is the architect of all disasters. God *causes* tragedies to punish us for our sins, they argue.

Few Americans are so extreme in their views. Yet, in the wake of Hurricane Katrina, such sentiments received widespread attention. Perhaps Hurricane Katrina was punishment for our sins, televangelist John Hagee mused. "All hurricanes are acts of God, because God controls the heavens. I believe that New Orleans had a level of sin that was offensive to God. . . . And I believe that the Hurricane Katrina was, in fact, the judgment of God against the city of New Orleans."[2]

And Hagee was far from alone. Given the number of reasons put forth for God's attack on New Orleans, it certainly seemed like a marked city. Among the most commonly cited reasons for God's anger were the prevalence of abortion in the United States; recent gay marriage legislation; the war in Iraq; U.S. failure to sign the Kyoto accords regulating greenhouse gas emissions; U.S. cooperation in Israel's decision to remove Jewish settlers from Gaza; the prevalence of occultists, witches, and practitioners of voodoo in New Orleans; rampant government corruption in New Orleans; New Orleans's reputation as a place that celebrates decadence via gambling, prostitution, drunkenness, and Mardi Gras; and God's desire to stop the "Southern Decadence" celebration, which was scheduled for days after Katrina hit.[3]

While some believers debated the source of God's wrath, others refused to believe that God would cause a tragedy as a warning to sinners. John Shelby Spong, a retired Episcopal bishop from New Jersey, countered such claims with strong words:

> The idea of God sitting on a throne above the clouds manipulating the weather in order to punish sinners is so primitive and so naive that it is staggering to the educated imagination. . . . It is surely not a God of Love who punishes New Orleans' poorest citizens with a hurricane that New Orleans' wealthiest citizens could and did manage to escape at least with their lives, because they had cars.[4]

Though a vast majority would second Spong's statement, 17 percent of Americans assert that God at times *causes* disasters as a warning to sinners.

God the Enabler

Most Americans are uncomfortable with the idea that God would directly *cause* a disaster. Instead, more Americans are willing to suggest that God sometimes *allows* bad things to happen. In this way, God enables evil but never causes it.

This idea of God as an enabler is most clearly expressed in the story of Job. In this biblical story, God compliments Job, saying that he is "blameless and upright . . . a man who fears God and shuns evil." Satan scoffs at God. Job is a righteous man, Satan says, only because God has blessed and protected him. Remove those blessings, he argues, and Job will quickly turn on God. Accepting the challenge, God says to Satan, "Everything he has is in your hands, but on the man himself do not lay a finger." Satan enthusiastically uses his free rein to kill members of Job's family, drive him to poverty, destroy all of his possessions, and afflict Job with boils, rashes, and sores.[5] Through it all, Job refuses to curse God's name.

In Job's case, God does not directly cause his misery. Still, God steps back and allows evil to occur. Perhaps this seems like a minor semantic difference. Some would argue that turning your back, knowing that something bad is about to happen, is just as bad as committing the act yourself. Yet Americans see a big difference when it comes to God. Nearly a third (27 percent) of Americans believe that God allows, but never causes, tragic events.[6] This way, they avoid the conclusion that God forces innocent people to suffer horribly. Still, their belief in an all-powerful God leads them to accept that God must *allow* terrible things to happen—including not only natural disasters but also man-made tragedies such as the terrorist attacks of 9/11 or the Oklahoma City bombing. Consequently, they look for the silver lining in a tragedy to indicate the reason for God's inaction while also remaining alert to his small blessings.

For example, on the third anniversary of 9/11, the Trinity Broadcasting Network (TBN), Cornerstone TV, and several other Christian broadcasting networks aired *Day of Miracles: True Miraculous Stories of 9/11*, which featured dozens of tales of people escaping seemingly certain death through divine intervention. Some claimed that God held up the Twin Towers for an extra thirty minutes so that people could escape. Others posited that divinely created traffic jams reduced the number of people in the buildings.[7] Similarly, in *Where Was God at 9:02 a.m.?* (the time when a bomb ripped apart the Alfred P. Murrah Federal Building in Oklahoma City), Robin Jones recounts stories of people who claim they were saved by God from that horrific terrorist attack. Jones reports that "those who survived will swear God was with them. There is no reason to doubt it. God was right there in those first few minutes, when so-called chance took some and spared others."[8]

Such tales of hope and survival do not focus on the thorny question of why a God powerful enough to hold up a building still allowed it to be attacked in the first place. Instead, they look for comfort by finding a role for God in tragedy or finding a grander purpose behind the event. As Katherine, a young secretary from Kansas City and believer in a Benevolent God, told us:

> I've seen several of those specials on survivors of September 11 or the family members of people that survived September 11 and yes, it is horrible and horrendous. I can't imagine the pain and suffering that they've gone through. But I bet that if it was to be examined closely you could find a reason for it in each of their lives. Something that changed or needed to be changed or shown. . . . I believe there has got to be a reason. . . . I believe in God.

Katherine's perspective is common among believers in a Benevolent God—always seeing the little miracles even within instances of enormous chaos and suffering. But for believers in an Authoritative God, Katherine's opinion does not delve deeply enough into God's motivations. These believers tend to wonder what has angered God and what he is asking of us. Frederick, a twenty-six-year-old Pentecostal and believer in an Authoritative God, explained:

> I believe God allows things [such as Hurricane Katrina]. I believe God was in control of that. I believe he could have stopped it. I also believe

God allowed it. I believe it got the whole country's attention. I believe the whole country prayed. I believe 9/11 . . . I believe you know that was an act of terrorism. God's not a terrorist, but I believe God wants us to be aware of the times we're living in and how much we need him. So, I believe that was very much a wake-up call to America.

Frederick recognizes the tragedy of Katrina and the attacks of 9/11 but concludes that God allowed these things to give us a punishing jolt—a reminder of the evils of terrorism or the evils of an immoral society. Similarly, Clyde, a seventy-four-year-old retired banker from Kansas City, expresses a related sentiment: "I think God may allow certain things to happen. . . . He allows them to happen [as a] warning, maybe . . . it could be a warning. 'Listen up people, you're not here by yourself. There's somebody greater than you.'"

God the Innocent

Most Americans (around 60 percent) feel that God plays no role in tragic events. They provide a variety of reasons for God's absence. Some talk about the importance of free will; they theorize that God does not intervene directly in our affairs, because to do so would remove our choice to either believe or not believe. "If God is like Superman flying around and saving people," Judy, a pastor's wife from Ocean Shores, Washington, told us, "we are forced to believe."

Other believers take the long view of God's creation and explain disasters as a natural part of the ebb and flow of life. For them, God set the natural order in motion and then removed himself to let it unfold. Francis, a twenty-nine-year-old Episcopalian from California and believer in a Distant God, summarized this view concisely:

God set up the earth in a certain way and it renews itself. . . . So things like hurricanes and tsunamis and earthquakes, you know, these are ways that the earth corrects itself. And God's got such a long span view of what's going on. . . . Creation is working itself out. Now, with that said, I think that humans have made a lot of impact on it and I think that the intensity of the natural disasters that we're seeing now is largely a result of humans. . . . There's too many of us for one thing,

we're overpopulated, and we're damaging the planet in ways that cause
it to get more violent towards us. But I would not place that on God.
I would say that's our fault, that's stuff we've done.

For both Francis and Judy, the very idea that God plans or instigates
specific natural disasters contradicts their core beliefs. The fact that their
God is not actively intervening in daily events does not diminish their
faith but strengthens it.

A person's interpretation of the cosmic meaning of disasters like
Hurricane Katrina follows logically from her image of God.[9] Naturally,
Americans with an Authoritative God are the most likely to state that
God causes a disaster; the idea that God is both engaged and judgmental leads logically to the conclusion that bad things are a sign of his
wrath. This tendency to believe that God warns us or calls us to action
most clearly distinguishes those with an Authoritative God from people
with all other conceptions of God. Indeed, believers in an Authoritative
God tend to imagine a world in which evil forces lurk everywhere and
we are engaged in a constant spiritual struggle between good and evil.
This has far-reaching consequences.

Pervasive within certain strands of Christianity is the rhetoric of
"spiritual warfare," in which life events, major disasters, and the
unfolding of world history are viewed as part of a continual struggle
between the forces of good and evil—a cosmic spiritual battle in which
we are pawns.[10] Fears of an impending spiritual showdown are reflected
in popular Christian fiction such as Frank Peretti's *This Present Darkness*
(1986) and *Piercing the Darkness* (1989). Within Peretti's books, the
forces of good use prayer and angelic intervention to battle the forces
of Satan. Although these books are novels, some religious groups take
their message very seriously and pass out copies of the books to their
congregations.[11] When asked whether his work is fact or fiction, Peretti
stated, "Right now, it's half and half—half fictional device, half reality.
I think in a few years it will be more reality than fiction. . . . We're
heading for some real confrontation."[12]

The tendency among those with an Authoritative God to view the
world as a spiritual battleground is reflected in their beliefs about supernatural forces of evil and the end of the world. Believers in an
Authoritative God are far more likely to believe in Satan, demons, the

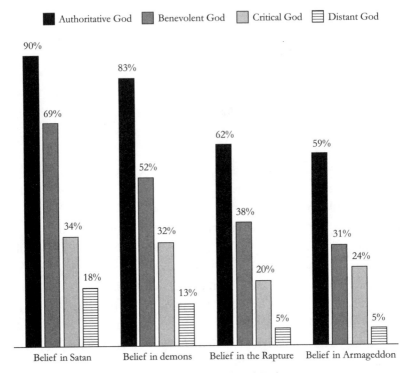

Figure 6.2. God and Evil

Rapture (the second coming of Jesus, when they expect true believers to rise up to heaven), and Armageddon, a final battle between good and evil before the day of judgment (see figure 6.2).

Those with a Distant God are the most skeptical about the existence of evil emanating from beings such as Satan or demons. They similarly do not believe in a cataclysmic end of times in which evil will be ultimately vanquished. Instead, they view tragic events and disasters in our own time as either the result of human action, natural randomness, or dumb luck. Believers in a Critical God tend to share this general worldview. And for both types of believers, natural and man-made disasters are not the product of some supernatural war between good and evil.

Believers in a Benevolent God are more likely to feel God's hand in daily events but tend to dismiss or ignore the issue of why God lets tragedy occur. Instead, these believers focus on the good that God brings and feel that the world will be better if we retain this optimistic view of events. Those with an Authoritative God clearly stand apart. For them, the world is full of evil. In fact, many believers in super-natural evil feel that these forces explain why good people often suffer.[13]

Beliefs about whether the world will end in Armageddon or the Rapture guide Americans in their response to tragedies and have become a significant component in determining their attitudes about foreign policy and world affairs.[14] In addition, beliefs about spiritual warfare are known to strongly influence the political activities of believers, such as their willingness to engage in rallies, petitions, pickets, and other polit-ical and social movements.[15] This can lead to very aggressive behavior toward the perceived earthly sources of evil.

Disaster as a Call to Warfare

On August 26–27, 1883, an apocalyptic series of eruptions began on the volcanic island of Krakatoa, at the time a part of the Dutch East Indies. As Simon Winchester notes in his masterful retelling of the events, the explosion produced the loudest sound in recorded history.[16] Lava flows and raining debris killed at least 3,000 nearby residents. The collapse of the island produced a tsunami that claimed nearly 40,000 more.

Spurred by questions about the meaning of such a disaster, the local population, mostly Muslim, began to develop a simmering resent-ment toward the occupying Christians. A mullah active in Banten town in nearby Java, Hajji Abdul Karim, *knew* why the eruption had occurred. Islamic theology includes the concept of the Mahdi, a savior who will appear in the world during its last days to save the righteous. Before the Madhi's arrival, God would demonstrate his great displeasure with the world via a series of cataclysms, Karim warned, and Krakatoa was just such an event: "Has not three-quarters of the island of Krakatoa disap-peared? Are you blind to these deeds brought about by God? Be humble for the Almighty! Pay for your sins! Can you still doubt, said the *mullahs*, now that you know that Abdul Karim has predicted this?"[17] Karim's message resonated within a certain segment of the Muslim community of western Java, and the attachment of this spiritual meaning to the tsunami of Krakatoa inspired a violent uprising against Dutch Christian colonists.

People convinced of God's anger can respond forcefully to perceived warnings from God if they agree on who or what is to blame for God's wrath. Hajji Abdul Karim provided an explanation for the devastating tsunami that decimated Krakatoa—God was angry with their deviation from Islamic values—and the population responded by attacking their Christian invaders. Similarly, the historian Philip Jenkins argues that climate changes and the Black Death in the thirteenth and fourteenth centuries set off a rash of violence against minority populations throughout Europe and Asia. Jenkins notes that within Europe, "in a climate of death and horror, people cast about for scapegoats. . . . The Church formally declared witchcraft a heresy in 1320, and people were soon being executed for devil-worship and black magic. And governments, desperate to find safe outlet for their subjects' rage, condoned mob attacks on religious minorities." Interestingly, Jenkins finds that "Christians suffered as well, at the hands of Muslims in Asia and the Middle East strained by some of the same circumstances that were affecting Europe."[18] The common thread tying together these disparate instances of violence was the belief that dire problems could be solved by attacking people who displeased God.

Modern-day ethnic and political violence can also be motivated by beliefs about God's wrath. Genocidal violence in the former Yugoslavia and in Darfur have occurred along religious lines. As Daniel Chirot and Clark McCauley argue, a major motivation in many mass political killings is a "fear of pollution," or the idea that a religious, ethnic, or ideological tradition is threatened by contaminants—people who are religiously, ethnically, or ideologically different.[19] If people believe that a catastrophe is a sign that God is displeased with a certain group, then violence toward that group is thought to be divinely ordained. As such, believers in an Authoritative God, believing that it is God's will, are sometimes driven to aggressive action.

Violence against perceived agents of evil indicates the important ties among beliefs about spiritual warfare, the meaning of tragedies, and earthly warfare. As mentioned earlier, many believers in an Authoritative God attributed the devastation of Hurricane Katrina to the sinful ways of our country or, more specifically, New Orleans. God, they think, was angry about homosexuality. The devastating attacks of 9/11 produced an even more pointed reaction among believers in spiritual warfare. Most Americans sought religious answers in the face of 9/11.[20] But for believers in an Authoritative God, the meaning of the tragedy and agents of evil were very clear—Islamic terrorism was a devilish cancer to be pursued and fought at all costs. These feelings could easily be channeled into an overtly religious foreign policy. President Bush provided just such a framing for the Iraq War, drawing heavily on the idea of spiritual warfare.

The War in Iraq as a Spiritual Battle

"If you truly believe in the Scriptures, you will see your son again," promised George W. Bush. The president was comforting Robert Lehmiller, whose son was killed fighting in Iraq. Other families who have met President Bush after losing a relative in the war similarly report that their conversations turned immediately to faith.[21] In public life and from what we know about his private side, President Bush's religious devotion is closely linked to his ideas about foreign policy. Even before the Iraq War began, the Bush presidency infused discussions of the War on Terror with religious language—labeling Iraq as part of an "axis of evil" and invoking God as an ally in "our struggle." An astonished Mahmoud Abbas, the Palestinian prime minister, reported that George W. Bush personally told him that the wars in Iraq and Afghanistan were his "mission from God."[22]

The extent to which the commingling of spiritual warfare and foreign policy appeals to Americans depends on their belief in an Authoritative God. These believers can effortlessly weave world events and national policy into a larger battle between good and evil. Patty, a middle-aged administrative assistant from the Midwest, bluntly asserted that "there is a special blessing for people that support Israel. And a curse to those that do not support them, and as things keep going in the political system, I don't think that it's going to be too much longer before we are not supporting Israel, and when that happens there will be consequences!" As a strong believer in an Authoritative God, Patty is convinced that the United States is a Christian nation and that our foreign policy must support God's cosmic battle against evil, which includes supporting Israel and the Iraq War. Other believers in an Authoritative God tend to share Patty's view. In the fall of 2007, these

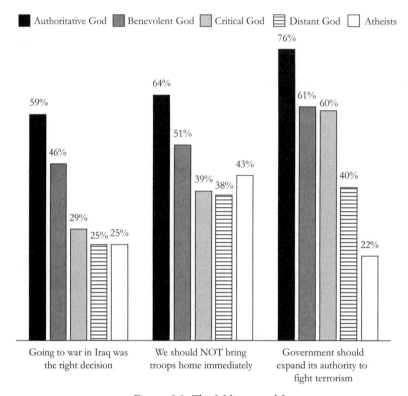

Figure 6.3. The Military and Iraq

believers were much more likely to think that "going to war in Iraq was the right decision," that "we should not bring home our troops immediately," and that "the government should extend its authority to fight terrorism" (figure 6.3). Although a majority of Americans initially supported the Iraq War, most turned against it as the war lingered on and death tolls mounted. By 2007, the most die-hard advocates of the war tended to be religiously devout individuals with an Authoritative God.[23]

Many of these believers saw the events of 9/11 as a wake-up call that, at the very least, raised burning questions about God's plan. For those who felt that 9/11 was a divine call to action, George W. Bush offered direction. Framing the War on Terror and the Iraq War as existential fights against evil, Bush defined the enemy of American values as the enemy of God. The administration powerfully argued that 9/11 had put us on the offensive against an evil that had been ignored for far too long. As he famously asserted, "Either you are with us, or you are with the terrorists."[24] This kind of language appealed to believers who think that God has laid out the moral world in very stark terms and calls on us to fight evil at every turn. Most important, President Bush's rhetoric clearly tied his foreign policy agenda to a calling from God.

On average, Christians who believe in an Authoritative God firmly believe that the United States is favored by God. They are likely to think that we should officially "declare the United States a Christian nation," that the "success of the United States is part of God's plan," that "people should be made to show respect for American traditions," and that "the government should advocate Christian values" (figure 6.4).[25] For these believers, the ubiquitous phrase "God bless America" means quite literally that God sides with the United States in its pursuits. Sandy, a working-class mother in the Midwest and believer in an Authoritative God, put it this way: "America has a special place in God's heart.

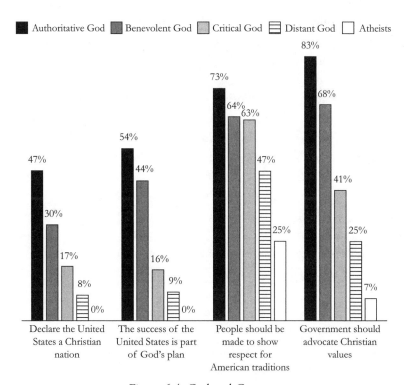

Figure 6.4. God and Country

We should be the leaders. We should teach the world. I was talking to my daughter about this yesterday. She said, 'I think the reason we should lead other countries is because they want something, to be free, and they need to know that God loves them no matter what.'" Sandy approved of President Bush's handling of the Iraq War because she felt that our international purpose should adhere strongly to our national religious mission. Essentially, she wanted the government to use its power and resources to save souls, and she felt strongly that President Bush agreed.

For believers like Sandy, patriotism and faith in an Authoritative God are inseparable, and the combination of these two faiths leads to very ardent support for U.S. military dominance. The religious aspect of attitudes about the Iraq War and trust in George W. Bush is clear.[26] Believers in an Authoritative God were the most likely to stick with the Bush administration as its popularity flagged. Harold, a young waiter who lives not far from Bush's former residence in the town of Crawford, Texas, defended the former president because of their shared faith. Harold passionately argued, "I really believe in the president. Being a believer, I believe he had God's favor on him in those elections. I believe God protects him. I believe that God is directing him and trying to talk to him every bit he can."

For Harold and many other believers in an Authoritative God, President Bush's unswerving commitment to military action in Iraq fits with their sense that this is not simply another war but rather a fight against evil that is demanded by God. Their patriotism is synonymous with their religious faith, and after 9/11, President Bush created a clear national religious mission that gave direction to those Americans who see little distinction between proselytizing and foreign policy.

Julie, a school cafeteria worker in Arkansas, summed up a common perspective among believers in an Authoritative God:

This nation was formed and based on believing in God, and I think that God is upset now with what the liberals are doing, like the ACLU trying to take religion and Christianity out of the picture. I think we're a blessed land, the most blessed land in the whole world because we have so many freedoms that so many countries don't have. . . . It's just like a friend of mine who goes to Cuba on missionary work each year says—there is no medicine in their stores, no Tylenol for babies with fever. There is nothing on the shelves. But we're moving away from where we began, and if we continue in that way, we may have the wrath of God at some point.

When asked specifically about the Iraq War, Julie explained, "I've had a lot of friends and relatives that have fought in that war and have become hurt. But God is very pleased that we helped the people of Iraq." Julie's commitment to the war is based not on an ignorance of its costs but rather on a firm faith that we are fighting a spiritual battle that must be continued regardless of the sacrifice. Believers who equate American foreign policy in Iraq with a larger spiritual war have a commitment that is as unwavering as President Bush's.

But devout believers who do not see military conflicts as an extension of spiritual warfare believe that former President Bush actually strayed from our perceived religious mission. Yolanda, a West Coast graduate student and believer in a Benevolent God, worries greatly about how God views our actions in Iraq and the supposed devotion of President Bush. Yolanda warns,

> I think that President Bush's actions have shown that he is not walking in "the Kingdom." He is just caught up in the power structures, which require him to do these things like lie and go to war . . . perhaps what he is doing he doesn't think it is his fault and he thinks he can still have a relationship with God. But he is in a position where he cannot really listen to God.

Yolanda feels that contemporary politics, especially the messiness of war, is part of a profane world that fall short of the ideals of her Benevolent God. In turn, she is hostile to the religious rhetoric of President Bush and firmly opposed the war. Similarly, Justin, a young high school teacher in Kansas, pondered how his Benevolent God would feel about the Iraq War, saying, "I don't think God is behind us in this. There is a bumper sticker that says, 'Who would Jesus bomb?' You just got to think about that. Jesus wouldn't stand for this! I think he would be outraged."

The God of Warfare

Ideas about war go hand in hand with ideas about God. When a person strongly believes that the world is faced with true evil and that God may punish us for failing to fight those forces, she will be highly motivated to heed the call. Believers in an Authoritative God tend to think that great disasters are either caused or allowed by God, but in either case, they feel that tragedies are divine warning signs. And disasters that occur in the United States are especially significant because these believers tend to feel that America is favored and closely watched by God.

The attacks of 9/11 were disturbing to all Americans, but believers in an Authoritative God saw this tragedy as evidence of a spiritual battle they were convinced was already at play. President Bush provided them with a framework to understand what God was communicating and what he wanted us to do. Still, the circumstances that led to the Iraq War were historically specific and could have unfolded much differently, had a different person been president. Believers in an Authoritative God may have rejected the foreign policy agenda of a president who did not frame military action within a religious discourse that fit their conception of spiritual warfare. They might have distanced themselves from the profane world of politics because it had no clear religious direction.

Consequently, the rhetoric of religious and political leaders is crucial in directing how believers in an Authoritative God will interpret and respond to tragedy. These believers live in a world in which they are engaged in ongoing spiritual warfare, and when called upon, they will respond. But how they respond depends on the way evil is defined and where it is located. Once it has been located, these believers will confidently and assertively support its annihilation.

Americans with Benevolent, Critical, and Distant Gods are hesitant, if not loath, to think of earthly conflicts and disasters in spiritual terms. Believers in a Benevolent God may support war, but they do not tend to think that God plays a role in destruction, although he might provide protection for faithful soldiers. They also tend to look away from the evils of the world and focus on God's love and mercy. Brice, a young and active member of the Church of Christ, sheepishly admitted, "I try not to follow [the Iraq War] terribly much, just because I don't want to know about the terrible things that happen in the world. But, for the most part, I think the United States stands up for what's right, and so I'm sure that God smiles on that." Like some other believers in a Benevolent God, Brice focuses predominantly on the good, which in turn reflects her image of an endlessly loving yet actively engaged God.

Believers in Critical and Distant Gods find the spiritual import of world affairs shocking and even antagonistic to their faith. They tend to be unconvinced by arguments that promote our involvement in spiritual warfare or, conversely, advocate our concentrated attention on God's wondrous gifts. Instead, these believers look for policies that concretely respond to real-world problems while still not undermining their basic beliefs in freedom and democracy. Some will be hawks, and others will be doves; regardless, they will tend not to offer religious justifications for their ideas. Still, God remains an important part of their worldview, just not one who has detailed opinions about current events or is constantly intervening in our affairs.

In troubled times, particularly after great disasters, believers look to God for guidance and attempt to understand what God wants. What we hear from God is sometimes astoundingly different, and it leads to vastly opposed opinions about foreign policy and international warfare.

In the future, we expect a simple principle to hold. Americans with an Authoritative God will be most likely to support a war and aggressive government policies following a great disaster, provided that the war is perceived as a spiritual battle against Satan or his minions. In the case of the Iraq War, the tragedy of 9/11 combined with the religious rhetoric of President Bush assured that those with an Authoritative God would be the most supportive of the war effort.

SEVEN

God—Present and Future

To what extent does God interact with the world?

To what extent does God judge the world?

These two important questions have never been directly or systematically asked of the American public. So we asked them and a host of other questions aimed at tapping into how Americans see God. We were unsure what we might find. Would Americans be able to answer these questions? They could and did. Would Americans respond differently to these questions, or would we just hear the same vague and general responses from most? We discovered that Americans differ radically in their beliefs about how closely God guides and judges their lives. These two dynamic dimensions of belief reveal four distinct images of God:

1. *The Authoritative God—one who is both engaged and judgmental*
2. *The Benevolent God—one who is engaged but not judgmental*
3. *The Critical God—one who is not engaged but judgmental*
4. *The Distant God—one who is not engaged or judgmental*

But most important, do these different Gods matter? Unequivocally, yes. A person's God is a direct reflection of his level of moral absolutism, his view of science, his understanding of economic justice, his concept of evil, and how he thinks we should respond to it. And these powerful relationships exist regardless of where he lives, the color of his skin, the amount of money he makes, how many years he has spend in school, or the church he attends.

Simply put, America's four Gods lie at the heart of our moral, cultural, and political disagreements. If we hope to explain the root of our culture wars and what form they might take in the future, we need to look closely at our beliefs about God.

God and the Present

At present, there are countless confusions about our culture wars. Still, we tend to agree that there are some basic worldview differences from which a host of more specific moral and political disagreements stem. But what is the main crux of these differences? On this question, there is much debate. There are simple stereotypes promoted by popular pundits who seek to foster disgust of an other—stereotypes that tend to exaggerate urban/rural, white-collar/blue-collar, and godly/godless distinctions. Of these, only the godly/godless division directly indicates a difference in belief; the other distinctions erroneously take for granted that our different outlooks are tied to our geography or our employment. There are also more complex typologies of worldviews proposed by intellectuals and academics who eschew blunt stereotypes in order to better understand our diversity. These proposed categories tend to be more abstract and more difficult to recognize in discussions with average Americans. By considering these different depictions of our culture wars, we hope to demonstrate how our investigation into beliefs about God can shed some light on previously obscured topics (while also indicating which topics remain in darkness).

Too often, pundits tell us the wrong story about our culture wars. They erroneously contend that that the godly are loyal conservatives and that the godless are loyal progressives. What is unique about this perspective is that political activists and pundits on both the left and the right share it.

Conservative political and religious leaders often equate spiritual devotion with cultural, social, and political conservatism. The religious pundit Pat Robertson is unafraid to anoint someone as "God's candidate," and conservative commentators like Ann Coulter relish the opportunity to label the Democratic Party "godless." Angered at the use of religious rhetoric to propagate conservative policies and attack scientific research, a group of public intellectuals, popularly known as the New Atheists, felt it was time to fight what they saw as the hypocrisies and irrationalities of religiosity.[1] But in making an argument for the rational and ethical superiority of atheism, they look past the reality of our times and offer an argument that appears surprisingly similar to that of conservative pundits—namely, the claim that progressivism is compatible only with atheism.

Oxford professor Richard Dawkins develops an attention-grabbing argument against the existence of God in *The God Delusion* (2006). He joins other prominent science professors making similar arguments in works such as *God: The Failed Hypothesis* (2007), *Unintelligent Design* (2003), and *The Ghost in the Universe: God in Light of Modern Science* (2002). In *God Is Not Great: How Religion Poisons Everything*, Christopher Hitchens takes the advocacy of atheism a step further by arguing that a society without religion would be ethically superior. Equating all religion with naïve superstition, Hitchens bluntly states that "religion has run out of justifications. Thanks to the telescope and the microscope, it no longer offers an explanation of anything important."[2]

Although the arguments of the New Atheists are certainly engaging, they tend to misrepresent the current relationships among science, progressivism, and belief in God. Today, Democrats and cultural progressives are overwhelmingly likely to believe in God. Many professional scientists are also devout believers.[3] In sum, a large swath of America is religiously devout, politically liberal, *and* scientifically savvy—three things we are told cannot go together.

Considering these facts, we can see how the New Atheists ironically bolster religious conservatives' attempts to frame their culture war as a crusade against secularism. At present, disenchanted enclaves of atheists do not signal the dawn of a new secular age but rather provide stark indicators that religious faith is overwhelmingly dominant.[4] We are a secular nation only to the extent that the Constitution ensures that there is no official national religion. Beyond this legal separation of church and state—and most likely because of it—we are a very religious people.[5] Despite what pundits on both left and right exclaim, the American public is not engaged in a battle between the secular and the religious.

While trying to steer past misleading stereotypes and crass political agendas, academics still place Americans into one of two cultural camps. These stark ideological dichotomies reflect the dominance of our two major political parties. The Republican side of the public is defined in various ways: "traditionalists," "orthodox," "evangelical/fundamentalists," "utilitarian individualists," or a host of other labels aimed at distilling into one category the essence of American conservatism.[6] The Democratic side of this equation is called the opposite—"cosmopolitans," "humanists," "progressives," "ecumenicals," or some similar term intended to evoke the converse of American conservatism. In creating these ideological categories, researchers and theorists hope to identify the key philosophical disputes that divide Americans. James Hunter's division of America into "progressive" and "orthodox" camps provides keen insight into how basic differences in conceptions of moral authority determine our social and political divisions. Cognitive scientist George Lakoff describes the moral worldview of conservatives as that of a "Strict Father" and liberal morality as that of a "Nurturant Parent." These categories indicate moral differences by referencing different parenting styles that are easily recognizable—the strict parent who applies the rod to instill moral order versus the nurturant parent who praises and rewards appropriate moral behavior. But regardless of the labels Hunter, Lakoff, and others develop, most researchers adhere to the core idea that our culture wars are over rudimentary moral disagreements.

Still, many individuals and groups don't fit neatly into one of two categories. There are moral traditionalists who advocate progressive economic and social policies—think of religiously orthodox African Americans who advocate conservative moral codes yet consistently vote as Democrats. And there are Republicans who passionately promote conservative economic policies while not caring a bit about abortion or gay marriage. In his analysis of groups that upset easy categorization, sociologist Fred Kniss argues for a "multiparty conception of American religion" and identifies ways in which the philosophical differences between our two major political parties are unable to fully account for moral and theological diversity in America.[7] Kniss, in developing a fourfold typology to replace the typical two-party typologies, bases his categories on elementary moral differences. And herein lies a problem.

While researchers are quite right to look at our moral differences and Kniss is correct to object to simple two-party explanations, the difficulty in these attempts to better explain our culture wars is a problem of assessment. How do we know when a person is a "utilitarian individualist" or an "ecumenical humanist"? Perhaps a person's moral philosophy can be surmised from her party affiliation or church membership. But we know too well that these groups do not control the thoughts of their members, and we can never assume a person is in full agreement with her party or church. Therefore, we have to ask individuals. But researchers don't ask Americans direct questions such as "Is the collective or the individual the center of moral authority?" We cannot, mainly because most of us simply do not have ready-made responses to such abstract questions. Consequently, the problem of understanding a person's moral philosophy is complicated by the fact that most people cannot clearly express it.

Talking about God solves this basic dilemma. When we talk about God, we are actually addressing the moral and philosophical issues that are of such interest to researchers. In this way, images of God give substance to the theoretical frameworks proposed by many researchers. But in talking about God, Americans use different language to express their moral attitudes. And this language requires some explication. Here is one example.

Cathy and Belle live in different parts of the country but share a common complaint: they both believe that America is experiencing a moral crisis. Cathy, a twenty-nine-year-old graduate student from Pasadena, California, lamented, "God's opinion of the United States is that you have this grand experiment and it has, like all earthly kingdoms, deteriorated." In faraway Lake Village, Arkansas, Belle, a forty-nine-year-old cafeteria worker, seemingly echoed Cathy's sentiment, bemoaning that "our nation was formed and based on believing in God, and I think that he is really upset now." While the statements of Belle and Cathy appear similar, they take on vastly different meanings when we reconsider what each woman means when she says "God." Belle believes in an Authoritative God; Cathy's God is Distant.

Someone who believes in an engaged God thinks that a transcendent moral authority is present in the world. As a consequence, prudence requires that we defer to this moral authority. Those with a less engaged God feel that we can never know God's true thoughts and that we need to rely on our God-given moral and intellectual powers to make decisions. Also, conceiving of a judgmental God indicates that an individual feels that moral codes are absolute. The opposite is true of individuals who believe in a nonjudgmental God and tend to shy away from stark judgments.

Because Cathy believes in a nonjudgmental and less engaged God—the Distant God—her comments must be interpreted metaphorically. In fact, when she says that God thinks the American experiment has deteriorated, she means that we have too often substituted inflexible religious dogma for our God-given reason. For Cathy, human reason provides us with a moral compass that should guide our actions independently of the claims of biblical literalists and those who purport to speak for God. She feels that Americans have lost the essence of God, who is our inward source of moral strength and is not to be found in some dogmatic religious code. More specifically, she expressed her displeasure with the Iraq War and other Bush administration policies because, in her view, our national agenda during the Bush years was based on a misguided sense of religious righteousness. By better understanding Cathy's Distant God, we can see that her moral philosophy relies on self-analysis and the questioning of worldly authority.

Belle has an engaged and judgmental God. For her, God's laws are revealed in the Bible, and his will is carried out by his earthly followers. Because Belle believes that God commands us to ban abortion and discourage homosexuality, she is in favor of conservative policies on these issues. Belle fears that "liberals" and the American Civil Liberties Union are violating God's clear commandments and that we risk harsh punishments for their folly. She also believes that God necessarily had a guiding hand in establishing American dominance in world affairs. Consequently, any attack on Americans is an affront to God. Belle also worries that President Obama has never properly tied his policies to God's larger plan. By better understanding Belle's Authoritative God, we can see that her moral philosophy is generated out of a devotion to a transcendent authority whose wishes are clearly stated in religious text.

In a general sense, the Authoritative God and the Distant God fit well within a typical two-party typology—an Authoritative God appears compatible with typical depictions of conservative morality, and a more liberal morality seems consistent in a universe with a Distant God. But as our analyses demonstrate, these two Gods are not the only Gods. Believers in a Critical God recognize a strict moral code but feel they are on their own in navigating the cruel world. In turn, they tend to have little faith that social policies can do much to upend the harsh realities of a universe fraught with injustices and injuries. On the other hand, believers in a Benevolent God posit a universe where divine grace is bountiful. But mimicking this largesse with social policy proves difficult—it assumes an idealized society where competition for resources is rare and unnecessary. Consequently, the attitudes of believers in Benevolent and Critical Gods, while in stark contrast, are both likely to drift outside the political philosophies of the left and the right.

Clearly, our fourfold God typology is artificial to the extent that the diversity of beliefs about God is infinite.[8] Yet these four Gods provide us with new ways to assess the moral worldviews of Americans. First, when talking about God's engagement, Americans indicate the extent to which they feel the hand of a transcendent moral authority guiding us. Essentially, discussions of God's engagement elicit Hunter's categories of moral authority—an engaged God indicates belief in a traditional transcendent authority; a less engaged God designates belief in individual moral autonomy.

Second, when talking about God's judgment, Americans demonstrate the extent to which they think we are engaged in a cosmic battle between good and evil. Those with a judgmental God feel that evil is clearly defined and that we are obliged to eradicate it by any means necessary. By contrast, those with a less judgmental God are not as confident of what evil is and what to do about it. In effect, beliefs about God's judgment gauge the extent to which Americans adopt a Strict Father morality or a Nurturant Parent morality—the moral perspectives described by George Lakoff. Specifically, those with a judgmental God favor strict penalties and assert that we should never spare the rod when confronting evil. In turn, Americans with a nonjudgmental God prefer to stress what is good as a means to diminish evil.

Our four Gods help us assess two important dimensions of our moral philosophies: (1) the extent to which we rely on transcendent authority and (2) the ways we think best address evil. Consequently, we look to images of God to understand the present moral worldviews of Americans, and we should also think about how images of God change in order to predict what our moral worldviews might look like in the future.

God and the Future

Our conceptions of God change—both over the course of history and during our lifetime. Are there trends in *how* they change? In *Discovering God*, sociologist Rodney Stark argues that humans always *adapt* their images of God according to what best fits their current needs and experiences.[9] According to Stark, we are naturally inclined to favor a loving God: people hope for a God who cares for them and desires to help them. Why would anyone want a God who was indifferent or even hurtful? In the United States, this is evidently true. Belief in a loving God unites us more than anything else we found.

Stark also asserts that people favor "Gods of infinite scope and absolute power."[10] This explains a general trend toward monotheism throughout history. Images of the divine date back to the first records of human life, beginning with a plethora of gods and goddesses.[11] Over time, collections of gods and goddesses coalesced into an image of a single God. Judaism firmly posits a single living God whose essence is infinite in scope.[12] Christianity and Islam sprang from this Jewish understanding of a single living God. Today, monotheisms dominate the global religious landscape.

Just as Americans agree that God is loving, Americans tend to think of God as infinite in scope and absolute in power. In general, religious choice in the United States is essentially limited to monotheism versus atheism, with very little discussion of polytheistic or nontheistic alternatives. Even Americans who think that God is in everything—a core tenet of pantheism—are more comfortable talking about God as a distinct being.

But beyond this master trend toward a loving and infinite God, how are Americans adapting their image of God to changing times? In *American Gospel*, Jon Meacham argues that "there is no doubt . . . that the Founders lived and consciously bequeathed a culture shaped and sustained by public religion, one that was not Christian or Jewish or Muslim or Buddhist but was simply transcendent, with reverence for the 'Creator' and for 'Nature's God.'"[13] Meacham's description of the Founding Fathers' God as "Nature's God" most closely resembles a Distant God—a God who created the universe but left humans to apply their own reason to moral, scientific, and political concerns.

If we were to assume that citizens of the newly formed United States shared the religious beliefs of the Founding Fathers, we would conclude that belief in Authoritative, Benevolent, and Critical Gods has dramatically increased since then—around a third of us now believe in an Authoritative God. More likely, the Founding Fathers were outliers. They were a select few—cosmopolitan men with substantial wealth and extensive education—and they were quite progressive in their thinking on a whole host of topics. There is, in fact, some evidence that Americans have moved closer to the kind of God our Founding Fathers envisioned, a trend that may continue.

One possible sign of this trend is that the number of Americans who say that they have no religious preference is growing. While they still believe in God (for the most part), these Americans belong to no religious organization and refuse to identify as followers of a specific tradition.[14] Americans with "no religion" tend to be believers in a Distant God. As such, they express views that may appear secular because they offer secular justifications for their moral positions and defer to academic science in their understanding of the natural world. In many ways, these unaffiliated believers resemble the Founding Fathers, who often found traditional religion lacking. Still, it would be a mistake to call this "atheism-lite," simply because organized religion may not properly address these people's spiritual yearnings.

Americans who no longer identify with a particular religious group still tend to describe themselves as "spiritual." Again, this suggests a move toward an individualistic spirituality that is not attached to any particular denomination or church. Sociologist Robert Wuthnow argues that in the United States "denominationalism has become less significant."[15] The declining significance of denominations, along with a drop in the number of religiously affiliated Americans, suggests that belief is in flux. Most likely, this indicates a move toward a more Distant

God—a God who does not demand strict orthodoxy but instead favors individual spiritual seeking.

But we should not place our bets on the ultimate victory of the Distant God, because some strong countertrends are at play. Evangelicalism is the most conspicuous and successful transdenominational religious movement in America.[16] Americans from a wide range of denominational families identify with this movement. Self-identified evangelicals speak passionately about their faith journeys and tell stories of daily interactions with God and Christ. In fact, a person who was unfamiliar with Christianity and listened to our interviews with evangelicals might come away with the idea that they shared a close personal friend named Jesus and wonder how this sociable and helpful man traveled around so much.

Nearly half of Americans who call themselves evangelicals believe in an Authoritative God, and a quarter believe in a Benevolent God. American evangelicalism stresses an intense personal relationship with God, and sociologist Christian Smith argues that this, in turn, contributes greatly to the success and growth of the movement.[17] Smith's argument fits with the fact that church attendance and participation are closely connected to belief in an engaged God. Indeed, evangelical theology appears tailor-made for modern Americans seeking a closer bond with God as they navigate a complex world. Consequently, God's engagement with the individual, rather than God's judgment, might be the fundamental strength of American evangelicalism. Vital religions have always motivated individuals by offering them spiritual intimacy, rather than threats of punishment in the afterlife. The success of the nondenominational evangelical movement demonstrates this. Thus, evangelicalism will most likely continue to grow by stressing God's engagement.

These diverse trends—toward waning church attendance for some, the growth of evangelicalism among others—suggest that conceptions of God will remain varied and vibrant for years to come. While the big trend may be toward less traditional spirituality, the American landscape provides a lot of room for the cultivation and perpetuation of ancient faiths. In fact, the freedom to choose one's faith may secure the continued vitality of traditional images of God.

What might the future look like for an America with changing Gods? Let's look at a few "what if" scenarios.

Future Culture Wars

Changes in religious belief would have large-scale and immediate ramifications for American culture. That said, religious beliefs do not exist in a vacuum. Our beliefs and our circumstances influence each other. Clearly, there is no single starting point when talking about cultural change, and we must be careful not to claim that changes in images of God will *cause* changes in social, political, or economic life. Nonetheless, conceptions of God tap some deep underlying currents in the culture. So we can speculate on how America would respond to changes in conceptions of God.

Throughout this book, we have emphasized four areas of disagreement that are closely tied to our image of God: (1) our moral absolutism, (2) our understanding of science, (3) our reaction to inequality, and (4) our responses to evil. We all try to pull the nation in the direction of our imagined ideal community, whether through community activism, voting, or our interactions with others. What would happen if belief in God changed?

The Future of American Values

Shortly before the 2004 presidential election, the Republican National Committee appealed directly to moral absolutists in Arkansas with a startling mass mailing. The front of the envelope pictured a man kneeling and placing a ring onto the finger of another man. Across this photo was plastered the word "ALLOWED." Opposite this photo was a picture of a Bible marked "BANNED." An additional warning read: "This will be Arkansas . . . if you don't vote," and recipients were urged to read the enclosed letter "if you want to stop *them*."[18] This kind of political tactic, which frames public policy as a choice between depravity and decency, is highly compatible with the moral absolutism of believers in a judgmental God. But if we move away from the Authoritative God and toward the Benevolent God, we could expect that this kind of political tactic will lose some of its overall potency, because fewer believers will respond favorably to such a clear demarcation between good and evil.

In distinct contrast, if a Distant God becomes more popular, we would see more advocacy of freedom to make one's own decisions about a wide range of moral topics. Therefore, we could expect strong advocacy of abortion rights and civil liberties for gays and lesbians. Also, currently unpopular policies like legalization of marijuana and euthanasia might gain traction with the general public. Consequently, a change in images of God will not only shift the balance of power on current hot-button issues but also refocus public debate on fresh concerns. Specifically, laws concerning marijuana and euthanasia could become key political talking points in the future.

Overall, the potential decline of belief in Authoritative and Critical Gods would lead to less emphasis on harsh criminal sentencing. Regardless, we foresee a continued debate about the extent to which society should impose moral restrictions on specific behaviors. Those with a Benevolent God will still strongly advocate laws governing social and sexual behaviors, even though they will be more lenient about the consequences. As a result, we might expect a potentially toned-down debate about the most sensitive sexual and cultural issues of the day.

The Future of Science

Former President George W. Bush famously advised public schools to "teach the debate" between intelligent design and evolution. Bush's proposal was sympathetic to religious believers who feel embattled and threatened by modern science. But the world's major religious traditions have demonstrated an amazing ability to either incorporate or become compatible with modern science, and many American religious believers see no contradiction between their religious faith and belief in evolution. Others, however, feel that scientific claims often overstep the boundaries of science and begin to tread on the toes of religious faith. What determines whether American believers embrace or oppose current scientific theories lies in the extent to which they feel that God manipulates the natural order. While President Bush wanted public schools to "teach the debate," this debate is really about competing views of God's role in the world rather than competing scientific theories.

For believers in the Authoritative and Benevolent Gods, God sits above the natural order and is never subject to the laws of nature. They tend to feel that scientists ignore the elevated position God holds in the cosmos and, consequently, believe that science advances antireligious theories of the natural order. By contrast, believers in the Critical and Distant Gods see God as an integral part of the natural order and feel that scientific theories reveal the true essence of the divine. For these believers, science does not threaten their faith but rather provides a richer and more interesting path to God.

Popular attitudes toward evolution, climate change, and stem-cell research are all based on how Americans perceive the agenda and integrity of scientific and medical professionals. Those who view changes in medicine and science as infringing on God's role in the world distrust the academic and medical communities and tend to respond favorably to those who question mainstream science.

With more believers in a Benevolent God, we should continue to see pressure put on scientists to consider the role of God in their studies. They would also continue to advocate the teaching of intelligent design and/or creationism in public schools. Nonetheless, believers in a Benevolent God will continue to support scientific funding and, given time, may even come to view many of the more controversial statements of professional scientists as valid. Meanwhile, more believers in a Distant God ensure a continued trust in the endless possibilities of science. Scientific funding will be ample, and believers will continue to rely on scientists to solve their medical and environmental problems.

Perhaps one of the most religiously charged issues in our future will be the role of religious authority in science. Americans who believe in an engaged God are leery of academic scientists and worry that they advance a latent antireligious agenda in their research. While all Americans say they value science, the role of God in scientific understanding remains a contested problem and is likely to remain a powerful one if current trends in belief hold.

The Future Economic Order

Liberation theology has never taken deep root in American soil. This religious tradition, mainly associated with the Roman Catholic Church, combines a Christian ethic with a Marxist focus on political activism and economic equality. Americans say that they empathize deeply with the poor but are also firm believers in the capitalist system and the ability of free markets to benefit us all. God, in turn, is not at the center of class-based struggles in the United States.

But our image of God is still deeply rooted in our economic status. Simply put, Americans with lower incomes tend to imagine an angrier God. While we predict a movement away from judgmental or angry images of God, this could reverse if income inequality increases. In fact, continued poverty, disenfranchisement, and economic frustration may ensure that images of an Authoritative God or a Critical God remain quite popular.

Although we do not expect that future class wars will emerge from religious disagreements, how Americans want to fight poverty is very much premised on different images of God. Those with less judgmental Gods, particularly the Benevolent God, believe that the government is suited for addressing economic inequality. Those who see God in more judgmental terms (Authoritative and Critical) tend to prefer that government fund religious organizations as a holistic approach to poverty.

Faith-based initiatives directly address this distinction. This program recognizes that the most active advocates of communities in need are often local congregations. Undeniably, religious calling can be a powerful motivator in fighting poverty.[19] Supporters view the faith-based program as a way to mobilize highly motivated and organized people to help their communities. Critics feel that it threatens the separation of church and state and is a clear show of favoritism toward religion.

If there is a reduction in belief in a judgmental God, we will see less call for the government to fund social services provided by religious organizations. And believers in a Benevolent God will remain on the forefront of religious-based community activism, even as they eschew federal funding.

The Future World Order

On some level, politicians want us to believe that God is on our side and, more subtly, on their side. Both Republicans and Democrats now freely refer to God and specifically tie God to the interests of the United States. How do Americans feel about this? The lack of public outcry against the use of God in political rhetoric indicates that we have come to accept this as a normal part of our political dialogue. But how

Americans interpret the meaning of the phrase "God bless America" is filtered through the prism of their conception of God.

Americans who believe in a more judgmental God are the most likely to think that God favors the United States over all other nations. Political rhetoric that divides the world into good and evil advances this potent call to action and is often used to justify military engagement, strong responses to crime, and the death penalty. As one believer told us, the American soldier and the executioner are faithfully responding to their religious calling. But if belief in Authoritative and Critical Gods wanes, religious justifications of warfare may also be less appealing to Americans.

Believers in a Benevolent or Distant God tend to prefer political or strategic motivations for warfare; they are averse to the notion of a cosmic struggle between good and evil. For this reason, future American leaders may find religious rhetoric less useful for advocating aggressive foreign policy.

Keep Your Eye on God

We need to keep a close eye on changing images of God to maintain a sense of where moral and policy disagreements will be most intense and how we might ease them.

We expect that our disagreements over God's engagement will most likely increase. Currently, most Americans feel that God is very active in our lives, but trends toward a more Distant God would indicate a growing chasm in public belief. This may lead some believers to become more averse to arguments for intelligent design and to political references to God and less sympathetic to the moral absolutism of traditional religious doctrine. In turn, those with an engaged God will feel more embattled and potentially more vigorous in their demands to see God referenced in the public square. But in the end, those with a more engaged God may have to accept their God being pushed out of the public square and the fact that discussions of how God influences the universe will not be considered in the theories of modern scientists. Instead, believers in a more engaged God may become more isolated in their demands for a science that accounts for their religion and for social policy drawn directly from their religious doctrines.

In fact, this growing disagreement makes public allusions to God treacherous. Currently, politicians pepper their speeches with God talk in hopes of displaying their moral fervor and their opponent's moral inadequacies. Without doubt, Americans view leaders who espouse values and perspectives compatible with their own as godly, righteous, and moral. But when a public figure advances a contrary opinion or is affiliated with an unfavorable political party or group, that leader's religiosity, moral fiber, and honesty are seriously questioned. For instance, many political liberals feel that former President Bush was not only misguided but also insincere in his religious devotion. Similarly, conservatives routinely question the religious authenticity of President Obama when he openly asserts his Christian faith. The religious and moral grounding of our social, economic, and policy disputes makes pragmatic and conciliatory discussions about policies difficult and rare. Rather than debate policy, we debate the morality of individuals. And if their image of God does not match our own, we conclude that they are either godless or fanatical.

With regard to the future political ramifications of God, we need to keep close watch on changes in attitudes about God's judgment. Our current economic crisis could lead some Americans to posit a more judgmental God, simply because hardship appears to be related to this image of God. That said, we also sense that images of a very judgmental God are most likely on the decline. If this turns out to be the case, political rhetoric premised on our collective fight against evil will become less potent. But if larger portions of the American public begin to envision a more judgmental God, the time is ripe for political and religious leaders to exploit growing tendencies to lash out at evil in our midst. Warmongering and hard-line attacks against hated minorities and immigrants could become more acceptable.

We need to keep an eye on changing images of God because the effect these images have on us can be a blessing but can also turn tragic. They are a blessing when a shared sense of a loving God brings together a community. Tragedy comes when we disagree so fundamentally about who God is and what God wants that we stir up conflict. This tragedy was recognized by Pam, a woman we spoke with who, more than anything, wants to bring people of various faiths to a common understanding of God. After 9/11, Pam, an active Presbyterian, became committed to learning more about Islam and even started an interfaith group to discuss religious reconciliation. Pam explained her profound sadness at not being able to convince her Muslim acquaintances that they worshipped the same God. At one intense moment, Pam pleaded, "We believe in one God. It is the same God. It is not Allah for you and God for me." But after bitter words were exchanged, Pam concluded that "there were definitely two Gods in that room that night."

Trying to coax a person with different beliefs to share your God (or lack of belief in God) can be misguided and often insulting. Consequently, the tragedy of our many Gods is that we fail to fully understand each other. Elites often benefit by exploiting these differences and mutual misunderstandings. They can drive wedges into communities and suck resources into conflicts that could be avoided. While elites and pundits often utilize the differences between our Gods to expand their pocketbooks and their influence, the similarities of our Gods—namely, the loving aspect—will keep our shared moral philosophy alive. A morality directly related to a loving God fosters respect for one another and charity and ensures that our differences will not spiral out of control. A perfectly harmonious existence is clearly a dream, but at least it is a dream common to all of our Gods.

THE GOD QUESTIONNAIRE

This test poses the same questions about God answered by respondents of the Baylor Religion Survey (BRS).[1] Because the God Questionnaire assumes some belief in the supernatural, atheists were not asked to supply answers in our national survey, but we nevertheless invite nonbelievers to read through and think about the questions. Also, we feel that our questions are applicable to individuals from various religious traditions, so that Muslims, Jews, and Christians should be able to respond without problem. Of course, all survey questions force you to choose responses that may not fully communicate the complexity of your personal beliefs. So simply provide the best answer available. With this clear limitation in mind, the God Questionnaire is a painless and hopefully illuminating exercise that will help you better understand our discussion as we proceed. You can also take the God Questionnaire online at www.Americasfourgods.com if you want your score automatically tallied and compared to the scores of other Americans.

---

1. The BRS contains more than 400 questions, so for the purpose of brevity, we have included only those items directly related to conceptions of God. Remember that your experience in answering these questions is not the same as it was for survey respondents. You have probably been thinking about your image of God since starting this book. Survey respondents did not know they would be asked questions about God and were, in fact, presented with questions on a wide variety of religious and nonreligious topics. As such, survey respondents are likely to have provided more spontaneous or reflexive answers to the God questions than you will. Survey researchers are also well aware of the importance of *context* when administering surveys. People can respond differently to questions, depending on the order in which they are presented and differences in the way they are worded. Taking a block of questions out of the broader context of the survey may influence your answers in ways we cannot anticipate.

Please answer the following questions to the best of your ability. There is no right or wrong answer.

For each item please check one box only.

A. God's Judgment

How well do you feel that each of the following words describes God?	Very well	Somewhat well	Undecided	Not very well	Not at all
1. Loving	☐	☐	☐	☐	☐
2. Critical	5	4	3	2	1
3. Punishing	5	4	3	2	1
4. Severe	5	4	3	2	1
5. Wrathful	5	4	3	2	1

Even if you might not believe in God, based on your personal understanding, what do you think God is like?	Strongly Agree	Agree	Undecided	Disagree	Strongly Disagree
6. Angered by human sin	5	4	3	2	1
7. Angered by my sins	5	4	3	2	1

B. God's Engagement

How well do you feel that each of the following words describes God?	Very well	Somewhat well	Undecided	Not very well	Not at all
8. Distant	1	2	3	4	5
9. Ever-present	5	4	3	2	1

Even if you might not believe in God, based on your personal understanding, what do you think God is like?	Strongly Agree	Agree	Undecided	Disagree	Strongly Disagree
10. Removed from worldly affairs	1	2	3	4	5
11. Removed from my personal affairs	1	2	3	4	5
12. Concerned with the well-being of the world	5	4	3	2	1
13. Concerned with my personal well-being	5	4	3	2	1
14. Directly involved in worldly affairs	5	4	3	2	1
15. Directly involved in my affairs	5	4	3	2	1

Who Is Your God?

Your image of God depends on whether you are higher (above the average) or lower (at the average or below) on two perceived qualities of God's character—God's judgment and God's engagement.

God's Judgment

To compare your attitudes about God's judgment with the general public, you need to compute your Judgment score. The first block of questions in the God Questionnaire (under "A. God's Judgment") gauges your beliefs about God's judgmental qualities. The first item refers to your beliefs about God's love. As we discussed in chapter 1, this perceived aspect of God's personality is not particularly revealing. Note that questions 2–7 have a number from 1–5 printed in the background of each checkbox. For example, if you answered "very well" when asked how well the word "critical" describes God, you received a 5 on question 2. To determine your score for God's Judgment, add up the numbers behind your answers for questions 2–7. Your score should be somewhere between 6 and 30. If you would like to keep this number handy for future reference, write your score in the box next to "God's Judgment" on the God Questionnaire.

Those with higher scores on the Judgmental God index tend to imagine a God who often dislikes what he sees. The closer your own score is to 30, the more judgmental, wrathful, and angry you tend to imagine God to be. The average Judgmental God score for BRS respondents was 17, with the majority of respondents falling between 11 and 23. What this means is that most Americans fall between the two extremes—believing God to be neither extremely judgmental nor completely forgiving. The closer your Judgmental God score is to 17, the more in line you are with the American average. People who fall in the middle of the Judgmental God scale may ascribe some judgmental qualities to God but may be uncertain as to what form that judgment takes.

God's Engagement

To determine how you feel about God's level of contact with the world, you need to score the second half of the God Questionnaire, which will provide you with a score for God's Engagement. Add together the numbers printed behind each possible answer for questions 8–15. Pay careful attention to these numbers because they reverse, depending on the question asked. For example, if you said that "Distant" describes God very well, you should add 1 to your score. But if you said that "Ever-present" describes God very well, add 5 to your score. Your final score for God's Engagement should be between 8 and 40.

While God's level of anger and judgment proved to be a divisive issue, with most falling in between the two possible extremes, respondents to the Baylor Religion Survey were in stronger agreement regarding God's engagement with the world. Most Americans believe God to be very engaged with and active in the world. The closer to 31 your score for God's Engagement is, the more similar you are to the average American.

Armed with your scores for God's Judgment and God's Engagement, you can determine which of the four Gods you believe in.

Who Is Your God?

God's Judgment Score		God's Engagement Score		Your God
High (18 to 30)	AND	High (32 to 40)	=	TYPE A
Low (6 to 17)	AND	High (32 to 40)		TYPE B
High (18 to 30)	AND	Low (8 to 31)	=	TYPE C
Low (6 to 17)	AND	Low (8 to 31)	=	TYPE D

If your score for God's Judgment is at 17 or below, check the boxes marked "Low" under God's Judgment. If your score for God's Judgment is at 18 or higher, check the boxes marked "High" under God's Judgment. In a similar vein, check the boxes marked "High" under God's Engagement if your score is at 32 or above and the "Low" boxes otherwise. Your God type is the one for which you checked both boxes. So if you checked "High" for God's Judgment and "High" for God's

Engagement, you have a Type A God. If you checked "Low" for God's Judgment but "High" for God's Engagement, you have a Type B God, and so forth.

Based on the pattern of responses to these questions on the Baylor Religion Survey, we brainstormed a name for each God type. With a greater propensity to judgment and engagement, we labeled the Type A God *Authoritative*. The Type B God, who shows a lower tendency toward judgment but high levels of engagement, we titled *Benevolent*. The God who does not engage in the world but remains judgmental of it, we called *Critical*. Finally, we labeled a God who is considered neither very judgmental nor very involved in the world *Distant*. Note that our labels for each God type are merely our attempt to capture its unique qualities. Such labels are *not* meant to imply that a person who views God as Authoritative imagines him as having no Benevolent qualities. Indeed, as noted before, almost everyone imagines God to be a loving being, and in our interviews, people with an Authoritative image of God provided many stories of God demonstrating his benevolence. Even people who imagine God as Distant sometimes offer accounts of God's intervention in their lives or believe that God may become angered by certain world events. For an issue as nuanced and complex as personal theology, no categorization scheme can hope to perfectly capture the opinions of everyone. Rather, our God types are meant to be used relative to one another. Someone with an Authoritative image of God views God as more judgmental, on average, than a person who holds a Benevolent view of God. Compared with others, people with a Distant image of God were least likely to imagine a deity who judges or engages with the world.

Remember also that while they are not included in our typology, some Americans are atheists. Atheists are certain that God does not exist. For them, God is a wholly fictional human creation and is not even useful as a metaphor for some supernatural realm. Therefore, they do not provide responses to questions concerning God. Nevertheless, we include atheists in our study of God because we find that their nonbelief is as important in defining their worldview as another person's belief in God.

APPENDIX

Data, Methods, and Findings

For readers concerned about methodological issues, this appendix provides details on the sources of our data—two waves of the Baylor Religion Survey and a series of qualitative interviews—and the statistical analyses that lie behind our presentation.

The Baylor Religion Survey

Funded by the Templeton Foundation, the Baylor Religion Survey (BRS) is an in-depth survey of religious beliefs and attitudes administered to the U.S. general population. Most other national surveys, such as the General Social Survey and National Election Study, include limited questions on religion.[1] That is not to say that the developers of these surveys do not feel religion is important. Rather, it is a question of focus. The Baylor Religion Survey was designed to try to fill this gap with the inclusion of dozens of new religion questions. Most important for the purposes of this book, the BRS includes more than two dozen questions that ask respondents to characterize God's personality.

This book utilizes data from the first two waves of the Baylor Religion Survey. Wave 1, collected in the fall of 2005, consists of a random sample of 1,721 Americans. Wave 2, collected in the fall of 2007, provides responses from a random sample of 1,648 Americans. In the interests of space, we have not reproduced the full survey booklets for each wave in this volume. Interested readers can view the questionnaires at the Web site for Baylor's Institute for Studies of Religion (ISR): http://www.isreligion.org/research/surveysofreligion/. Researchers can also download the Baylor Religion Survey at http://thearda.com.

Data Collection

The Gallup Organization administered the Baylor Religion Survey. Of course, many items on the BRS are similar or identical to those on existing surveys, such as the General Social Survey, the National Election Study, and the many surveys conducted by the Pew Forum. But new questions, such as the image of God module, had never before appeared on a national survey and were field-tested by both Baylor University and the Gallup Organization.

Even though the BRS includes many religion questions, it was *not* administered only to highly religious people or to a certain type of religious person. The Gallup Organization called a random sample of people around the country to solicit their participation in the survey. Every person in the United States with a phone had an equal chance of being selected for the survey. While Americans are overwhelmingly Christian, people of non-Christian religions and atheists completed the survey as well.[2]

For both waves, Gallup used a mixed-mode sampling design (telephone and self-administered mailed surveys). The recruitment and administration of the BRS can be broken down into three distinct phases: (1) initial recruitment through random-digit dialing, (2) phone interviews on a randomly selected subsample of participants to determine bias in initial refusals; and (3) the mailed survey. Given the number of different stages in the process, we will focus on Wave 1 in our description here and present a table to summarize both waves.

The Gallup Organization conducted phone recruitment requesting participation in a survey project designed to "investigate the values and beliefs of Americans." The Gallup Organization did not indicate that the BRS was specifically about religion or that Baylor University was involved in the study, for fear that this might bias the response rate. The random-digit telephone sample was drawn from telephone exchanges serving the continental United States. To avoid various other sources of bias, a random-digit procedure designed to provide representation of both listed and unlisted (including not-yet-listed) telephone numbers was used. The design of the sample ensures representation of all telephone numbers by randomly generating the last two digits of numbers selected on the basis of their area code, telephone exchange, and bank order.

The mailed survey was a sixteen-page booklet with a cover page titled "The Values and Beliefs of the American Public—A National Study."[3] Questionnaires included a cover letter explaining the study's objectives and a number to call if participants had any questions or comments. In appreciation of their participation, potential mail survey respondents were offered a $5 incentive to complete the self-administered questionnaire and return it to the Gallup Organization. A follow-up reminder postcard was sent to all those who did not respond to the initial survey mailing.

For Wave 1, the Gallup Organization contacted 7,041 households by phone, and 3,002 people agreed to participate in the study. The response rate for the initial recruiting phase is calculated according to the American Association for Public Opinion Research (AAPOR) RR1 definition: RR1 = 3,002 / 7,041 = 42.6 percent. Of the 2,603 surveys mailed, 1,721 were completed and returned. Consequently, the return rate for the mailed surveys is 66.1 percent (1,721 / 2,603). When these three phases of data collection (initial recruitment, phone interviews, and mailed surveys) are pooled to calculate the response rate for the mixed-mode method per AAPOR RR1, it becomes 24.4 percent (1,721 / 7,041 = 24.4 percent).[4] Using the same formula, the response rate for the mixed-mode method per AAPOR RR1 for Wave 2 is 24.94 percent (1,648 / 6,604).

$$RR1 = \frac{I}{(I + P) + (R + NC + O) + (UH + UO)}$$

I = complete interviews; P = partial interviews; R = refusals and break-offs; NC = noncontact; O = other; UH = unknown if household occupied; UO = unknown, other. This response rate for multimethod surveys accounts for nonresponse at all levels of data collection.

The Gallup Organization asserts that these response rates fit within the normal parameters for reliable national survey data. In addition, all demographic variables compare favorably with other national surveys. To search for such bias, we compared our respondents to those of the 2004 General Social Survey on key religious indicators such as attendance and denomination. The respondents to the two surveys were quite similar. For example, there was no evidence of a systematic bias toward more conservative denominations in the BRS. For the thirty-seven groups for which comparisons are possible between the BRS and GSS, the two surveys differ by less than 1 percent.[5] The largest differences were for Catholics (the GSS had 4 percent more), Baptists (5 percent more in the GSS), and those with no religion (14.8 percent in the GSS, 11 percent in the BRS). Other religion indicators were equally comparable. Respondents to both surveys attend at about the same rate, with BRS data having a slightly higher number that never attend.

With the exception of being slightly more educated on average than GSS respondents (16 percent of BRS respondents have had some graduate study, compared with 10 percent in the GSS), our sample also looked very similar to the GSS with regard to employment status, marital status, and education. In sum, for the most part, differences between the BRS and GSS were small and certainly not sufficiently worrisome to suggest we have an overly religious sample that does not represent the general population.[6] We are confident that the BRS data can be used to present a portrait of current religious beliefs in the United States.

The Gallup Organization created weights for each wave using a ratio estimation program. By using a statistical algorithm, the overall (marginal) distributions, as well as the interrelationships among several variables, are simultaneously adjusted by assigning weights to individual respondents in order to bring all of the distributions into alignment with population parameters, or "true distributions" of these variables and their relationships with one another. The Gallup Organization used the most recent national data available from the Bureau of the Census Current Population Survey for gender, race, region, age, and education. In the first step of the weighting, a full weighting matrix of region by gender by age by education is derived from the CPS information. The second step involved a full weighting matrix of region by gender by race. All of our analyses are weighted using these constructed weight variables.

The God Interviews

Examining the results of the BRS provided us with some fascinating insights into American religion in general and American beliefs about

God in particular. It should be noted here that our conclusions about national trends are based on our quantitative data. But at the same time we realized that answers on a questionnaire do not tell a complete story about how people imagine God. Opinions about God are often vague, abstract, and highly personal, and survey data alone cannot adequately capture the many nuances of American beliefs. Therefore, we supplemented our national survey data with a series of in-depth one-on-one interviews that helped us clarify and expand on our theories about why certain statistical relationships exist.

There were two types of interviews completed: individual interviews and focus groups. With regard to the former, the authors and a team of three trained graduate students conducted the interviews. The authors attempted to have as much geographic, racial, and religious diversity in the interviews as possible. In most cases, we used convenience sampling. We selected cities or regions to conduct interviews where we had a contact person who was a starting point for soliciting interviews. Through snowball sampling, we collected other interviews as needed. In some cases, we used an alternate method of soliciting interviews. For example, we did not have any contacts along the coast of Washington that we could use to solicit interviews. One of the authors gave an interview to a coastal newspaper that described the project and requested that those interested in being interviewed contact him. We also did not have existing contacts in Boston, Pasadena, or Kansas City, and we cold-called churches to seek interviews in those locations. As interviews were completed, we continually reevaluated our basic demographic distributions and regional distribution and determined new locations and interviewee characteristics as needed. For example, if we noted that we had few interviews with Roman Catholics, we specifically looked for Catholics in a targeted region.

When including both individual and focus group interviewees, the total number of respondents for this project was 106. Seventy of these interviews were conducted one-on-one in the following states and cities: Massachusetts (Boston, Newport, 2), Rhode Island (Providence, 5), Texas (Dallas, Houston, Waco, 18), Arkansas (Lake Village, 1), Florida (Bradenton, Holmes Beach, Orlando, St. Augustine, Tampa, 14), California (Glendale, Pasadena, San Fernando, Woodland Hills, 12), Kansas (Kansas City, 14), and Washington (Copalis Beach, Moclips, Ocean Shores,

Lynnwood, 4). Those respondents were of the following races: Caucasian (60; 86 percent), Hispanic (2), Asian (3; 4 percent), and African American (7; 10 percent), split between males (32; 46 percent) and females (38; 54 percent). Interviewees ranged in age from 19 to 79, with an average age of 47.

Respondents were from a wide array of religious traditions and denominations. Forty-three percent (30) of the interview subjects identified with an evangelical denomination (for example: Pentecostal, nondenominational, Southern Baptist, and Seventh-Day Adventist). Seventeen percent (12) of our subjects identified as Catholic, and 29 percent (20) identified with a Mainline denomination (including the United Church of Christ, Disciples of Christ, Presbyterian Church [U.S.A.], Anglicans, and Episcopalians). The remaining respondents were Jewish (2, 3 percent) and of other religions (6, 9 percent), which included Buddhists, Greek Orthodox, and a respondent who identified himself as a "mystic."

The interviews themselves were semistructured. We asked the respondents broad questions about the nature of God and allowed them to elaborate as desired. Although we added or deleted items when we desired reflection on a specific issue, our common interview schedule consisted of the following eight topics:

Do you believe in God? [If not, do you believe that something exists beyond the physical world?]

Please describe God as best you can. [Is God a "he" or a "she"? What does God look like? Can you describe God's personality?]

Is God active in your daily life? In what ways?

Are there specific things that you have experienced that you believe were acts of God?

Are there world events that you believe were acts of God?

How does God deal with sinners?

Is there divine justice? What is it and how it is accomplished?

Does God have an opinion about moral issues? [Abortion, homosexuality, the death penalty]

These items were used a guide for the interviewers, who were free to ask them in a different order if doing so helped the flow of conversation.

Interviewers were instructed to prompt for examples or personal experiences and were free to ask follow-up questions for clarification. All interviews were tape-recorded. On average, the interviews lasted for forty-five minutes.

Each interviewee was also given a survey containing the same block of questions about God that were included on the BRS. The interviewers did not mention the God typology or four God types during the interviews, and in no case did interviewees appear familiar with the God typology mentioned in media coverage. Once interviews were complete, the tapes were transcribed and questionnaire data entered, allowing us to determine the God type for each respondent who completed the survey. During interviews, the subjects were allowed to expand upon each topic as much as possible and correct or clarify themselves as desired. We did not, however, send final transcripts to each subject for approval.

In addition to these one-on-one interviews, we selected two groups to visit that would be used as illustrations in particular chapters. Twenty one-on-one interviews were conducted at the Westboro Baptist Church in Topeka, Kansas (see chapter 3). Another sixteen interviews were conducted at the Greater Exodus Baptist Church in Philadelphia (see chapter 5).

Although we attempted to interview a variety of different people, we must be clear that such interviews do not constitute a random sample. Consequently, we cannot use them to draw inferences about the beliefs of the general population. Thankfully, the Baylor Religion Surveys allow us to determine how the average American answers questions about God. Our work is not one of grounded theory. Yet we used the interviews to test hypotheses generated from our analysis of the BRS; in sum, this qualitative data indicate the mechanisms and internal logic that connect the opinions and attitudes about various conceptually disparate issues. And the interviews fully confirmed our assertions that a wide range of Americans think deeply about God and that their images of God influence how they think about a host of other topics.

The Analyses

Throughout the book, we do not present full regression tables, nor do we make a point of discussing the effects of control variables. But the reader can be assured that we do not claim a connection between God images and a particular outcome if that relationship disappears with the addition of key control measures. After all, there is little point in focusing on images of God if their effects can be accounted for by other variables.

In most models, we focused on two perceived qualities of God's character—God's perceived level of judgment/anger and God's level of engagement with the world. In our analyses, we refer to the first measure as "God's Judgment" and the latter as "God's Engagement." If we were more interested in *how* an outcome varied by God type, we performed analyses using dichotomous variables representing the four God types.[7]

In Wave 1, God's Engagement is a simple additive scale of eight items tapping the respondent's belief about God's interest and involvement in the world. Six of those items ask respondents their level of agreement (on a 5-point, Likert-type scale) with the following descriptions of God: "removed from worldly affairs," "removed from my personal affairs," "concerned with the well-being of the world," "concerned with my personal well-being," "directly involved in worldly affairs," and "directly involved in my affairs." Two additional items ask respondents how well the adjectives "Distant" and "Ever-present" describe God: "not at all," "not very well," "undecided," "somewhat well," or "very well." Items were flipped as necessary, such that higher scores equal higher levels of perceived engagement. The resulting scale ranged from 8 to 40 with a mean of 30.64 (alpha = .91).

We measured God's Judgment by summing six items. Respondents are asked if they agree that God is "angered by human sins" and "angered by my sins." They are also asked how well the adjectives "critical," "punishing," "severe," and "wrathful" describe God. As with the items regarding God's Engagement, all are on 5-point, Likert-type scales. The final scale has an alpha of .85. Scores range from 6 to 30, with a mean of 17.04.

Not all items from Wave 1 were reproduced in Wave 2; therefore, the God's Engagement measure differs slightly. Our measure of God's Engagement in Wave 2 consists of six items: God is "concerned with the well-being of the world," "concerned with my personal well-being," "directly involved in worldly affairs," and "directly involved in my affairs" and responses to the adjectives "Distant" and "Ever-present." Again, items were flipped as necessary, such that higher scores equal higher levels of perceived engagement. The Wave 2 God's Engagement scale ranges from 7 to 35, with an alpha of .88. God's Judgment was created in an identical manner in both waves. The alpha score for God's Judgment in Wave 2 remained at .85.

We created the typology of four different God types used throughout the book by splitting variables at their mean. Those who were above the mean on God's Judgment were considered "high" on God's judgment. Those with scores above the mean on God's Engagement were considered to have "high" values. The four God types correspond to the four possible combinations of these two split variables. Some readers may wonder why we did not simply focus on the two variables of God's Judgment and Engagement in the text. We did so for several reasons. First, the four God types line up nicely with the way in which God is discussed in popular discourse and therefore provide a useful heuristic tool. As we discussed in chapter 6, some public figures have spoken of a God that causes tsunamis and hurricanes to punish humans for their sins. An image of God as *Authoritative* captures such a worldview quite well. Clearly, the *Distant God* captures the God of Benjamin Franklin and the deists quite well. Our interviews supported the notion that these two characteristics of God's perceived personality tend to coalesce into a unified image of God in the minds of believers rather than acting as separate variables. In other words, people talked very differently about God if they see "him" as angry but disengaged than if they see him as engaged but not angry. Finally, we desire our work to be accessible to readers who are not trained in the use of statistics in the social sciences. In our opinion, it is easier to grasp the concept of different personality profiles of God than it is the interaction of two conceptually distinct but related measures. Table A.1 provides the frequencies for each God type in Waves 1 and 2.

It was also important to ensure that images of God are not simply a proxy for other religion measures such as church attendance, denomination, or biblical literalism. Therefore, we included key demographic and religious controls in our models. Biblical literalism is included as a dichotomous variable comparing those who believe that the Bible should be "taken literally, word-for-word, on all subjects" with all

Table A.1 Images of God in Baylor Religion Survey, Waves 1 and 2

	Wave 1	Wave 2
Atheist	71 (5.2%)	68 (4.8%)
Authoritative God	429 (31.4%)	401 (28.2%)
Benevolent God	315 (23.0%)	317 (22.3%)
Critical God	219 (16.0%)	297 (20.9%)
Distant God	333 (24.4%)	340 (23.9%)
Missing	354	225
Total	1,721	1,648

others. Attendance is included as a simple frequency ranging from "Never" to "Several times a week." To control for religious family, we utilized the RELTRAD classification system developed by Steensland and colleagues (2000).[8] The RELTRAD system places denominations into the groupings Evangelical Protestant, Mainline Protestant, Black Protestant, Catholic, Jewish, Other religion, and None/no religion. In our analyses, we entered RELTRAD as a series of dummy variables, with Evangelical as the contrast category.

We also include controls for age, race, education, income, gender (0 = female), and marital status. Marital status is a dichotomous variable comparing people who are married (1) to all others. Race compares whites (1) to other races. Education has six categories—eight years or less of schooling, some high school, high school diploma, some college or vocational school, college degree, postgraduate degree. Family income has seven categories: $10,000 or less, $10,000–$20,000, $20,000–$35,000, $35,000–$50,000, $50,000–$100,000, $100,000–$150,000, and $150,000 and over. Family income was logged in our analyses.

We also include a control for political ideology. For analyses using Wave 2, we utilize a seven-category variable with responses ranging from "Extremely conservative" to "Extremely liberal." Unfortunately, this item does not exist in Wave 1; therefore, for Wave 1 analyses, we use a seven-category variable with the responses "Strong Democrat," "Moderate Democrat," "Leaning Democrat," "Independent," "Leaning Republican," "Moderate Republican," and "Strong Republican."

Before conducting our analyses, we took several steps to recover missing data. First, we examined our race variables and found that a large amount of missing data was created by individuals neglecting to check "no" on individual race items. In other words, a person who checked that "yes" they were white but failed to check "no" to all of the other race categories was being counted as missing. By considering a nonresponse a "no" we recovered 144 cases in Wave 2. Further, we used predicted values to replace missing values for income based on a regression using other demographic characteristics (gender, age, education, race, and marital status). This recovered an additional seventy-six cases in Wave 2. We ran each model with and without these altered variables, and their inclusion does not change the pattern of results. We could have recovered more cases if we had attempted to use predicted values for biblical literalism, church attendance, or images of God. We were concerned, however, about using predicted values for the key religion measures central to our arguments, and we elected not to do so.

The introduction and chapters 1 and 7 primarily present simple frequencies. In the following sections, we provide the key analyses that informed the major conclusions of chapters 2–6.

Chapter 2: God, Self, and Society

In chapter 2, we examined several sources of conceptions of God: child-rearing, personality types, religious identity, and personal identity. Hence, table A.2 presents our analysis of how demographic factors, religious background, and personality characteristics relate to one's image of God.

Immediately clear is that a complicated set of factors are associated with different conceptions of God. If you are very conservative, you are more likely to conceive of an Authoritative God; those with very liberal leanings tend toward a Distant God. Yet politics tell us nothing about those with Benevolent and Critical Gods. Females and younger people tend toward a Benevolent God. Religious background, parenting practices, and personality also have significant effects on different ways of imagining God, as outlined in chapter 2.

Chapter 3: God and Morals

The Baylor Religion Survey Wave 2 includes two questions related to the perceived source of homosexuality. First we ask respondents their

Table A.2 Predicting God (Baylor Religion Survey, Wave 2)

	Authoritative God	Benevolent God	Critical God	Distant God
Demographics				
Gender (0 = Female)	1.129 (.159)	**.585 (.157)****	**1.527 (.160)****	.921 (.160)
Age	**1.008 (.005)***	**.990 (.005)***	1.002 (.005)	1.002 (.005)
Married	**1.066 (.179)**	**.940 (.176)**	**.890 (.171)**	**.940 (.176)**
Income	.724 (.188)*	1.668 (.198)**	.519 (.181)**	2.096 (.230)**
Education	.954 (.076)	.954 (.075)	**.875 (.077)***	**1.157 (.076)***
Race (0 = Nonwhite)	.671 (.250)	**.563 (.241)****	.955 (.253)	**2.159 (.291)****
Political Conservatism	**1.239 (.058)****	.999 (.056)	.984 (.054)	**.853 (.055)****
Religion†				
Catholic	**.345 (.209)****	**1.980 (.211)****	1.318 (.215)	**1.581 (.225)***
Black Protestant	.785 (.388)	1.149 (.405)	1.260 (.465)	.229 (1.263)
Mainline Protestant	**.488 (.206)****	**1.815 (.217)****	**1.518 (.219)***	1.150 (.233)
Jewish	**.377 (.713)**	.430 (.829)	1.635 (.512)	1.267 (.480)
Other Religions	**.232 (.354)****	**2.405 (.295)****	.558 (.419)	**2.339 (.322)****
No Religion	**.045 (.947)****	.884 (.445)	**.501 (.306)***	.820 (.287)
How Religious?	**1.824 (.132)****	**1.609 (.134)****	.828 (.121)	.862 (.120)
Biblical Literalist? (0 = No)	**1.455 (.183)***	.903 (.202)	**.583 (.244)***	**.370 (.349)****
Church Attendance	**1.128 (.034)****	**1.138 (.037)****	**.870 (.037)****	**.795 (.041)****

continued

Table A.2 continued

	Authoritative God	Benevolent God	Critical God	Distant God
Parenting				
Church Attendance at 12	**1.069** **(.036)***	1.022 (.035)	1.031 (.034)	**.935** **(.034)***
Parents Spanked	**1.487** **(.153)****	.865 (.157)	1.077 (.163)	**.593** **(.173)****
Parents Praised	**0.595** **(.265)***	.781 (.245)	**1.637** **(.244)***	1.415 (.251)
Personality				
Extraversion	1.045 (.037)	1.026 (.036)	**.913** **(.038)****	1.052 (.037)
Agreeableness	.946 (.053)	**1.176** **(.054)****	.919 (.052)	.940 (.053)
Conscientiousness	.980 (.052)	1.073 (.051)	.952 (.052)	1.015 (.053)
Emotional Stability	1.003 (.045)	1.048 (.045)	**.906** **(.045)***	1.016 (.045)
Openness	1.015 (.055)	1.009 (.055)	**.910** **(.053)***	1.047 (.056)
Constant	**−3.076** **(.820)****	**−4.750** **(.814)****	**3.403** **(.841)****	−2.018 **(.862)****
N	1,253	1,253	1,253	1,253

* = $p < .05$; ** = $p < .01$.
† Contrast category for religious tradition = Evangelical Protestant.
Logistic regression analyses. Odds ratios presented with standard errors in parentheses.

level of agreement with the statements "People are born as either homosexual or heterosexual" and "People choose to be homosexuals." We find that people with more active and judgmental views of God are less likely to believe that people are homosexual by nature. However, God's perceived level of judgment does not have a direct effect on the belief that homosexuality is a choice (see table A.3).

Both God's Judgment and God's Engagement lead to more absolutist attitudes toward gay marriage (see table A.4). A question on the BRS Wave 1 asks respondents if gay marriage is "not wrong at all," "only

Table A.3 Images of God and the Origins of Homosexuality (Baylor Religion Survey, Wave 2)

	People are born as either homosexual or heterosexual	People choose to be homosexuals
Demographics		
Gender (0 = Female)	**−.160 (.068)****	**.206 (.072)****
Age	**.071 (.002)****	**−.063 (.002)***
Married	−.008 (.075)	**.073 (.079)****
Income	.044 (.081)	−.029 (.086)
Education	.022 (.032)	**−.071 (.034)****
Race (0 = Nonwhite)	−.002 (.108)	−.042 (.115)
Political Conservatism	**−.232 (.024)****	**.246 (.025)****
Religion Controls†		
Catholic	**.126 (.093)****	**−.073 (.098)***
Black Protestant	**.116 (.192)****	.034 (.203)
Mainline Protestant	**.134 (.094)****	**−.102 (.100)****
Jewish	.046 (.237)	−.024 (.255)
Other Religions	**.062 (.141)***	−.036 (.149)
No Religion	**.082 (.139)****	−.036 (.147)
Biblical Literalist? (0 = No)	**−.175 (.092)****	**.072 (.097)***
Church Attendance	**−.126 (.015)****	**.100 (.015)****
Images of God		
God's Judgment	**−.066 (.006)***	.035 (.006)
God's Engagement	**−.068 (.007)***	**.109 (.007)****
Constant	4.265 (1.131)	1.573 (1.199)
N	1,254	1,255
R²	.335	.290

* = p < .05; ** = p < .01.
† Contrast category = Evangelical Protestant.
OLS regression analysis with standardized coefficients presented. Standard errors are in parentheses. Responses to each item were on a standard Likert-type scale, "strongly disagree," "disagree," "undecided," "agree," "strongly agree."

wrong sometimes," "almost always wrong," and "always wrong." Respondents clumped at "not wrong at all" (30 percent) and "always wrong" (59 percent); therefore, we dichotomized this item, comparing those who believe gay marriage is always wrong with all others. The results of a logistic regression are presented in table A.4.

Table A.4 Images of God and Belief That Gay Marriage Is "Always Wrong" (Baylor Religion Survey, Wave 1)

	Gay marriage is "always wrong"
Demographics	
Gender (0 = Female)	1.997 (.167)**
Age	1.024 (.005)**
Married	.933 (.176)
Income	.959 (.206)
Education	.790 (.075)**
Race (0 = Nonwhite)	.909 (.269)
Political Conservatism	1.555 (.045)**
Religion Controls†	
Catholic	.463 (.221)**
Black Protestant	2.411 (.551)
Mainline Protestant	.401 (.218)**
Jewish	.341 (.477)*
Other Religions	.384 (.375)**
No Religion	.151 (.370)**
Biblical Literalist? (0 = No)	4.337 (.310)**
Church Attendance	1.141 (.035)**
Image of God	
God's Judgment	1.061 (.014)**
God's Engagement	1.046 (.014)**
Constant	−4.457 (.726)**
N	1,296

* = p < .05; ** = p < .01.
† Contrast category = Evangelical Protestant.
Logistic regression analyses. Odds ratios presented with standard errors in parentheses.

God's Judgment will view gay marriage as always wrong, as does God's Engagement.

In the following analyses, we examine how God's perceived judgment and engagement relate to belief that abortion is "always wrong" in particular circumstances using logistic regression. In each model, we contrast people who believe that abortion is "always wrong" in the given situation with those who believe that it is "almost always wrong," "only wrong sometimes," or "not wrong at all." As we discuss in chapter 3, images of God are related to attitudes toward abortion differently, depending on the circumstances (see table A.5).

Chapter 4: God and Science

In chapter 4, we note that the most salient feature of God's perceived character with regard to science is Engagement. Those with an engaged God imagine a creator who is distinct from nature and able to shape the world directly. Those with a less engaged God imagine a creator who is, perhaps, part of nature itself. To capture these two conceptions of God, we combine respondents with a highly engaged God (Authoritative or Benevolent). Those with less active Gods (Critical or Distant) are also combined. In the following analyses, we search for differences in views regarding science by God type by entering a dichotomous variable that contrast those with an engaged God with all others. All of the following analyses use data from the Baylor Religion Survey, Wave 2.

We use OLS regression to predict several attitudes about the intersection of faith and science. First, respondents are asked their level of agreement with the statements "Science will eventually provide solutions to most of our problems" and "We rely too much on science and not enough on faith." Those with engaged Gods (Authoritative or Benevolent) exhibit considerably more skepticism regarding science (see table A.6).

We further asked respondents their level of agreement with the statements that "Science and religion are incompatible" and "Science helps to reveal God's glory." Those with Authoritative or Benevolent God types are most likely to believe that science is a window into God's plans yet see an incompatibility between scientific and religious worldviews.

Table A.5 Images of God and Belief That Abortion Is "Always Wrong" under Particular Circumstances (Baylor Religion Survey, Wave 1)

	The baby may have a serious defect	The woman's health may be in danger	The preg-nancy is a result of rape	The family cannot afford the child	The woman does not want the child
Demographics					
Gender (0 = Female)	1.052 (.169)	.714 (.206)	.935 (.177)	1.285 (.158)	1.277 (.156)
Age	**.991 (.005)***	.994 (.007)	.996 (.006)	.995 (.005)	**.989 (.005)***
Married	1.344 (.191)	1.408 (.237)	1.151 (.200)	1.224 (.170)	1.133 (.167)
Income	**.704 (.200)***	.735 (.235)	**.669 (.206)***	**.621 (.194)****	**.599 (.193)****
Education	.951 (.077)	.867 (.095)	**.851 (.081)***	**.832 (.072)****	**.799 (.071)****
Race (0 = Nonwhite)	.851 (.299)	.758 (.365)	.781 (.307)	1.193 (.261)	**1.544 (.258)***
Political Conservatism	**1.305 (.046)****	**1.178 (.058)****	**1.139 (.049)****	**1.276 (.041)****	**1.236 (.041)****
Religion Controls†					
Catholic	**1.790 (.216)****	**2.116 (.263)****	**1.591 (.227)***	1.074 (.213)	1.167 (.212)
Black Protestant	.974 (.490)	.777 (.615)	1.317 (.488)	.973 (.455)	1.008 (.456)
Mainline Protestant	**.489 (.239)****	**.528 (.324)***	**.435 (.263)****	**.515 (.205)****	**.588 (.205)****
Jewish[1]	—	—	1.116 (.673)	.605 (.472)	.562 (.474)
Other Religions	.663 (.453)	**.208 (.911)***	**.200 (.631)****	.599 (.372)	.659 (.369)
No Religion	**2.233 (.481)***	1.223 (.868)	**2.476 (.498)***	**.529 (.361)***	.673 (.336)
Biblical Literalist? (0 = No)	**1.835 (.195)****	**3.598 (.227)****	**3.337 (.194)****	**2.012 (.245)****	**2.947 (.262)****

continued

Table A.5 continued

	The baby may have a serious defect	The woman's health may be in danger	The pregnancy is a result of rape	The family cannot afford the child	The woman does not want the child
Church Attendance	1.336 (.039)**	1.303 (.051)**	1.244 (.039)**	1.168 (.033)**	1.174 (.033)**
Images of God					
God's Judgment	1.037 (.014)**	.993 (.017)	1.001 (.015)	1.039 (.014)**	1.050 (.014)**
God's Engagement	1.096 (.017)**	1.091 (.024)**	1.133 (.019)**	1.134 (.014)**	1.111 (.014)**
Constant	−6.658 (.821)**	−6.100 (1.060)**	−6.002 (.881)**	−4.677 (.700)**	−3.826 (.679)**
N	1,291	1,288	1,288	1,295	1,296

[1] Jewish respondents could not be included in the first two models as convergence was not achieved. There are forty-one Jewish respondents. All forty-one disagree that abortion is "Always Wrong" when the baby may have a serious defect or when the woman's health may be in danger. There is disagreement among Jewish respondents with regard to the last three circumstances, allowing their inclusion in the models.
* = $p < .05$; ** = $p < .01$.
† Contrast category = Evangelical Protestant; convergence not achieved if Jewish respondents in model.
Logistic regression analyses. Odds ratios presented with standard errors in parentheses.

Two items ask respondents about the debate over the theory of evolution. We find that those with Authoritative or Benevolent God images are less convinced by evolution and more likely to believe that creationism should be taught in public schools (see table A.7).

We also use logistic regression to examine who supports scientific research. People who believe in Authoritative or Benevolent Gods are more likely to believe that embryonic stem-cell research is "always wrong." People with Authoritative and Benevolent Gods are also less likely to believe that the government is spending "too little" supporting scientific research (see table A.8).

Table A.6 Faith and Science & Faith in Science (Baylor Religion Survey, Wave 2)

	We rely too much on science and not enough on faith	Science will eventually provide solutions to most of our problems	Science and religion are incompatible	Science helps to reveal God's glory
Demographics				
Gender (0 = Female)	−.040 (.058)	.041 (.060)	.005 (.058)	.025 (.066)
Age	.002 (.002)	−.034 (.002)	.045 (.002)	.018 (.002)
Married	.009 (.065)	**−.075 (.066)****	.011 (.065)	−.052 (.073)
Income	**−.139 (.070)****	**.057 (.072)***	**−.133 (.070)****	.022 (.079)
Education	**−.075 (.028)****	−.036 (.028)	**−.157 (.028)****	**.121 (.031)****
Race (0 = Nonwhite)	**−.065 (.095)****	.035 (.097)	**−.073 (.095)***	−.033 (.106)
Political Conservatism	**.138 (.021)****	**−.136 (.021)****	−.027 (.021)	**.097 (.023)****
Religion Controls†				
Catholic	−.002 (.082)	**.086 (.083)****	.011 (.082)	**−.073 (.092)***
Black Protestant	−.022 (.171)	**.069 (.174)***	**.071 (.171)***	**−.063 (.192)***
Mainline Protestant	−.019 (.084)	**.085 (.085)****	−.011 (.083)	−.035 (.094)
Jewish	**−.070 (.201)****	.042 (.205)	.032 (.201)	**−.094 (.226)****
Other Religions	−.036 (.125)	**.058 (.126)***	−.027 (.126)	−.042 (.139)
No Religion	**−.126 (.109)****	**.138 (.111)****	**.066 (.109)***	**−.242 (.122)****

continued

Table A.6 continued

	We rely too much on science and not enough on faith	Science will eventually provide solutions to most of our problems	Science and religion are incompatible	Science helps to reveal God's glory
Biblical Literalist? (0 = No)	.188 (.082)**	−.109 (.083)**	.039 (.081)	−.024 (.092)
Church Attendance	.205 (.013)**	−.177 (.013)**	−.070 (.013)*	.088 (.014)**
Images of God				
(Authoritative/ Benevolent)	.175 (.071)**	−.111 (.073)**	−.161 (.071)**	.248 (.080)**
Constant	2.782 (1.015)	3.696 (1.036)	3.640 (1.012)	1.934 (1.138)
N	1,316	1,319	1,312	1,315
R²	.424	.251	.127	.245

* = p < .05; ** = p < .01.
† Contrast category = Evangelical Protestant.
OLS regression analyses with standardized coefficients presented. Standard errors are in parentheses. Responses to each item were on a standard Likert-type scale, "strongly disagree," "disagree," "undecided," "agree," "strongly agree."

Chapter 5: God and Mammon

In chapter 5, we examine how images of God are related to views on economic issues. An item on BRS Wave 2 asks respondents how important it is to care for the sick and needy if one is to be a good person. Two further items from BRS Wave 1 ask level of agreement with the statement "The federal government should distribute wealth more evenly" and whether the government should fund faith-based initiatives. Using logistic regression, we examine how various factors influence these views on how economic and social problems are best addressed (see table A.9). A final model examines how different conceptions of God and our control variables influence whether a person identifies himself or herself as a Republican.

Table A.7 Images of God and Human Origins (Baylor Religion Survey, Wave 2)

	Humans evolved from primates over millions of years	Creationism should be taught in public schools
Demographics		
Gender (0 = Female)	.020 (.060)	.001 (.068)
Age	−.020 (.002)	**−.050 (.002)***
Married	−.037 (.067)	.011 (.076)
Income	.032 (.072)	.019 (.082)
Education	**.108 (.029)****	**−.072 (.033)****
Race (0 = Nonwhite)	.015 (.097)	−.035 (.111)
Political Conservatism	**−.218 (.021)****	**.248 (.024)****
Religion Controls†		
Catholic	**.165 (.084)****	**−.073 (.096)***
Black Protestant	.039 (.175)	.008 (.199)
Mainline Protestant	**.121 (.086)****	**−.092 (.098)****
Jewish	**.086 (.216)****	**−.059 (.237)***
Other Religions	**.044 (.127)***	**−.081 (.146)****
No Religion	**.151 (.111)****	**−.174 (.127)****
Biblical Literalist? (0 = No)	**−.132 (.084)****	**.064 (.095)***
Church Attendance	**−.209 (.013)****	**.108 (.015)****
Images of God		
(Authoritative/Benevolent)	**−.238 (.073)****	**.121 (.083)****
Constant	**3.659 (1.040)****	**2.525 (1.184)****
N	1,312	1,312
R^2	.528	.284

* = $p < .05$; ** = $p < .01$.
† Contrast category for religious tradition = Evangelical Protestant.
OLS regression analyses with standardized coefficients presented. Standard errors are in parentheses. Responses to each item were on a standard Likert-type scale, "strongly disagree," "disagree," "undecided," "agree," "strongly agree."

Table A.8 Images of God and Support for Science (Baylor Religion Survey, Wave 2)

	Embryonic stem-cell research is "always wrong"	The government is spending "too little" on science
Demographics		
Gender (0 = Female)	.929 (.173)	1.079 (.132)
Age	**.985 (.005)****	1.005 (.004)
Married	.935 (.196)	.876 (.145)
Income	**.628 (.195)****	.960 (.161)
Education	.900 (.084)	**1.261 (.062)****
Race (0 = Nonwhite)	.822 (.277)	.898 (.213)
Political Conservatism	**1.686 (.069)****	**.751 (.046)****
Religion Controls†		
Catholic	1.208 (.221)	1.154 (.186)
Black Protestant	.696 (.431)	1.517 (.376)
Mainline Protestant	.704 (.243)	**1.363 (.187)***
Jewish	.680 (.753)	**2.852 (.459)***
Other Religions	**.141 (.522)****	1.389 (.273)
No Religion	.515 (.544)	**2.488 (.238)****
Biblical Literalist? (0 = No)	**2.740 (.190)****	.896 (.198)
Church Attendance	**1.252 (.037)****	**.932 (.029)****
Image of God		
(Authoritative/Benevolent)	**1.717 (.212)****	**.601 (.156)****
Constant	–3.315 (.574)**	–.043 (.419)
N	1,287	1,310

* = p < .05; ** = p < .01.
Logistic regression analyses. Odds ratios presented with standard errors in parentheses.

Conceptions of God are related to these issues in different ways. Those with more engaged Gods (Authoritative or Benevolent) are more likely to believe that caring for the sick and needy is very important than are those with Critical or Distant Gods. They are also more likely to identify as Republican, controlling for other factors. Those with

Table A.9 Images of God and Economic Policy (Baylor Religion Survey, Waves 1 & 2)

	Caring for the sick and needy is "very important"	The government should distribute wealth more evenly	The government should fund faith-based initiatives	Identifies as Republican
Demographics				
Gender (0 = Female)	**.786** **(.128)***	.859 (.134)	1.222 (.150)	**1.411** **(.134)****
Age	**1.022** **(.004)****	.988 **(.004)****	.980 **(.005)****	1.006 (.004)
Married	1.163 (.147)	**1.604** **(.156)****	1.064 (.168)	1.267 (.155)
Income	**.753** **(.161)***	**.306** **(.182)****	**.458** **(.175)****	**3.232** **(.188)****
Education	**.898** **(.061)***	**.792** **(.065)****	.973 (.069)	**.850** **(.064)****
Race (0 = Nonwhite)	.825 (.211)	1.279 (.218)	**.465** **(.249)****	**2.090** **(.241)****
Political Preference	**.787** **(.047)****	**.543** **(.052)****	**1.211** **(.041)****	—
Religion Controls†				
Catholic	**2.013** **(.186)****	**1.763** **(.190)****	.942 (.200)	**.486** **(.184)****
Black Protestant	1.110 (.407)	**6.080** **(.463)****	**2.564** **(.437)***	**.156** **(.490)****
Mainline Protestant	1.078 (.182)	1.034 (.191)	1.054 (.198)	**.595** **(.184)****
Jewish	1.305 (.434)	1.494 (.436)	**.191** **(.825)***	**.417** **(.460)***
Other Religions	**1.674** **(.275)***	.857 (.285)	**.477** **(.419)***	.635 (.276)
No Religion	.895 (.231)	**1.597** **(.250)***	**.200** **(.432)****	**.203** **(.299)****

continued

Table A.9 continued

	Caring for the sick and needy is "very important"	The government should distribute wealth more evenly	The government should fund faith-based initiatives	Identifies as Republican
Biblical Literalist? (0 = No)	1.508 (.186)*	1.575 (.192)**	1.978 (.183)**	2.478 (.187)**
Church Attendance	1.125 (.028)**	.972 (.029)	1.124 (.032)**	1.135 (.028)**
Images of God††				
Benevolent God	.789 (.179)	1.472 (.184)*	.616 (.186)**	.947 (.180)
Critical God	.523 (.185)**	1.030 (.198)	1.093 (.209)	.709 (.197)*
Distant God	.465 (.185)**	.974 (.197)	.497 (.235)**	.605 (.198)**
Constant	1.136 (.438)**	5.092 (.506)**	.481 (.471)	−2.624 (.454)**
N	1,262	1,267	1,267	1,275

* = p < .05; ** = p < .01.

† Contrast category for religious tradition = Evangelical Protestant; †† Contrast category = Authoritative God.

Logistic regression analyses are used. Odds ratios are presented with standard errors in parentheses. Models 1, 2, and 4 use data from the Baylor Religion Survey, Wave 2. The question about faith-based initiatives was not asked in Wave 2, therefore model 3 utilizes date from Wave 1. Political preference is the only variable that is not directly comparable between Waves 1 and 2. In Wave 1 political preference ranges from strong Democrat (low) to strong Republican (higher values). In Wave 2, political preference ranges from extremely liberal (low) to extremely conservative (high). Political preference is not used as a predictor in the final model that predicts Republican identification.

Benevolent Gods show a special propensity to believe that the government should distribute wealth more evenly. Those with more judgmental Gods (Critical and Authoritative), however, prefer the use of faith-based initiatives for solving social problems.

Next we examine how images of God are related to beliefs about God's hand in one's personal fortunes. Two questions from BRS Wave

2 ask respondents their level of agreement with the statements "God rewards the faithful with major successes" and "God punishes sinners with terrible ways." Some people disagreed with both statements, suggesting that they believe God does not play a role in their personal fortunes and misfortunes. Others believe that God may reward the faithful but disagree that God might punish with misfortune. Finally, a third group agrees with both statements, suggesting that God is an architect of one's fortunes and misfortunes. A very small group of respondents (3.2 percent) believe that God only punishes and never blesses. This group was combined with the third group. A series of logistic regression analyses demonstrate that a person's God type impacts how people conceive of their personal fortunes (see table A.10).

In particular, those with less engaged Gods (Critical and Distant) tend to believe that their fortunes are their personal business—God does not bless or curse them. Authoritative God believers stand apart, with all other God types being significantly less likely to imagine a God who would personally punish a sinner with misfortune.

Chapter 6: God and Evil

In chapter 6, we shift our focus to a different aspect of God's perceived character. Two questions on Wave 2 of the Baylor Religion Survey ask respondents their level of agreement with the statements "God sometimes *allows* major tragedies to occur as a warning to sinners" and "God *causes* major tragedies to occur as a warning to sinners." We created a variable that indicates whether the respondent agrees or strongly agrees with either statement. In other words, we compare respondents who believe that God either causes tragedies, allows tragedies, or both, with people who do not think that God plays a role in tragic events. It is immediately clear that those with an Authoritative God are the most likely to believe that God plays *some* role in tragedy (see table A.11).

An item in Wave 2 of the Baylor Religion Survey asks respondents their level of agreement with the statement "Going to war in Iraq was the right decision" using a standard Likert-type scale. In addition to asking about party affiliation, the Wave 2 survey also asks respondents to describe themselves politically on a scale ranging from "extremely liberal" to "extremely conservative." We use this liberal-conservative

Table A.10 Images of God and Our Fortunes (Baylor Religion Survey, Wave 2)

	God does not bless with fortune or curse with misfortune	God only blesses with fortune, never curses with misfortune	God may bless with fortune and/or curse with misfortune
Demographics			
Gender (0 = Female)	.802 (.145)	1.069 (.158)	1.299 (.186)
Age	**1.011 (.004)****	.999 (.005)	**.986 (.006)****
Married	1.090 (.160)	1.224 (.182)	**.676 (.203)***
Income	1.087 (.172)	.918 (.193)	.975 (.199)
Education	**1.214 (.068)****	**.842 (.076)***	.901 (.090)
Race (0 = Nonwhite)	**1.488 (.227)***	1.179 (.260)	**.471 (.267)****
Political Conservatism	1.007 (.051)	.912 (.056)	**1.132 (.068)***
Religion Controls†			
Catholic	1.013 (.191)	1.201 (.216)	.787 (.251)
Black Protestant	**.395 (.438)***	1.760 (.412)	1.173 (.411)
Mainline Protestant	1.005 (.196)	**1.452 (.217)***	**.536 (.280)***
Jewish	1.331 (.585)	.672 (.749)	.935 (.701)
Other Religions	.927 (.288)	1.240 (.314)	.943 (.399)
No Religion	**3.016 (.411)****	**.322 (.566)***	.435 (.549)
Biblical Literalist? (0 = No)	**.502 (.182)****	**2.071 (.194)****	1.090 (.215)
Church Attendance	**.920 (.030)****	**1.106 (.033)****	1.014 (.038)
Images of God††			
Benevolent God	1.029 (.179)	**2.603 (.189)****	**.214 (.264)****
Critical God	**2.600 (.206)****	**.455 (.263)****	**.531 (.241)****
Distant God	**5.217 (.244)****	**.559 (.274)***	**.071 (.450)****
Constant	−1.296 (.484)**	−1.043 (5.45)*	.479 (.599)
N	1,179	1,179	1,179

* = p < .05; ** = p < .01.
† Contrast category = Evangelical Protestant; †† Contrast category = Authoritative God.
Logistic regression analyses with standard errors in parentheses.

Table A.11 Image of God and God's Role in Tragic Events (Baylor Religion Survey, Wave 2)

	God allows tragedies to occur as a warning to sinners	God causes tragedies to occur as a warning to sinners
Demographics		
Gender (0 = Female)	−.019 (.065)	.017 (.062)
Age	−.029 (.002)	−.006 (.002)
Married	−.031 (.073)	.013 (.069)
Income	**−.095 (.079)****	**−.126 (.075)****
Education	.018 (.031)	−.029 (.030)
Race (0 = Nonwhite)	−.047 (.106)	**−.072 (.101)***
Political Conservatism	**.190 (.023)****	**.078 (.022)***
Religion Controls†		
Catholic	.008 (.091)	−.013 (.086)
Black Protestant	−.036 (.186)	−.033 (.178)
Mainline Protestant	−.033 (.092)	−.025 (.088)
Jewish	−.022 (.230)	−.008 (.220)
Other Religions	.010 (.137)	−.031 (.130)
No Religion	**−.098 (.132)****	**−.073 (.126)***
Biblical Literalist? (0 = No)	**.145 (.089)****	.026 (.085)
Church Attendance	.041 (.014)	−.015 (.013)
Image of God		
Benevolent God	**−.253 (.090)****	**−.213 (.086)****
Critical God	**−.129 (.099)****	−.004 (.095)
Distant God	**−.386 (.104)****	**−.274 (.099)****
Constant	3.249 (1.098)	3.088 (1.050)
N	1,243	1,247
R²	.352	.165

* = p < .05; ** = p < .01.
† Contrast category = Evangelical Protestant.
OLS regression analyses with standardized coefficients presented. Standard errors are in parentheses. Responses to each item were on a standard Likert-type scale, "strongly disagree," "disagree," "undecided," "agree," "strongly agree."

Table A.12 Images of God and Support for the War in Iraq (Baylor Religion Survey, Wave 2)

	Going to war in Iraq was the right decision
Demographics	
Gender (0 = Female)	−.002 (.071)
Age	**−.086 (.002)****
Married	.042 (.079)
Income	**.091 (.085)****
Education	.016 (.033)
Race (0 = Nonwhite)	.024 (.114)
Political Conservatism	**.499 (.025)****
Religion Controls†	
Catholic	**−.092 (.097)****
Black Protestant	**−.099 (.202)****
Mainline Protestant	**−.116 (.099)****
Jewish	−.022 (.250)
Other Religions	−.028 (.148)
No Religion	**−.135 (.146)****
Biblical Literalist? (0 = No)	.030 (.096)
Church Attendance	−.011 (.015)
Image of God	
God's Judgment	.017 (.006)
God's Engagement	**.083 (.007)****
Constant	
N	1,256
R²	.402

* = p < .05; ** = p < .01.
† Contrast category = Evangelical Protestant.
OLS regression analyses with standardized coefficients presented. Standard errors are in parentheses.

continuum as our measure of political conservatism when performing analyses with Wave 2 data. We find that people who have a more engaged view of God were significantly more supportive of the war in Iraq, but views of God's anger do not have a significant effect (see table A.12).

Table A.13 Images of God and Nationalism (Baylor Religion Survey, Wave 2)

	The United States should declare itself a Christian nation	The success of the United States is part of God's plan	People should be made to show respect for American traditions	The U.S. government should advocate Christian values
Demographics				
Gender (0 = Female)	−.073 (.066)**	−.017 (.061)	−.074 (.065)**	−.038 (.064)
Age	.092 (.002)**	−.055 (.002)*	.076 (.002)**	.074 (.002)**
Married	.009 (.073)	.003 (.067)	−.003 (.071)	.022 (.071)
Income	−.105 (.079)**	−.089 (.073)**	−.001 (.077)	−.060 (.077)*
Education	−.051 (.031)*	−.045 (.028)	−.164 (.030)**	−.050 (.030)*
Race (0 = Nonwhite)	−.042 (.106)	.022 (.097)	−.014 (.103)	−.059 (.103)*
Political Conservatism	.224 (.023)**	.201 (.021)**	.265 (.023)**	.230 (.023)**
Religion Controls†				
Catholic	−.045 (.091)	−.022 (.083)	.073 (.088)*	−.035 (.088)
Black Protestant	−.023 (.187)	.055 (.172)*	.016 (.183)	−.023 (.182)
Mainline Protestant	.022 (.092)	−.028 (.084)	.058 (.090)	−.042 (.089)
Jewish	−.030 (.232)	−.021 (.212)	−.057 (.232)*	−.073 (.225)**
Other Religions	−.035 (.137)	−.030 (.126)	−.057 (.134)*	−.107 (.133)**
No Religion	−.081 (.136)**	−.099 (.124)**	−.099 (.133)**	−.134 (.132)**
Biblical Literalist? (0 = No)	.148 (.090)**	.132 (.082)**	.019 (.088)	.072 (.087)**
Church Attendance	.054 (.014)	.040 (.013)	−.007 (.014)	.114 (.014)**

continued

Table A.13 continued

	The United States should declare itself a Christian nation	The success of the United States is part of God's plan	People should be made to show respect for American traditions	The U.S. government should advocate Christian values
Images of God				
God's Judgment	.088 (.006)**	.058 (.005)*	.098 (.006)**	.082 (.006)**
God's Engagement	.185 (.007)**	.345 (.006)**	.030 (.006)	.257 (.006)**
Constant	.623 (1.104)	.507 (1.012)	2.708 (1.081)	.843 (1.072)
N	1,250	1,254	1,253	1,251
R^2	.359	.443	.225	.454

* = $p < .05$; ** = $p < .01$.
† Contrast category = Evangelical Protestant.
OLS regression analyses with standardized coefficients presented. Standard errors are in parentheses. Responses to each item were on a standard Likert-type scale, "strongly disagree," "disagree," "undecided," "agree," "strongly agree."

Our final series of analyses in chapter 5 examines the relationship between images of God and beliefs about the nature of the United States. Using standard Likert-type scales, respondents to BRS Wave 2 were asked if we should "declare the United States a Christian nation." Both God's Judgment and God's Engagement are significant predictors of this belief. God's Engagement is also the strongest, significant predictor of belief that the "success of the United States is part of God's plan" (see table A.13).

With regard to images of God, it appears that the belief that "people should be made to show respect for American traditions" is driven by views of God's judgment. Those who imagine God in more judgmental terms show more agreement with this statement, regardless of how engaged they believe God to be. However, both images of God are, once again, significant predictors of the belief that the "government should advocate Christian values."

Further Resources

For those who wish to further examine how images of God impact behaviors and attitudes, there are several resources available.

First, the Baylor Religion Survey, Wave 1, is now a public data source. You can download the full data set and view supporting materials and methodological information at the Web site of the Association of Religion Data Archives (www.thearda.com). The ARDA archives a host of quality religion surveys, all available for free download and analysis.

Second, the Baylor Institute for Studies of Religion maintains its own Web site on the Baylor Religion Survey. For announcements, research reports, and other material related to this ongoing project, visit http://www.isreligion.org/research/surveysofreligion.

Finally, we have developed a Web site related to this book project. Users can complete the God Questionnaire online (see postscript). As we collect responses and comments on the questionnaire, we will post results, feedback, and announcements on www.Americasfourgods.com.

NOTES

Introduction

1. According to David Domke and Kevin Coe, authors of *The God Strategy: How Religion Became a Political Weapon in America*, this is a phenomenon that really picked up steam during the Reagan administration. Since 1980, the total number of references to God in major presidential speeches has increased 120 percent over the preceding half-century.

2. Robert Bellah (1967, 11) famously described the close tie between American national culture and religion as our pervasive *civil religion*, explaining that "the American civil religion was never anticlerical or militantly secular. On the contrary, it borrowed selectively from the religious tradition in such a way that the average American saw no conflict between the two. In this way, the civil religion was able to build up without any bitter struggle with the church powerful symbols of national solidarity and to mobilize deep levels of personal motivation for the attainment of national goals."

3. Nietzsche, *The Gay Science*, 109.

4. While the specifics of their theories differ radically, classical social theorists such as Émile Durkheim, Karl Marx, Max Weber, and Talcott Parsons generally agreed that religion would disappear due to the effects of modernization (see Gorski 2000).

5. Taylor 2007, 13.

6. Ibid., 21.

7. Ibid., 25.

8. Throughout the book, we will refer to our interview subjects by name; however, these names are altered slightly to ensure the anonymity of the person.

9. Bishop and Cushing 2008.

10. Prothero (2007) introduces and measures the concept that we can be more or less literate in our religious knowledge.

11. Prothero 2007.

12. Gingrich 2006.

13. Coulter 2006, 22.

14. These studies are known as the Baylor Religion Surveys and contain the most detailed set of questions about God that have ever been administered to a national sample of Americans. Those interested in an overview of the methods and sampling for our survey and interviews should turn to appendix 1 for relevant details. Detailed sampling and methodological information about the Baylor Religion Survey is also available at the Association of Religion Data Archives (http://www.thearda.com).

15. Whitehead and Palmer-Boyes (2009) show viewing God as a "he" is significantly associated with more conservative views of gender roles and is among the most powerful predictors of gender role attitudes.

16. John Lofland and Rodney Stark (1965) conducted a landmark study on the conversion process. Similar to the stories of conversion we heard, Lofland and Stark noted that converts describe their own experience as beginning with an intimate encounter with God or a dramatic realization about God. But by following their subjects through the process of conversion, Lofland and Stark discovered something that precedes any change in beliefs—a change in friendship networks. Simply put, converts acquire new beliefs about God only after they are immersed in a group of friends who also hold these beliefs. This insightful discovery highlights the importance of our social circumstances in determining our ultimate beliefs. Nonetheless, it is never enough just to hang out with people who have different conceptions of God. Many individuals with close friends in cults still stop short of becoming true believers and eventually drift away from the group. Only when a person embraces the beliefs of those around him is he "reborn" into a new identity and purpose. At the end of the day, while conversions tend to be instigated by social circumstances, they occur only when a person's story of God has been altered dramatically.

17. Smith 2003, 64.

18. See Greeley 1988, 1989, 1991, 1993, and 1995.

19. Greeley 1995, 124.

20. *What Do We Imagine God to Be?* edited by Pierre Hegy (2007) is a wonderful book that rigorously looks at the many different ways that God affects us.

21. Hunter 1991.

22. See Wuthnow 1988, 1996; Hunter 1991; Guinness 1993; Evans 1997; Smith 1998.

23. Hunter 1991, 44; also see Glazer 1987; Warner 1988; Woodrum 1988; Hadden and Shupe 1989; Jelen 1991; Kirkpatrick 1993.

24. See Davis and Robinson 1996a, 1996b; DiMaggio, Evans, and Bryson 1996; Evans 1997, 2003; Fiorina, Abrams, and Pope 2005; Jelen 1997; Norvel 1974; Olson 1997; Williams 1997.

25. Mead 1934.
26. Geertz 1973, 24.

Chapter 1

1. Bellah, Madsen, Sullivan, Swidler, and Tipton 1985, 221.
2. From *Boyhood* by Leo Tolstoy.
3. Miles 1995.
4. Ibid., 237.
5. The John 3:16 movement can be traced back to Rollen Stewart, a born-again Christian who began attending sporting events in the 1980s wearing a rainbow-colored wig and carrying a sign reading simply "John 3:16." Stewart was arrested in 1992 after a bizarre standoff. On September 2, 1992, Stewart picked up two day laborers and drove them to a hotel near the Los Angeles airport. He took the two men up to a room, where he walked in on a chambermaid. Stewart drew a gun. The two laborers fled, and the chambermaid locked herself in a bathroom. After a standoff with the police, Stewart was captured and given three life sentences for kidnapping. Stewart's story is outlined in an excellent 1997 documentary directed by Sam Green, *The Rainbow Man/John 3:16*.
6. Amazon.com offers an even wider selection, adding John 3:16 key chains, gift baskets, ceramic tiles, bumper stickers, wristbands, napkin holders, charms, and posters. And the hamburger chain In-N-Out Burger includes a barely visible reference to John 3:16 on the bottom of its paper cups.
7. God's love is perhaps one of the strongest areas of agreement among U.S. religious believers. The majority of males and females, Democrats and Republicans, whites, African Americans, and those of other races, college graduates and high school graduates, and evangelical Christians and Catholics all believe God to have loving qualities. Certainly there are some statistically significant differences. Females are more likely to believe God is loving (90.2 percent) than males (79.7 percent). Nearly all African American respondents to our survey (99.1 percent) believe God is loving, compared with 84.3 percent of whites. Belief that God is loving tends to decrease as education increases. Those with a postgraduate education, for example, are less likely to see God as loving (78.6 percent) than those with a high school diploma (88.4 percent). And although still in the majority, believers in a loving God are less likely to affiliate with the Democratic Party (83.8 percent) than they are with the Republicans (91.5 percent).

   While significant in a statistical sense, such differences are not very interesting in a sociological sense. In our analyses, we find that belief in God as a loving being tends to mirror belief in the existence of God in the first place. Females (97.9 percent) are more likely to believe in God than are males

(93.5 percent). Belief in God also tends to decrease as education increases, with high school graduates demonstrating more belief (98.3 percent) than those with a postgraduate education (92.7 percent). Of the blacks in our sample, 100 percent believed in God, compared with 95.5 percent of whites. Republicans (98.6 percent) are slightly more likely to believe in God than are Democrats (94.7 percent).

8. "BTK Sentenced to 10 Life Terms: Victims' Families Confront Confessed Serial Murderer" 2005.

9. We measured God's perceived level of judgment for BRS respondents using the same six questions presented on the "God Test." Respondents to the BRS were asked if they agree that God is "angered by human sins" and "angered by my sins." They are also asked how well the adjectives "critical," "punishing," "severe," and "wrathful" describe God. Scores range from 6 to 30, with a mean of 17.04 and a standard deviation of 6.431. All the items are on 5-point, Likert-type scales. The final scale has an alpha of .85.

10. *Where Is God When It Hurts?* (2002), *Disappointment with God* (1997), *Finding God in Unexpected Places* (2005), and *Reaching for the Invisible God* (2000).

11. Yancey 2000, 113–114.

12. Six of those items ask respondents their level of agreement with the following descriptions of God: "removed from worldly affairs," "removed from my personal affairs," "concerned with the well-being of the world," "concerned with my personal well-being," "directly involved in worldly affairs," and "directly involved in my affairs." Two additional items ask respondents how well the adjectives "distant" and "ever-present" describe God. Active God scores range from 8 to 40, with a mean of 31 (30.64). The Active God measure is a simple additive scale with items reverse-coded if necessary. Alpha = .91. This means that, in effect, the average American believes God to be relatively interested in the world and its events.

13. Spencer 2005.

14. "Town Is Warned of God's Wrath" 2005.

15. Transcript from an interview between Jerry Falwell and Pat Robertson. The interview was taped on September 13, 2001, and aired the following day on the *700 Club*.

16. Quotes are from a phone interview with SQuire Rushnell that took place on July 17, 2007.

17. Ibid.

18. Ibid.

19. "Pope to Dealers: You'll Answer to God" 2007; Wade and Pullella 2007.

20. Owen 2007.

21. Ibid.

22. Franklin 1728.

23. Tillich 1957.

Chapter 2

1. Youtz 1907, 428.
2. Fowler 1981, 128; Harms 1944; Ladd, McIntosh, and Spilka 1998. See also Rizzuto 1979.
3. Newberg and Waldman 2009, 102.
4. Vergote and Aubert 1972; Vergote and Tamayo 1981; Vergote et al. 1969.
5. Birky and Ball 1987; de Roos et al. 2004; Dickie et al. 1997, 2006; Gleason 1975; Hertel and Donahue 1995; Tamayo and Desjardins 1976.
6. As Stark and Finke (2000, 115) note: "Even in the extremely diverse, unregulated, and very competitive American religious economy, most people remain within the religious organization into which they were born, and most of those who do shift from one organization to another remain within the religious tradition into which they were born—even including conversions across the Christian-Jewish divide, fewer than 1 percent of Americans convert." On nonbelievers, see Baker and Smith 2009.
7. As James Fowler explains, our childhood religious belief is "powerfully and permanently influenced by examples, moods, actions, and stories of the visible faith of primally related adults." Fowler 1981, 133.
8. When asked, "Outside of attending religious services, about how often do you read the Bible, Koran, Torah or other sacred book?" 37 percent of respondents indicated that they did so at least once a month. Source: Baylor Religion Survey, Wave 2, 2007. When asked how often they participate in religious education programs, such as Bible study or Sunday school, 38 percent of respondents indicated that they participate at least once a month. Source: Baylor Religion Survey, Wave 2, 2007.
9. Baylor Religion Survey, Wave 2 (2007). Respondents were asked: "Please indicate if you have ever had any of the following experiences . . . I felt called by God to do something"; 44.6 percent of respondents said they had had this experience.
10. Newberg and Waldman 2009, 83.
11. For instance, Kellstedt, Green, Smidt, and Guth (1996) have advocated creating a four-tier Evangelical categorization: essentially, breaking Evangelicals into the core (mainly conservative Republicans), second tier (slightly more liberal), third tier (more Mainline Protestant), and fourth tier (black Protestants and Roman Catholics). Smith 1998, 131.
12. In 2000, Steensland and colleagues proposed a new method for classifying religious traditions which was based on both doctrine and historical changes in religious groups. In their typology individuals are placed in one of the following categories: Evangelical Protestant, Black Protestant, Mainline Protestant, Catholic, Jew, Other, and No Religious Affiliation. (See Steensland et al. 2000 for full discussion.)
13. Hunter 1988; Roof and McKinney 1987; Wuthnow 1988.

14. Ammerman 1997, 358.
15. Daniel was given the distributions about his congregants' answers and was unable to match individual congregants to their responses.
16. Emerson and Smith 2000, 136.
17. Abraham Lincoln's second inaugural address, March 4, 1865, reprinted in *Inaugural Addresses of the Presidents of the United States* (U.S. Congress Joint Congressional Committee on Inaugural Ceremonies, 1989).
18. Religious wars tend to focus on disagreements about who has the one true God (see Armstrong 2000 and Stark 2001a). Large-scale conflicts concerning atheism really only emerged during the Soviet era (see Froese 2008), and most Communist regimes today have abandoned a virulent advocacy of atheism.
19. Pew Research Center 2006.
20. In fact, the close tie between religious and political ideology has led many theorists to describe the American ideological spectrum as an amalgamation of both—often placing conservative Protestants on one end and liberal Jews on the other. Roof and McKinney (1987, 224) describe this tendency, which has solidified in the public and academic imagination in the past couple of decades.
21. In the 2008 elections, Democratic candidates were extremely sensitive to this issue: Hillary Clinton, Barack Obama, and John Edwards all accepted invitations to discuss their personal faith at a televised forum sponsored by a liberal evangelical organization. This was a clear change of strategy for Democrats, who, with the clear exception of Jimmy Carter, have generally avoided public references to faith. In fact, Clinton, Edwards, and Obama attempted to outdo one another in demonstrating how faith would guide their political leadership: Clinton asserted that it is "absolutely essential that you be grounded in your faith," while Edwards minced no words in testifying that "I have a deep and abiding love for my Lord, Jesus Christ."
22. The Evangelical Manifesto Steering Committee 2008.
23. During the 1980s, conservative Christian leaders formed an innovative coalition with the Republican Party. Prior to this alliance, a Democrat, Jimmy Carter, captured the bulk of the evangelical vote in the 1976 presidential election by successfully demonstrating his religious integrity, even though he held liberal stances on most social issues. And African Americans, many of whom are vehemently opposed to gay marriage and abortion for religious reasons, still vote Democratic to this day. But in recent decades, the GOP has successfully captured the loyalty of millions of devout white Christians because, we are told, they believe in the same sacred things. Pat Robertson, Jerry Falwell, and James Dobson were all openly supportive of Bush. Indeed, Robertson believed that God himself supported Bush. Robertson made this comment on November 4, 2004, during an interview on the Fox News Channel's *Hannity & Colmes*.

24. Hout and Fischer 2002.

25. Pitirim Sorokin (1998, 107) puts this best: "To many a downright empiricist, such an admission of the truth of faith may appear equivalent to the injection of ignorance, superstition, and the like into the social sciences. Yet if they are real empirical observers of themselves, of their fellow men, of the structure and development of science, philosophy, religion, ethics, and the fine arts, they cannot deny either this source of cognition or the existence of the aspect of reality discovered through it. It is as much an empirical datum or fact as any other datum or fact and equally unquestionable."

26. James 1961, 73.

27. See the appendix for specific statistical analyses.

Chapter 3

1. Sociologist Jeni Loftus (2001) examined U.S. attitudes toward homosexuality using data from the General Social Survey. By 1998, she found, approximately 27.4 percent of the U.S. population found homosexuality to be "not wrong at all." Using the 2004 General Social Survey, we found that the percentage who accept homosexuality had increased to 30 percent.

2. "Times Topics: Same-Sex Marriage, Civil Unions, and Domestic Partnerships" 2009.

3. Herek and Capitanio 1995.

4. Considered another way, more than a fourth of Americans (26.6 percent) consider abortion to be always wrong in a particular circumstance (such as the woman simply not wanting a child) but never wrong in another (such as in the case of rape).

5. We looked at five circumstances (when the baby has a serious defect, when the woman's health is in danger, when the pregnancy is the result of rape, when the family cannot afford a child, and when the woman does not want the child) and calculated the percentage of respondents who said abortion was "always wrong" in all instances.

6. See Fiorina et al.'s (2005) analysis of abortion attitudes over the past four decades.

7. Years of survey research and many case studies have found that how often a person attends church, the type of religious group to which a person belongs, and whether a person takes the Bible literally impact views on abortion. These effects tend to be rather simple in nature. Those who attend church more often have more restrictive views on abortion in all circumstances. Biblical literalists are *always* less supportive of abortion, whether the reason behind that abortion is rape, the possibility of a serious birth defect, or any other. Similarly, members of religious traditions that tend to be more conservative in nature, such as evangelicals, are nearly always more absolutist on abortion issues than their Mainline counterparts.

8. See Cook, Jelen, and Wilcox 1992; Harris and Mills 1985; Jelen 1988; Jelen and Wilcox 1997; Luker 1984; Petersen 2001; Woodrum and Davison 1992.

9. As sociologists and statisticians, we have available a technique that allows us to remove from consideration factors we know to have confounding results on our findings. Church attendance, religious tradition, view of the Bible, and demographic characteristics such as race and gender are all strongly related to one's image of God. Removing the effects of church attendance, race, gender, and a host of other factors reveals a complex relationship between God and the circumstances of abortion (see figure 3.2).

10. For example, although Distant God believers are generally more tolerant of abortion than other God types, they could not be characterized as approving of abortion. A majority of those with a Distant God (53.4 percent) believe that abortion is at least sometimes wrong (if not always) when the reason is that the family cannot afford the child. A twenty-three-year-old female from Florida with a Distant God told us, "I don't think we could ever know that," when asked how God feels about abortion. Source: Baylor Religion Survey, Wave 2 (2007).

11. "Mr. Rogers," host of *Mister Rogers's Neighborhood* on PBS, was, in fact, the Reverend Frederick McFeely Rogers, ordained in the Presbyterian Church USA. He passed away in February 2003.

12. WBC theology is, in fact, a very strict version of five-point Calvinism, the history of which is beyond the scope of this chapter. The five tenets of strict five-point Calvinism are (1) total depravity: mankind is unworthy of God's favor; (2) unconditional election: God has chosen certain people to go to Heaven, and this choice is not based on merit, as no person is worthy in God's eyes; (3) limited atonement: Jesus sacrificed himself to atone for the sins of those chosen as elect; (4) irresistible grace: those who are chosen by God will be unable to resist the "call"; and (5) perseverance of the saints: all whom God calls to him will work for him until the end and will not be frustrated by worldly concerns. For a more detailed overview of this theology, see Steele, Thomas, and Quinn 2004.

13. The quote is from a press release that has been removed from the WBC Web site as of this writing. The monograph was previously publicly available at: http://www.godhatesfags.com/fliers/feb2004/Monograph_2-14-2004.pdf.

14. This news release, titled "Thank God for the Utah Mine Disaster," dated August 11, 2007, was obtained from the Westboro Baptist Church. The disaster referenced in this release occurred on August 6, 2007, when a portion of the Crandall Canyon mine in Utah collapsed, trapping six miners. The collapse is believed to be the result of seismic activity. As of this writing, the bodies of the miners have not been recovered.

15. Durkheim 1982 [1893].

16. Erikson 1966.

17. In fact, atheists or the irreligious are some of the least trusted and most despised individuals in America today, mainly because they are generally believed to be without moral foundation and certainly going to hell (see Edgell, Gerteis, and Hartman 2006).

18. Thomas Jefferson (1822), "Religion and the University," a letter to Dr. Thomas Cooper.

19. Meacham 2006, 28. If John Adams had access to contemporary data, he would find that atheists are as likely to volunteer in their community as religious believers and are no more likely than believers to get divorced or have criminal records.

20. Edgell et al. (2006) show that atheists are one of the most disliked minorities in the United States.

Chapter 4

1. President Clinton is quoted in the *New York Times* coverage of the event ("Reading the Book of Life; White House Remarks on Decoding of Genome" 2000).

2. Ibid.

3. Michael Dexter, director of the Wellcome Trust (a British charitable organization), said in a London news conference regarding the project: "This is an outstanding achievement not only of our lifetime, perhaps in the history of mankind." Dexter was quoted in CNN coverage of the discovery ("Rough Map of the Human Genome Completed" 2000). Wellcome's Sanger Institute sequenced a third of the human genome.

4. Collins 2006, 30.

5. Ibid., 3.

6. On the back cover of Dawkins 2006, J. Craig Venter offers the praise: "Richard Dawkins is the leading soothsayer of our time. Through his exploration of the gene-based evolution of life, his work has had a profound effect on so much of our collective thinking, and *The God Delusion* continues his thought-provoking tradition." Dawkins returns the favor, describing Venter as a "brilliant (and non-religious) 'buccaneer of science'" (Dawkins 2006, 99).

7. Ecklund and Scheitle (2007) utilize data from the Religion among Academic Scientists survey (2005) to examine field-specific differences in religious beliefs. When asked about their belief in God, 24.9 percent of academics in the natural sciences (physics, biology, and chemistry) said that they believe in God "sometimes," believe in God with "some doubt," or have no doubts about God's existence. A slightly higher percentage of respondents in the social sciences (sociology, economics, political science, psychology), 30.6 percent, believe in God sometimes, with some doubt, or with no doubts.

8. We refer to Americans' "faith" in science because most Americans have a rudimentary knowledge of science at best. Accordingly, the average person must take the statements and innovations of professional scientists, medical specialists, and academic researchers on faith, because he or she does not have the educational background necessary to critically engage the professional scientific community. Therefore, Americans must determine for themselves how their faith in science and their faith in God coexist.

9. Gould 1998, 271.

10. Dawkins 2003.

11. Einstein 2000, 204.

12. Spinoza 1955 [1677]. See Note for Proposition 15 in the proof "Concerning God."

13. Indeed, the tendency for religious movements to conform to their sociocultural environment is one of the key observations in the sociology of religion. Given a long enough time span, every religion tends to remove more and more of its rules and restrictions and conform more to societal mores. This very process of accommodation, however, often leads new, stricter sect movements to split off from established churches. See Stark and Bainbridge (1985) for an excellent overview of this process.

14. Leibniz 1961.

15. Gould 1983, 253–262.

16. Thirty-five percent of believers in an active God think that "scientists are hostile to religion"; only 13 percent of believers in Spinoza's God feel the same way.

17. This finding comes from a Princeton study reported in the *New York Times* (Tierney 2007).

18. Ibid.

19. Tourist resources for Glen Rose report that the most likely candidate for the brontosaurus tracks was a dinosaur named *Pleurocoelus*.

20. The Web site of the Texas Natural Science Center (of the University of Texas at Austin) provides an overview of the tracks: "Some scientists think that the footprints actually document a battle between the theropod and the sauropod" (http://www.utexas.edu/tmm/exhibits/trackway/index.html).

21. Quote from *Creation Live!* a video purchased at the Glen Rose Creation Evidence Museum. Young and Edis (2006) and Stenger (2007) trace the modern Young Earth creationism movement to Henry Morris and Jon Whitcomb. In 1960, Whitcomb and Morris published *The Genesis Flood*, which argued that the Bible provides a literally true account of the creation of the world. The book claims that the Earth is 6,000 to 10,000 years old and that its geological features can be explained by the great flood of Noah's time. See also Sarfati 1999.

22. Several books with titles such as *Missionaries and Monsters* (Gibbons 2006) and *Dinosaurs: Dead or Alive?* (O'Donnell 2006) recount claims of

encounters with living dinosaurs. Answers in Genesis and the Creation Science Foundation, two groups promoting creationism, issued a joint statement questioning many of the claims made by Baugh. The groups believe that Baugh's bad science will turn people away from creation accounts: "It is sad that Carl Baugh will 'muddy the water' for many Christians and non-Christians. Some Christians will try to use Baugh's 'evidences' in witnessing and get 'shot down' by someone who is scientifically literate. The ones witnessed to will thereafter be wary of all creation evidences and even more inclined to dismiss Christians as nut cases not worth listening to." The statement has been preserved online at http://paleo.cc/paluxy/whatbau.htm.

23. For example, the museum offers a reproduction of the "Zapata track." This is an alleged human footprint found in New Mexico in Permian rock.

24. Heffner, Heffner, and Baugh 2001, 26.

25. The Pew Research Center (2005) provides an excellent summary of recent surveys related to evolution and creationism. In their meta-analysis of survey data on the issue, Pew finds that "approximately 40%–50% of the public accepts a biblical creationist account of the origins of life, while comparable numbers accept the idea that humans evolved over time." Our own examination of surveys confirms this assertion. For example, the General Social Survey (2004) finds that 42.6 percent of respondents believe that God created man in his current form, and a CBS News Poll from 2005 found that 51 percent believe this.

26. *USA Today*/Gallup Poll conducted June 1–3, 2007 (*n* = 1,007). The question asked: "Next, we'd like to ask about your views on two different explanations for the origin and development of life on earth." Respondents were then asked to use the possible responses "definitely true," "probably true," "probably false," "definitely false," and "unsure" to indicate their certainty about "Evolution—that is, the idea that human beings developed over millions of years from less advanced forms of life" and "Creationism—that is, the idea that God created human beings pretty much in their present form at one time within the last 10,000 years."

27. For example, a *Newsweek* poll conducted March 28–29, 2007, found that, of the 43 percent of respondents who indicated belief in evolution, more than two-thirds (69 percent) believe that God guided the process.

28. Other key figures in the intelligent design movement include Philip Johnson, a Berkeley lawyer; Michael Behe, a biochemist and author of *Darwin's Black Box: The Biochemical Challenge to Evolution* (2006), and Michael Denton, author of *Evolution: A Theory in Crisis* (1986).

29. For example, Kenneth R. Miller, a professor of biochemistry at Brown University, notes that the type III secretory system used by bacteria to transmit proteins into a host cell is composed of a subset of the proteins that make up flagellum. This refutes the argument that each component part of

the flagellum could not operate without the others. See Miller 2004. For critical overviews of the intelligent design movement, see Young and Edis 2006, Dawkins 2006, and Brockman 2006.

Chapter 5

1. Wuthnow 1994, 220; North and Smietana 2008, 24.
2. As David Bostitis (2005) explains, African American support for the Democratic Party and its presidential candidates dates to the New Deal era, prior to which the majority of African Americans were Republican. See also Bolce and Gray 1979, Carmines and Stimson 1989, Dawson 1994, Harris 1994, Kidd et al. 2007, McDaniel and Ellison 2008, Smith and Seltzer 1992, Stanley and Niemi 2006, and Walton and Smith 2003.
3. Emerson and Smith 2000, 77.
4. Bartkowski and Regis 2003; Chaves 1999; Greenberg 2000; Katz 1996; Moberg 1974; Omri 2008; Schaefer 2003; Wilson and Janoski 1995; Wineburg 2001.
5. Then-Governor George W. Bush, as quoted in the foreword to Marvin Olasky's *Compassionate Conservatism* (2000, xii). David Frum, a conservative insider in the early Bush White House, also saw the importance of the salvation component of church-supplied welfare but reasoned that this spiritual component would make it difficult or nearly impossible to implement the program effectively. See *David Frum's Diary* from October 18, 2006, at frum.nationalreview.com for his explanation of why faith-based funding is untenable. Olasky 2000, 178.
6. The therapeutic effects of God imagery have been extensively explored in the treatment of personal traumas (see Moriarty 2007). The therapist asks the patient to imagine God as he or she remembers a trauma; in this way, the presence of God is expected to have a calming effect. This is the very technique described by Reverend Flores.
7. Some white conservative evangelicals and liberal Mainline Protestants still oppose faith-based funding. It may come as a surprise that a few believers in an Authoritative God oppose faith-based initiatives. But this is no surprise to Jay Hein, who is well aware of what he calls misperceptions within white evangelical circles. His Office of Faith-Based and Community Initiatives openly states that many conservative Christians have theological objections to getting government money for activities that they believe adherents should support, worries about becoming dangerously dependent on a distant funding source that may dry up tomorrow, or concerns about implementing government policies with which they might partially disagree. Most notably, many faith-based groups are concerned that the cost of federal funds is the putative divestiture of much or all of the religious character. See "How Much Federal Support for Faith-Based and Grassroots Charities?" 2001.

8. This sentiment is evident in Obama's (2008) speech to the East Side Community Ministry in Zanesville, Ohio:

> You see, while [faith-based outreach groups] are often made up of folks who've come together around a common faith, they're usually working to help people of all faiths or of no faith at all. And they're particularly well-placed to offer help. As I've said many times, I believe that change comes not from the top down, but from the bottom up, and few are closer to the people than our churches, synagogues, temples, and mosques. That's why Washington needs to draw on them. The fact is, the challenges we face today—from saving our planet to ending poverty—are simply too big for government to solve alone. We need all hands on deck.

See also Francis 2009; Meckler 2009; Zeleny and Luo 2008.

9. Barack Obama made the statement after an April 6, 2008, fundraiser at the Getty mansion in San Francisco. A tape of his comments became public.

10. Nearly a third of those with an Authoritative God are the most likely to believe that God sometimes punishes people with misfortune. Another third of Authoritative believers think that God may reward their faithfulness but prefer not to see misfortune as God's retribution. Taken together, this means that a majority of people with an Authoritative God view their life circumstances as at least partially God's doing.

It makes sense that people with an Authoritative God think that he somewhat determines the trajectory of their lives, since they view God as very "hands on" the world. People with a Benevolent God also view God as very active in world affairs but do not imagine God as judgmental. It follows that they do not like to think of God as cursing people. If they think that God is involved at all in our fortunes, it is through blessings (43 percent). Only a small minority (8 percent) of those with a Benevolent God think that God causes misfortune.

Those who imagine God as judgmental but reluctant to directly involve himself in world affairs (a Critical God) are comparatively unlikely to believe that God plays any role in their failures and successes (71 percent). The few who do tend to think that God's hand is revealed through curses (18 percent), not blessings (10 percent). Those with a Distant God simply do not see God as playing a role in our personal fortunes at all.

11. Tucker 1974, 54.

12. Sociologists of religion have often noted the tendency of stricter religious groups, often called sects, to focus on otherworldly over worldly rewards. See, for example, Stark and Finke 2000.

13. Frank 2005, 136.

14. Differences in opinions about God are highly predictive of how Americans feel about gay marriage regardless of their income. For instance, nearly all believers in an Authoritative God (around 80 percent) want to ban gay marriage whether they earn less than $35,000 a year or more than $100,000. Similarly, believers in a Distant God are unlikely to want to ban gay marriage in all income categories. At the end of the day, your income has no significant relevance to your attitudes toward gays, but your God is extremely important. Consequently, conservative moral policies bridge economic divides while exploiting religious ones. On economic and class divides, see Barker and Carman 2000; Cook and Barrett 1992; Gilliam and Whitby 1989; Hasenfeld and Rafferty 1989; Kelley and Evans 1993; Kluegel and Smith 1986.

15. Green, Guth, Smidt, and Kellstedt (1996, 187) are quick to point out a misconception that has plagued social science for much of the past half century, namely, that "religion was routinely dismissed as a proxy for underlying economic interests or resulting anxieties." Our findings demonstrate that social class is of primary importance in understanding economic attitudes, but that images of God play a key intervening role.

Chapter 6

1. We also asked our respondents their level of agreement with the statement "God rewards the faithful with major successes." Those who agree with this statement are much more likely to believe that God also causes disasters to occur (correlation = .393, $p < .01$). In other words, if you believe that God directly has a hand in good things, you also believe that God will punish you with bad things.

2. John Hagee is senior pastor at Cornerstone Church in San Antonio, Texas. Terry Gross interviewed Hagee on the September 18, 2006, edition of *Fresh Air* on National Public Radio. In the provided quote, Hagee was responding to the question "Do you still think that Katrina is punishment from God for a society that's becoming like Sodom and Gomorrah?"

3. See http://www.religioustolerance.org/tsunami04h.htm#quo for an excellent overview of the various reasons people gave for God's anger with the United States and/or New Orleans in particular that was said to have motivated Hurricane Katrina.

4. John Shelby Spong is a liberal Christian theologian, retired bishop of the Episcopal Diocese of Newark, New Jersey, and author of books such as *Rescuing the Bible from Fundamentalism*. The provided quote is from Spong's response to a question from a Fox News producer about comments by Pat Robertson about God's willingness to cause disasters.

The full text of his response is available here: http://www.dailykos.com/story/2005/11/16/18509/384.

5. With the exception of his wife. Job 1:8, 1:12 (NIV).

6. The Baylor Religion Survey, Wave 2 (2007), asks respondents their level of agreement with the statement "God sometimes allows tragedies to occur as a warning to sinners" and the statement "God sometimes causes tragedies to occur as a warning to sinners." Approximately 27 percent (27.4) of respondents agree or strongly agree with the first statement, but disagree or strongly disagree with the second.

7. For example, a search on Google for "Where was God during 9/11" on July 7, 2007, produced many hits. Many of these were sermons about 9/11 that included reports of miracles. The Web site "Where was God on 9/11?" provides a complete itinerary of God's actions on that day: http://www.swapmeetdave.com/United/Where.htm.

8. Jones 1995, 17.

9. In his analysis of the effects of Hurricane Ivan on Grenadian society, Leslie James argues that "catastrophies disintegrate the foundations of the world as it is known. They force human beings to examine their values and constructs of reality. These include constructs or images of God" (Hegy 2007: 167).

10. Governor Sarah Palin made headlines when running for vice president for her association with religious leaders who practice a brand of Pentecostalism known as "spiritual warfare" (see the *New York Times* story on October 25, 2008).

11. See Rabey 1988.

12. Peretti is quoted in Maudlin 1989, 58.

13. A line of research by Lupfer and colleagues examines whether people attribute life events to supernatural agents such as God and/or Satan (Lupfer, Brock, and DePaola 1992; Lupfer, Tolliver, and Jackson 1996; Weeks and Lupfer 2000). Such research finds that those with higher levels of religiosity (Weeks and Lupfer 2000) and conservative Christians (Lupfer et al. 1996) are more likely to view Satan and God as explanations for life's ups and downs. Attributing life events to the work of Satan was most likely to occur in negative circumstances (Lupfer et al. 1996).

14. See, for example, Altemeyer and Hunsberger 1992.

15. Wilcox, Linzey, and Jelen (1991) found that an individual's attitude toward the church's role in combating Satan predicted potential participation in social movements, rallies, or petitions and membership in the Moral Majority. Swatos (1988) found the belief that Satan is responsible for pornography to be related to the picketing of stores carrying erotic materials.

16. Winchester 2003.

17. Ibid., 333. Note that Winchester located the quote from an 1892 report on the social conditions of west Java written by a Dutch teacher named

R. A. van Sandick. Obviously, this passage represents Sandick's translation of Abdul Karim's words and therefore may not be exact.

18. Jenkins 2007.
19. Chirot and McCauley 2006.
20. Beyerlein and Sikkink 2008.
21. Stolberg 2007.
22. See Reichley 2002, 348. BBC2 aired a documentary series entitled "Elusive Peace: Israel and the Arabs" in 2005. The documentary includes an account of a private conversation in June 2003 between George Bush, Palestinian Prime Minister Mahmoud Abbas, and Abbas's foreign minister, Nabil Shaath. Shaath claims Bush stated, "I'm driven with a mission from God" and that he was inspired by God to begin the wars in Afghanistan and Iraq and to aid in the Palestinian-Israeli conflict. The report remains controversial, and the White House has not verified the veracity of Shaath's claims.
23. See Froese and Mencken 2009.
24. See the president's remarks in his "Address to a Joint Session of Congress and the American People" (2001).
25. A few believers in an Authoritative God also believe that the United States is godless or opposed to God's wishes. Islamic fundamentalists and Westboro Baptists fit this profile.
26. See Froese and Mencken 2009.

Chapter 7

1. Dawkins 2006; Hitchens 2007; Harris 2004, 2006; Mills 2006; Perakh 2003; Stenger 2007; Edis 2002.
2. See Stenger 2007; Perakh 2003; Edis 2002; Hitchens 2007, 282.
3. Stark and Finke 2000, 73.
4. Nonbelievers exist in a culture where belief is ubiquitous and where they are unavoidably defined in relation to belief in God. The religious historian Mircea Eliade (1957) puts it best: "Nonreligious man descends from *homo religious* and, whether he likes it or not, he is also the work of religious man." Nonbelievers are the "work of religious man" to the extent that they must blaze a trail that departs from our traditional religious culture. For example, Americans without faith in God are called "atheists" or "nonbelievers," and both terms express belief only in the negative sense—the absence or lack of belief.
5. Stark and Finke (2000) make the argument that American religious fervor is due to our religious pluralism. Because the U.S. government does not discriminate against religious groups, they are free to flourish and thrive; in turn, this religious freedom ensures that Americans can practice the religion they want. At the end of the day, freedom inspires devotion.

6. See James Wellman's (2008, 22) discussion of two-party dichotomies in American culture for a nice overview of the various attempts by social scientists to label and categorize the opposing sides of the culture wars.

7. For Kniss (1997), Americans differ not only in how they define moral authority but also in terms of how we define our moral project. The difference comes down to how *individually* or *collectively* we define our moral authority and project. "Conservatives" are those who appeal to collective moral authority yet see the individual as the moral project. The conservative stance on abortion fits nicely with this categorization: we collectively determine immorality of abortion and demand that the individual follow our moral code. "Liberals" typically appeal to individual moral authority yet see society as the moral project. Yet some groups, like the Mennonites, appeal to collective moral authority to advance a collectivist moral project.

8. Our four types of Gods should be considered ideal types in a Weberian sense of the term. Essentially, no individual actually believes in the exact God we describe. Still, these ideal types provide guidelines by which we can evaluate the extent to which an individual holds beliefs more in line with one type over the others.

9. Stark 2007, 10.

10. Ibid., 11.

11. Many of the earliest creation stories envision God as a goddess—a mother who gives birth to all life. The Goddess of Willendorf limestone idol from 19,000 B.C.E. depicts an exaggerated female figure with large breasts and hips. The Paleolithic period is rife with similar images of a Mother Goddess, known by those in ancient Samaria as Inana; in ancient Babylon as Ishtar; in Canaan as Anat; in Egypt as Isis; and in ancient Greece as Aphrodite (see Armstrong 1993). Ancient Hindu imagery from the Indus Valley, now modern-day India, shows deities with human characteristics, such as Vishnu, the sustainer of all things, and Krishna, his supreme incarnation. With thirty-three gods in the Vedic tradition, early Hindus pondered the paradox of God being at once many and also "one" (best emblemized in the god Shiva). Sikhs particularly stressed the concept of the oneness of God and later broke with Hindus over whether God could be manifested in many forms.

12. In the Old Testament, the spirit of Yahweh appears as fire and light (the burning bush and the pillar of fire providing guidance and protection), in the form of a cloud (providing shade and direction in the desert wilderness), and an audible voice that spoke to Moses, David, and many others who number among God's chosen. The first of the Ten Commandments decisively prohibits graven images because Judaism purports to reveal the one true God.

13. Meacham 2006, 233.

14. Hout and Fischer 2002. Hout and Fischer additionally report that most Americans "with no [religious] preference hold conventional religious beliefs, despite their alienation from organized religion."

15. Wuthnow 1988, 97.

16. Wuthnow 1988, 1996; Hunter 1991; Guinness 1993; Evans 1997; Smith 1998. Still, there are serious arguments among researchers as to how many evangelicals there are in the United States. This essentially comes down to a problem with measurement (see Hackett and Lindsay 2008 concerning measurement options).

17. Smith 1998.

18. The mailer was sent to voters in West Virginia and Arkansas by the Republican National Committee in September 2004. A copy of the mailing can be seen here: http://www.steveclemons.com/GOPMailer.htm. "Them" clearly referred to liberals, and the back of the mailing outlined a "liberal agenda" that included "Removing 'under God' from the Pledge of Allegiance," "Allowing teenagers to get abortions without parental consent," "Overturning the ban on the hideous procedure known as Partial Birth Abortion," and "Allowing same-sex marriages."

19. Of respondents to the Baylor Religion Survey, Wave 2, who reported belief in God, 46.2 percent report having volunteered at least one hour a week "through the community, through your place of worship," or "through the community not through your place of worship." The majority (54.7 percent) of those who have felt "called by God to do something" have engaged in volunteering in the past month, indicating that a perceived active relationship with God is associated with a desire, or even a requirement, to serve the community.

Appendix

1. The National Opinion Research Center (NORC) has conducted the General Social Survey (GSS) since 1972. The GSS was administered to random samples of the U.S. population on a yearly basis from 1972 to 1994 with the exceptions of 1979, 1981, and 1992. Starting in 1994, the survey has become biennial, with administration in 1994, 1996, 1998, 2000, 2002, 2004, 2006, 2008, and most recently 2010. The GSS provides in-depth coverage on particular topics through the use of rotating content modules and has included content modules on religion on several occasions. For example, in 1988, the GSS included a special module on religion with items related to religious socialization (e.g., religion in the family) and religious beliefs and behaviors.

2. For details of the methodology behind the Baylor Religion Survey, see Bader, Froese, and Mencken 2007.

3. A copy of the mailed survey instrument can be found at http://www
.isreligion.org/research/surveysofreligion/.

4. See the American Association for Public Opinion Research.

5. We were unable to definitively locate respondents in the GSS 2004 who
were Baha'i, Chinese folk religion, Christian & Missionary Alliance, Christian Science, or Salvation Army.

6. For a full report on how BRS respondents compare with the GSS, see Bader,
Froese, and Mencken 2007.

7. We used two methods to determine how a particular outcome varied by
God type. If we desired to control for other measures, we entered God type
into an OLS regression as a series of dummy variables (contrast category =
Authoritative God). We used ANOVA to examine simple differences between
God types on a particular outcome measure without controls.

8. Steensland et al. 2000.

REFERENCES

"Address to a Joint Session of Congress and the American People." 2001. The White House, September. Retrieved June 12, 2008 (http://georgewbush-whitehouse.archives.gov/news/releases/2001/02/20010228.html).

Allport, Gordon W. 1921. "Personality and Character." *Psychological Bulletin* 18: 441–455.

Altemeyer, Bob, and Bruce Hunsberger. 1992. "Authoritarianism, Religious Fundamentalism, Quest, and Prejudice." *International Journal for the Psychology of Religion* 2(2): 113–133.

Ammerman, Nancy. 1997. *Congregation and Community*. Piscataway, NJ: Rutgers University Press.

Armstrong, Karen. 1993. *A History of God: The 4000-year Quest of Judaism, Christianity and Islam*. New York: Knopf.

———. 2000. *The Battle for God*. New York: Knopf.

Arnett, Eric, and Robert May. 1998. "Big Spenders?" *Science* 281(5384): 1806–1807.

Asher, Herbert B. 1980. *Presidential Elections and American Politics: Voters, Candidates and Campaigns since 1952*. Homewood, IL: Dorsey.

Axelrod, Robert. 1967. "The Structure of Public Opinion on Policy Issues." *Public Opinion Quarterly* 31: 51–60.

Bader, Christopher D., Paul Froese, and F. Carson Mencken. 2007. "American Piety 2005: Content and Methods of the Baylor Religion Survey." *Journal for the Scientific Study of Religion* 46: 447–463.

Baker, Joseph O., and Buster G. Smith. 2009. "The Nones: Social Characteristics of the Religiously Unaffiliated." *Social Forces* 87: 1251–1264.

Baker, Wayne. 2005. *America's Crisis of Values: Reality and Perception*. Princeton, NJ: Princeton University Press.

Barker, David C., and Christopher Jan Carman. 2000. "The Spirit of Capitalism? Religious Doctrine, Values, and Economic Attitude Constructs." *Political Behavior* 22(1): 1–27.

Barker, Eileen. 1984. *The Making of a Moonie: Brainwashing or Choice*. Oxford: Basil Blackwell.

————. 1986. "Religious Movements: Cult and Anti-Cult since Jonestown." *Annual Review of Sociology* 12: 329–346.

Bartkowski, John P., and Helen Regis. 2003. *Charitable Choices: Religion, Race, and Poverty in the Post-Welfare Era.* New York: New York University Press.

Behe, Michael. 2006. *Darwin's Little Black Box: The Biochemical Challenge to Evolution,* 2nd ed. New York: Free Press.

Bellah, Robert. 1967. "Civil Religion in America." *Dædalus, Journal of the American Academy of Arts and Sciences* 96(1): 1–21.

Bellah, Robert, Richard Madsen, William Sullivan, Ann Swidler, and Steven Tipton. 1985. *Habits of the Heart.* Berkeley: University of California Press.

Benson, Peter, and Bernard Spilka. 1973. "God Image as a Function of Self-Esteem and Locus of Control." *Journal for the Scientific Study of Religion* 12: 297–310.

Beyerlein, Kraig, and David Sikkink. 2008. "Sorrow and Solidarity: Why Americans Volunteered for 9/11 Relief Efforts." *Social Problems* 55: 190–215.

Birky, Ian T., and Samuel Ball. 1987. "Parental Trait Influence on God as an Object Representation." *Journal of Psychology* 122: 133–137.

Bishop, Bill, with Robert Cushing. 2008. *The Big Sort: Why the Clustering of Like-Minded America Is Tearing Us Apart.* New York: Houghton Mifflin.

Bishop, George. 1999. "The Polls—Trends: Americans' Belief in God." *Public Opinion Quarterly* 63: 421–434.

Bobo, Lawrence. 1991. "Social Responsibility, Individualism, and Redistributive Policies." *Sociological Forum* 6(1): 71–92.

Bolce, Louis, and Susan Gray. 1979. "Blacks, Whites, and Race Politics." *Public Interest* 53: 61–75.

Borg, Marcus J. 2003. *The Heart of Christianity.* New York: HarperCollins.

Borowik, Irena. 2002. "The Roman Catholic Church in the Process of Democratic Transformation: The Case of Poland." *Social Compass* 49(2): 239–252.

Bositis, David A. 2005. *Blacks and the 2004 Democratic National Convention.* Washington, DC: Joint Center for Political and Economic Studies.

Brockman, John, ed. 2006. *Intelligent Thought: Science versus the Intelligent Design Movement.* New York: Vintage.

Brooks, Arthur C. 2006. *Who Really Cares.* New York: Basic Books.

Brooks, Clem. 2002. "Religious Influence and the Politics of Family Decline Concern: Trends, Sources and U.S. Political Behavior." *American Sociological Review* 67(2): 191–211.

Broughton, David, and Hans-Martien ten Napel, eds. 2000. *Religion and Mass Electoral Behavior in Europe.* London: Routledge.

Bruce, Steve. 1999. *Choice and Religion: A Critique of Rational Choice Theory.* New York: Oxford University Press.

"BTK Sentenced to 10 Life Terms: Victims' Families Confront Confessed Serial Murderer." 2005. CNN, August 18. Retrieved November 7, 2007 (http://www.cnn.com/2005/LAW/08/18/btk.killings/index.html).

Caldwell, Deborah. 2005. "Did God Send the Hurricane?" Beliefnet, September 1. Retrieved April 25, 2008 (http://www.alternet.org/katrina/24878?page=2).

Carmines, Edward G., and James A. Stimson. 1989. *Issues Evolution: Race and the Transformation of American Politics.* Princeton, NJ: Princeton University Press.

Casanova, Jose. 1994. *Public Religions in the Modern World.* Chicago: University of Chicago Press.

Chaves, Mark. 1999. "Religious Congregations and Welfare Reform: Who Will Take Advantage of 'Charitable Choice'?" *American Sociological Review* 64(6): 836–846.

———. 2004. *Congregations in America.* Cambridge, MA: Harvard University Press.

Cheney, Patrick, ed. 2004. *The Cambridge Companion to Christopher Marlowe.* New York: Cambridge University Press.

Chirot, Daniel, and Clark McCauley. 2006. *Why Not Kill Them All? The Logic and Prevention of Mass Political Murder.* Princeton, NJ: Princeton University Press.

Club for Growth. 2007. "Mike Huckabee's Record on Economic Issues." Retrieved April 17, 2008 (http://www.clubforgrowth.org/news/pr/?id=296).

Collins, Francis. 2006. *The Language of God: A Scientist Presents Evidence for Belief.* New York: Free Press.

Comte, Auguste. 1974 [1855]. *The Positive Philosophy.* Trans. Harriet Martineau. New York: AMS Press.

Conover, Pamela Johnston, and Stanley Feldman. 1981. "The Origins and Meaning of Liberal/Conservative Self-Identifications." *American Journal of Political Science* 25(4): 617–645.

Cook, E. A., Ted Jelen, and C. Wilcox. 1992. *Between Two Absolutes: Public Opinion and the Politics of Abortion.* Boulder, CO: Westview.

Cook, Fay Lomax, and Edith J. Barrett. 1992. *Support for the American Welfare State.* New York: Columbia University Press.

Cook, Judith A., and Dale W. Wimberly. 1983. "If I Should Die before I Wake: Religious Commitment and Adjustment to the Death of a Child." *Journal for the Scientific Study of Religion* 22: 222–238.

Coulter, Ann. 2006. *Godless: The Church of Liberalism.* New York: Crown Forum.

Davis, Nancy J., and Robert V. Robinson. 1996a. "Are the Rumors of War Exaggerated? Religious Orthodoxy and Moral Progressivism in America." *American Journal of Sociology* 102: 756–787.

———. 1996b. "Religious Orthodoxy in American Society: The Myth of a Monolithic Camp." *Journal for the Scientific Study of Religion* 35: 229–245.

———. 1999. "Their Brothers' Keepers? Orthodox Religionists, Modernists, and Economic Justice in Europe." *American Journal of Sociology* 104(6): 1631–1665.

Dawkins, Richard. 1986. *The Blind Watchmaker: Why the Evidence of Evolution Reveals a Universe without Design.* New York: W. W. Norton.

———. 2003. "You Can't Have It Both Ways: Irreconcilable Differences?" In *Science and Religion: Are They Compatible?* ed. Paul Kurtz, 205–209. Amherst, NY: Prometheus.

———. 2006. *The God Delusion.* Boston: Houghton Mifflin.

Dawson, Michael C. 1994. *Behind the Mule: Race and Class in African-American Politics.* Princeton, NJ: Princeton University Press.

Denton, Michael. 1986. *Evolution: A Theory in Crisis.* Chevy Chase, MD: Adler & Adler.

de Roos, Simone A., Jurjen Iedema, and Siebren Miedema. 2004. "Influence of Maternal Denomination, God Concepts, and Child-Rearing Practices on Young Children's God Concepts." *Journal for the Scientific Study of Religion* 43: 519–535.

Dickie, Jane R., Amy K. Eshleman, Dawn M. Merasco, Amy Shepard, Michael Vander Wilt, and Melissa Johnson. 1997. "Parent-Child Relationships and Children's Images of God." *Journal for the Scientific Study of Religion* 36: 25–43.

Dickie, Jane R., Lindsey V. Ajega, Joy R. Kobylak, and Kathryn M. Nixon. 2006. "Mother, Father, and Self: Sources of Young Adults' God Concepts." *Journal for the Scientific Study of Religion* 45: 57–71.

DiMaggio, Paul, John Evans, and Bethany Bryson. 1996. "Have Americans' Social Attitudes Become More Polarized?" *American Journal of Sociology* 102(3): 690–755.

Dionne, E. J. 2008. *Souled Out: Reclaiming Faith and Politics after the Religious Right.* Princeton, NJ: Princeton University Press.

Domke, David, and Kevin Coe. 2008. *The God Strategy: How Religion Became a Political Weapon in America.* New York: Oxford University Press.

Durkheim, Émile. 1982 [1893]. "Rules for the Distinction of the Normal and the Pathological." In *The Rules of Sociological Method*, ed. Steven Lukes, 85–107. New York: Simon and Schuster.

———. 1995 [1912]. *The Elementary Forms of Religious Life.* Trans. Karen Fields. New York: Free Press.

Ecklund, Elaine Howard, and Christopher P. Scheitle. 2007. "Religion among Academic Scientists: Distinctions, Disciplines and Demographics." *Social Problems* 54: 289–307.

Edgell, Penny, Joseph Gerteis, and Douglas Hartman. 2006. "Atheists as 'Other': Moral Boundaries and Cultural Membership in American Society." *American Sociological Review* 71: 211–234.

Edis, Taner. 2002. *The Ghost in the Universe: God in Light of Modern Science.* Amherst, NY: Prometheus.

Einstein, Albert. 2000. *The Expanded Quotable Einstein.* Ed. Alice Calaprice. Princeton, NJ: Princeton University Press.

Elder, Samuel A. 2007. *The God Who Makes Things Happen: Physical Reality and the Word of God.* Lincoln, NE: iUniverse.

Eliade, Mircea. 1957. *The Sacred and the Profane: The Nature of Religion.* New York: Harcourt.

Emerson, Michael, and Christian Smith. 2000. *Divided by Faith: Evangelical Religion and the Problem of Race in America.* New York: Oxford University Press.

Erikson, Kai T. 1966. *Wayward Puritans: A Study in the Sociology of Deviance.* New York: Macmillan.

The Evangelical Manifesto Steering Committee. 2008. *Evangelical Manifesto: A Declaration of Evangelical Identity and Public Commitment.* Washington, DC: Author. Retrieved May 20, 2008 (http://www.evangelicalmanifesto.com/docs/Evangelical_Manifesto.pdf).

Evans, John. 2003. "Have Americans' Attitudes Become More Polarized?—An Update." *Social Science Quarterly* 84: 71–90.

Evans, John H. 1997. "Worldviews or Social Groups as the Source of Moral Value Attitudes: Implications for the Culture Wars Thesis." *Sociological Forum* 12(3): 371–404.

Feldman, Stanley. 1988. "Structure and Consistency in Public Opinion: The Role of Core Beliefs and Values." *American Journal of Political Science* 32(2): 416–440.

Finke, Roger, and Rodney Stark. 1988. "Religious Economies and Sacred Canopies: Religious Mobilization in American Cities, 1906." *American Sociological Review* 53: 41–49.

———. 2006. *The Churching of America 1776–2005: Winners and Losers in Our Religious Economy.* New Brunswick, NJ: Rutgers University Press.

Fiorina, Morris P., Samuel J. Abrams, and Jeremy C. Pope. 2005. *Culture War? The Myth of a Polarized America.* New York: Longman.

Fowler, James W. 1981. *Stages of Faith: The Psychology of Human Development and the Quest for Meaning.* New York: HarperCollins.

Francis, David R. 2009. "Obama's Faith in Faith-Based Works." *Christian Science Monitor*, February 9 (http://www.csmonitor.com/2009/0206/p08s04-comv.html).

Frank, Thomas. 2005. *What's the Matter with Kansas? How Conservatives Won the Heart of America.* New York: Metropolitan.

Franklin, Benjamin. 1728. "Articles of Belief and Acts of Religion, First Principles." http://www.historycarper.com/resources/twobf2/articles.htm.

Froese, Paul. 2004a. "After Atheism: An Analysis of Religious Monopolies in the Post-Communist World." *Sociology of Religion* 65(1): 57–75.

———. 2004b. "Forced Secularization in Soviet Russia: Why an Atheistic Monopoly Failed." *Journal for the Scientific Study of Religion* 43(1): 35–50.

———. 2008. *The Plot to Kill God: Findings from the Soviet Experiment in Secularization.* Berkeley: University of California Press.

Froese, Paul, and Christopher Bader. 2008. "Unraveling Religious Worldviews: The Relationship between Images of God and Political Ideology in a Cross-Cultural Analysis." *Sociological Quarterly* 49(4): 689–718.

Froese, Paul, and F. Carson Mencken. 2009. "An American Holy War? The Connection between Religious Ideology and Neo-Conservative Iraq War Attitudes." *Social Science Quarterly* 90(1).

Galanter, Marc. 1980. "Psychological Induction into the Large-Group: Findings from a Modern Religious Sect." *American Journal of Psychiatry* 137: 1574–1579.

———. 1983. "Unification Church ('Moonie') Dropouts: Psychological Readjustment after Leaving a Charismatic Religious Group." *American Journal of Psychiatry* 140: 984–989.

Galanter, Marc, Richard Rabkin, Judith Rabkin, and Alexander Deutsch. 1979. "The 'Moonies': A Psychological Study of Conversion and Membership in a Contemporary Religious Sect." *American Journal of Psychiatry* 137: 1574–1579.

Geertz, Clifford. 1973. *The Interpretation of Cultures.* New York: Basic Books.

Gerring, John. 1997. "Ideology: A Definitional Analysis." *Political Research Quarterly* 50: 957–994.

Gibbons, William J. 2006. *Missionaries and Monsters.* Landisville, PA: Coachwhip.

Gilliam, Franklin D. Jr., and Kenny J. Whitby. 1989. "Race, Class and Attitudes toward Social Welfare Spending." *Social Science Quarterly* 70(1): 88–100.

Gingrich, Newt. 2006. *Rediscovering God in America: Reflections on the Role of Faith in Our Nation's History.* New York: Thomas Nelson.

Glazer, Nathan. 1987. "Fundamentalists: A Defensive Offensive." In *Piety and Politics: Evangelicals and Fundamentalists Confront the World,* ed. Richard John Neuhaus and Michael Cromartie. Washington, DC: Ethics and Public Policy Center.

Gleason, John J. 1975. *Growing Up to God.* New York: Abingdon.

Gockel, Galen. 1969. "Income and Religious Affiliation: A Regression Analysis." *American Journal of Sociology* 74(6): 632–647.

Gorski, Philip S. 2000. "Historicizing the Secularization Debate: Church, State and Society in Late Medieval and Early Modern Europe, ca. 1300–1700." *American Sociological Review* 65: 138–167.

Gorsuch, Richard L. 1968. "The Conceptualization of God as Seen in Adjective Ratings." *Journal for the Scientific Study of Religion* 7(1): 56–64.

Gould, Stephen Jay. 1983. *Hen's Teeth and Horse's Toes.* New York: W. W. Norton.

———. 1998. *Leonardo's Mountain of Clams and the Diet of Worms.* New York: Harmony.

Greeley, Andrew M. 1988. "Evidence That a Maternal Image of God Correlates with Liberal Politics." *Sociology and Social Research* 72: 150–154.

———. 1989. *Religious Change in America*. Cambridge, MA: Harvard University Press.

———. 1991. "Religion and Attitudes towards AIDS Policy." *Sociology and Social Research* 75: 126–132.

———. 1993. "Religion and Attitudes toward the Environment." *Journal for the Scientific Study of Religion* 32: 19–28.

———. 1995. *Religion as Poetry*. New Brunswick, NJ: Transaction.

Green, Donald, Bradley Palmquist, and Eric Schickler. 2002. *Partisan Hearts and Minds: Political Parties and the Social Identities of Voters*. New Haven, CT: Yale University Press.

Green, John, James Guth, Lyman Kellstedt, and Corwin Smidt. 2001. "Faith in the Vote." *Public Perspective* May–April: 33–35.

Green, John, James Guth, Corwin Smidt, and Lyman Kellstedt. 1996. *Religion and the Culture Wars: Dispatches from the Front*. New York: Rowman and Littlefield.

Greenberg, Anna. 2000. "The Church and the Revitalization of Politics and Community." *Political Science Quarterly* 115: 377–394.

Guinness, Os. 1993. *The American Hour: A Time of Reckoning and the Once and Future Role of Faith*. New York: Free Press.

Guth, James, John Green, Lyman Kellstedt, and Corwin Smidt. 1995. "Faith and the Environment: Religious Beliefs and Attitudes on Environmental Policy." *American Journal of Political Science* 39(2): 364–382.

Hackett, Conrad, and Michael Lindsay. 2008. "Measuring Evangelicalism: Consequences of Different Operationalization Strategies." *Journal for the Scientific Study of Religion* 47: 499–514.

Hadden, Jeffery K., and Anson Shupe, eds. 1989. *Secularization and Fundamentalism Reconsidered: Religion and Political Order*. Vol. 3. New York: Paragon House.

Harms, E. 1944. "The Development of Religious Experience in Childhood." *American Journal of Sociology* 50: 112–120.

Harris, Fredrick. 1994. "Something Within: Religion as a Mobilizer of African-American Political Activism." *Journal of Politics* 56(1): 42–68.

Harris, Richard J., and Edward W. Mills. 1985. "Religion, Values, and Attitudes toward Abortion." *Journal for the Scientific Study of Religion* 24: 137–154.

Harris, Sam. 2004. *The End of Faith: Religion, Terror, and the Future of Reason*. New York: W. W. Norton.

———. 2006. *Letter to a Christian Nation*. New York: Knopf.

Hart, Stephen. 1992. *What Does the Lord Require? How American Christians Think about Economic Justice*. New York: Oxford University Press.

Hasenfeld, Yeheskel, and Jane A. Rafferty. 1989. "The Determinants of Public Attitudes toward the Welfare State." *Social Forces* 67: 1027–1048.

Heffner, John W., Marilyn E. Heffner, and Martha Baugh. 2001. *What Was It Like in the Beginning?* Oklahoma City, OK: Hearthstone.

Hegy, Pierre, ed. 2007. *What Do We Imagine God to Be? The Function of "God Images" in Our Lives*. Lewiston, NY: Edwin Mellen.

Herek, Gregory M., and John P. Capitanio. 1995. "Black Heterosexuals' Attitudes toward Lesbians and Gay Men in the United States." *Journal of Sex Research* 32: 95–105.

Hertel, Bradley R., and Michael J. Donahue. 1995. "Parental Influences on God Images among Children: Testing Durkheim's Metaphoric Parallelism." *Journal for the Scientific Study of Religion* 34: 186–199.

Hill, Christopher. 1993. *The English Bible and the Seventeenth-Century Revolution*. London: Allen Lane.

Hinojosa, Victor, and Jerry Park. 2004. "Religion and the Paradox of Racial Inequality Attitudes." *Journal for the Scientific Study of Religion* 43(2): 229–238.

Hitchens, Christopher. 2007. *God Is Not Great: How Religion Poisons Everything*. New York: Hachette.

Hout, Michael, and Claude S. Fischer. 2002. "Why More Americans Have No Religious Preference: Politics and Generation." *American Sociological Review* 67: 165–190.

"How Much Federal Support for Faith-Based and Grassroots Charities?" 2001. Washington, DC: The White House. Retrieved January 25, 2008 (http://georgewbush-whitehouse.archives.gov/news/releases/2001/08/unlevelfield2.html).

Hunt, Larry, and Matthew Hunt. 2001. "Race, Region, and Religious Involvement: A Comparative Study of Whites and African Americans." *Social Forces* 80(2): 605–631.

Hunter, James Davison. 1988. "American Protestantism: Sorting Out the Present, Looking toward the Future." In *The Believable Futures of American Protestantism*, ed. Richard John Neuhaus, 18–48. Grand Rapids, MI: Eerdmans.

———. 1991. *Culture Wars: The Struggle to Define America*. New York: Basic Books.

Inglehart, Ronald, and Wayne Baker. 2000. "Modernization, Cultural Change, and the Persistence of Traditional Values." *American Sociological Review* 65: 19–52.

Inglehart, Ronald, and Pippa Norris. 2004. *Rising Tide: Gender Equality and Cultural Change around the World*. Cambridge: Cambridge University Press.

James, William. 1961. *The Varieties of Religious Experience*. New York: Collier.

Jelen, Ted G. 1988. "Changes in Attitudinal Correlates of Opposition to Abortion, 1977–1985." *Journal for the Scientific Study of Religion* 27: 211–228.

———. 1991. "Religious Belief and Attitude Constraint." *Journal for the Scientific Study of Religion* 29: 118–125.

———. 1997. "Culture Wars and the Party System: Religion and Realignment, 1972–1993." In *Cultural Wars in American Politics: Critical Reviews of a Popular Myth*, ed. Rhys Williams. New York: Aldine de Gruyter.

Jelen, Ted G., and Clyde Wilcox. 1997. "Attitudes toward Abortion in Poland and the United States." *Social Science Quarterly* 78: 907–921.

———, eds. 2002. *Religion and Politics in Comparative Perspective*. New York: Cambridge University Press.

———. 2003. "Causes and Consequences of Public Attitudes toward Abortion: A Review and Research Agenda." *Political Research Quarterly* 56(4): 489–500.

Jenkins, Philip. 2007. "Burning at the Stake: How Global Warming Will Increase Religious Strife." *New Republic*, December 10. Retrieved December 10, 2007 (http://www.tnr.com/politics/story.html?id=cb5d0a0e-0a09–49f2–8201–770e20750144).

Jessee, Dean C. 2002. *The Personal Writings of Joseph Smith*. Salt Lake City, UT: Deseret.

Johnson, Stephen D., and Joseph B. Tamney. 1982. "The Christian Right and the 1980 Presidential Election." *Journal for the Scientific Study of Religion* 21(2): 123–131.

Jones, Robin. 1995. *Where Was God at 9:02 A.M.?* Nashville, TN: Thomas Nelson.

Jones-Correa, Michael, and David Leal. 2001. "Political Participation: Does Religion Matter?" *Political Research Quarterly* 54(4): 751–770.

Katz, Michael B. 1996. *In the Shadow of the Poorhouse: A Social History of Welfare in America*. Basic Books.

Kelley, Jonathon, and M. D. R. Evans. 1993. "The Legitimation of Inequality: Occupational Earnings in Nine Nations." *American Journal of Sociology* 99(1): 75–125.

Kellstedt, Lyman, John Green, Corwin Smidt, and James Guth. 1996. "The Puzzle of Evangelical Protestantism: Core, Periphery, and Political Behavior." In *Religion and Culture Wars: Dispatches from the Front*, 240–266. Lanham, MD: Rowman & Littlefield.

Kellstedt, Lyman, and Corwin Smidt. 1996. "Measuring Fundamentalism: An Analysis of Different Operational Strategies." In *Religion and the Culture Wars: Dispatches from the Front*, ed. John Green, James Guth, Corwin Smidt, and Lyman Kellstedt. New York: Rowman and Littlefield.

Kidd, Quentin, Herman Diggs, Mehreen Farooq, and Megan Murray. 2007. "Black Voters, Black Candidates, and Social Issues: Does Party Identification Matter?" *Social Science Quarterly* 88(1): 165–176.

Kilbourne, Brock K. 1983. "The Conway and Siegelman Claims against Religious Cults: An Assessment of Their Data." *Journal for the Scientific Study of Religion* 22: 380–385.

Kirkpatrick, Lee A. 1993. "Fundamentalism, Christian Orthodoxy, and Intrinsic Religious Orientation as Predictors of Discriminatory Attitudes." *Journal for the Scientific Study of Religion* 32: 256–268.

Kirschenbaum, Aaron. 1993. "Fundamentalism: A Jewish Traditional Perspective." In *Jewish Fundamentalism in Comparative Perspective*, ed. Laurence J. Silberstein. New York: New York University Press.

Kluegel, James R., and Eliot R. Smith. 1986. *Beliefs about Inequality: Americans' Views of What Is and What Ought to Be*. New York: Aldine de Gruyter.

Kniss, Fred. 1997. "Culture Wars(?): Remapping the Battleground." In *Culture Wars in American Politics: Critical Reviews of a Popular Myth*, ed. Rhys H. Williams. New York: Aldine de Gruyter.

Kohut, Andrew, John C. Green, Robert C. Toth, and Scott Keeter. 2000. *The Diminishing Divide: Religion's Changing Role in American Politics*. Washington, DC: Brookings Institution Press.

Ladd, Keith L., Daniel N. McIntosh, and Bernard Spilka. 1998. "Children's God Concepts: Influences of Denomination, Age, and Gender." *International Journal for the Psychology of Religion* 8: 49–56.

Lakoff, George. 2002. *Moral Politics: How Liberals and Conservatives Think*. Chicago: University of Chicago Press.

Layman, Geoffrey. 1997. "Religion and Political Behavior in the United States." *Public Opinion Quarterly* 61: 288–316.

———. 2001. *The Great Divide*. New York: Columbia University Press.

Leibniz, Gottfried Wilhelm. 1961. *Discourse on Metaphysics*. New York: Barnes & Noble.

Lilla, Mark. 2007. "The Politics of God." *New York Times*, August 19. Retrieved May 22, 2008 (http://www.nytimes.com/2007/08/19/magazine/19Religion-t.html).

Lincoln, C. Eric, and Lawrence H. Mamiya. 1990. *The Black Church in the African-American Experience*. Durham, NC: Duke University Press.

Lofland, John, and Rodney Stark. 1965. "Becoming a World-Saver: A Theory of Conversion to a Deviant Perspective." *American Sociological Review* 30: 862–875.

Loftus, Jeni. 2001. "America's Liberalization in Attitudes toward Homosexuality, 1973 to 1998." *American Sociological Review* 66: 762–782.

Luker, Kristin. 1984. *Abortion and the Politics of Motherhood*. Berkeley: University of California Press.

Lupfer, Michael B., Karla F. Brock, and Stephen J. DePaola. 1992. "The Use of Secular and Religious Attributions to Explain Everyday Behavior." *Journal for the Scientific Study of Religion* 31: 486–503.

Lupfer, Michael B., Donna Tolliver, and Mark Jackson. 1996. "Explaining Life-Altering Occurrences: A Test of the 'God-of-the-Gaps' Hypothesis." *Journal for the Scientific Study of Religion* 35: 379–391.

MacIntyre, Alasdair. 1981. *After Virtue: A Study in Moral Theory*. Notre Dame, IN: University of Notre Dame Press.

Madeley, John. 1991. "Politics and Religion in Western Europe." In *Politics and Religion in the Modern World*, ed. George Moyser. London: Routledge.

Mallery, Paul, Suzanne Mallery, and Richard Gorsuch. 2000. "A Preliminary Taxonomy of Attributions to God." *Journal for the Psychology of Religion* 10(3): 135–156.

Manza, J., and C. Brooks. 1997. "The Religious Factors in U.S. Presidential Elections." *American Journal of Sociology* 103: 38–81.

Marty, Martin, and R. S. Appleby. 1991. *Fundamentalism Observed*. Chicago: University of Chicago Press.

Maudlin, Michael G. 1989. "'Holy Smoke! The Darkness Is Back.' *Christianity Today* Talks with Frank Peretti." *Christianity Today*, December 15, 58–59.

Maynard, Elizabeth A., Richard L. Gorsuch, and Jeffrey P. Bjorck. 2001. "Religious Coping Style, Concept of God, and Personal Religious Variables in Threat, Loss, and Challenge Situations." *Journal for the Scientific Study of Religion* 40: 65–74.

McCrae, Robert R., and Oliver P. John. 1992. "An Introduction to the Five-Factor Model and Its Applications." *Journal of Personality* 60: 175–215.

McDaniel, Eric L., and Christopher G. Ellison. 2008. "God's Party? Race, Religion, and Partisanship over Time." *Political Research Quarterly* 61(2): 180–191.

McViegh, Rory, and Christian Smith. 1999. "Who Protests in America: An Analysis of Three Political Alternatives—Inaction, Institutionalized Politics, or Protest." *Sociological Forum* 14(4): 685–702.

Meacham, Jon. 2006. *American Gospel: God, the Founding Fathers and the Making of a Nation*. New York: Random House.

Mead, George Herbert. 1934. *Mind, Self and Society*. Chicago: University of Chicago Press.

Meckler, Laura. 2009. "Faith-Based Program Gets Wider Focus." *Wall Street Journal*, February 5 (http://online.wsj.com/article/SB123379504018650159.html).

Miles, Jack. 1995. *God: A Biography*. New York: Vintage.

Miller, Alan, and Rodney Stark. 2002. "Gender and Religiousness: Can Socialization Explanations Be Saved?" *American Journal of Sociology* 107(6): 1399–1423.

Miller, Kenneth. 2004. "The Flagellum Unspun: The Collapse of 'Irreducible Complexity.'" In *Debating Design: From Darwin to DNA*, ed. William Dembski and Michael Ruse, 81–97. New York: Cambridge University Press.

Miller, Norm. 2005. "Embattled N.C. Pastor Resigns, Says He Was Misunderstood." Nashville, TN: Southern Baptist Convention, Baptist Press, May 11.

Mills, David. 2006. *Atheist Universe: The Thinking Person's Answer to Christian Fundamentalism*. Berkeley, CA: Ulysses.

Mitchell, Paul, Brendan O'Leary, and Geoffrey Evans. 2001. "Northern Ireland: Flanking Extremists Bite the Moderates and Emerge with Their Clothes." *Parliamentary Affairs* 54(4): 725–742.

Moaddel, Mansoor. 1996. "The Social Bases and Discursive Content on the Rise of Islamic Fundamentalism." *Sociological Inquiry* 66: 330–355.

Moberg, David O. 1974. *The Great Reversal: Evangelism versus Social Concern*. Philadelphia: Lippincott.

Moriarty, Glen L. 2007. "Cognitive Therapy, Depression, and Images of God." In *What Do We Imagine God to Be? The Function of "God Images" in Our Lives*, ed. Pierre Hegy, 243–254. Lewiston, NY: Edwin Mellen.

Morris, A. D. 1984. *The Origins of the Civil Rights Movement*. New York: Free Press.

Mouw, Ted, and Michael Sobel. 2001. "Culture Wars and Opinion Polarization: The Case of Abortion." *American Journal of Sociology* 106: 913–943.

Moyser, George, ed. 1991. *Politics and Religion in the Modern World*. London: Routledge.

Munson, Ziad. 2005. "God, Abortion, and Democracy in the Pro-Life Movement." In *Taking Faith Seriously*, ed. Mary Jo Bane, Brent Coffin, and Richard Higgins, 277–300. Cambridge, MA: Harvard University Press.

"N.C. Church Kicks Out Members Who Do Not Support Bush." 2005. *Washington Post*, May 8, A12.

Nelsen, Hart M., Neil H. Cheek Jr., and Paul Au. 1985. "Gender Differences in Images of God." *Journal for the Scientific Study of Religion* 24: 396–402.

Newberg, Andrew, and Mark Robert Waldman. 2009. *How God Changes Your Brain: Breakthrough Findings from a Leading Neuroscientist*. New York: Ballantine.

Nietzsche, Friedrich W. 2001. *The Gay Science: With a Prelude in German Rhymes and an Appendix of Songs*. Trans. Josephine Nauckhoff. Ed. Bernard A. O. Williams. New York: Oxford University Press.

Noll, Mark. 2005. *America's God: From Jonathan Edwards to Abraham Lincoln*. Oxford: Oxford University Press.

Norris, Pippa, and Ronald Inglehart. 2004. *Sacred and Secular: Religion and Politics Worldwide*. New York: Cambridge University Press.

North, Charles, and Bob Smietana. 2008. *Good Intentions: Nine Hot-Button Issues Viewed through the Eyes of Faith*. Chicago: Moody.

Norvel, Glenn. 1974. "Recent Trends in Intercategory Differences in Attitudes." *Social Forces* 52: 395–401.

Numbers, Ronald L. 2006. *The Creationists: From Scientific Creationism to Intelligent Design*. Cambridge, MA: Harvard University Press.

Oberschall, A. 1993. *Social Movements*. New Brunswick, NJ: Transaction.

O'Donnell, Phillip. 2006. *Dinosaurs: Dead or Alive?* Longwood, FL: Xulon.

Olasky, Marvin. 2000. *Compassionate Conservatism: What It Is, What It Does, and How It Can Transform America*. New York: Free Press.

Olson, Daniel. 1997. "Dimensions of Cultural Tension among the American Public." In *Cultural Wars in American Politics: Critical Reviews of a Popular Myth*, ed. Rhys Williams. New York: Aldine de Gruyter.

Omri, Elisha. 2008. "Faith beyond Belief: Evangelical Protestant Conceptions of Faith and the Resonance of Anti-humanism." *Social Analysis* 52(1): 56–78.

Owen, Richard. 2007. "Hell Real and Eternal: Pope." *Australian*, May 28. Retrieved September 30, 2007 (http://www.theaustralian.com.au/news/world/hell-is-real-and-eternal-pope/story-e6frg6so-1111113237028).

Pargament, Kenneth I., and June Hahn. 1986. "God and the Just World: Causal and Coping Attributions to God in Health Situations." *Journal for the Scientific Study of Religion* 25: 193–207.

Perakh, Mark. 2003. *Unintelligent Design.* Amherst, NY: Prometheus.

Peretti, Frank E. 1986. *This Present Darkness.* Wheaton, IL: Crossway.

———. 1989. *Piercing the Darkness.* Wheaton, IL: Crossway.

Petersen, Larry R. 2001. "Religion, Plausibility Structures, and Education Effects on Attitudes toward Elective Abortion." *Journal for the Scientific Study of Religion* 40: 187–203.

Pew Research Center for the People & Press. 2006. "Growing Number of Liberal Democrats." October 11. Retrieved July 25, 2008 (http://pewresearch.org/pubs/75/growing-number-of-liberal-democrats).

Pew Research Center Pollwatch. 2005. *Reading the Polls on Evolution and Creationism.* Retrieved June 20, 2008 (http://people-press.org/commentary/display.php3?AnalysisID=118).

"Pope to Dealers: You'll Answer to God." 2007. *USA Today,* May 12. Retrieved September 30, 2007 (http://www.usatoday.com/news/world/2007-05-12-pope-brazil_N.htm).

"President Bush Addresses NAACP Convention." 2006. *Washington Post,* July 20. Retrieved March 20, 2008 (http://www.washingtonpost.com/wp-dyn/content/article/2006/07/20/AR2006072000803.html).

Prothero, Stephen. 2007. *Religious Literacy: What Every American Needs to Know—And Doesn't.* New York: HarperCollins.

Rabey, S. 1988. "Spiritual Warfare, Supernatural Sales." *Christianity Today,* December 9, 69.

"Reading the Book of Life; White House Remarks on Decoding of Genome." 2000. *New York Times,* June 27. Retrieved March 3, 2008 (http://query.nytimes.com/gst/fullpage.html?res=9502E1D81230F934A15755C0A9669C8B63).

Regnerus, Mark, David Sikkink, and Christian Smith. 1999. "Voting with the Christian Right: Contextual and Individual Patterns of Electoral Influence." *Social Forces* 77(4): 1375–1401.

Regnerus, Mark D., and Christian Smith. 1998. "Selective Deprivatization among American Religious Traditions: The Reversal of the Great Reversal." *Social Forces* 76: 1347–1372.

Reichley, James. 2002. *Faith in Politics.* Washington, DC: Brookings Institution.

"Remarks of Senator Barack Obama as Prepared for Delivery." July 1, 2008. Zanesville, Ohio (http://i.usatoday.net/news/mmemmottpdf/obama-faith-speech-july-1-2008.pdf).

Richardson, James T. 1985. "The Active vs. Passive Convert: Paradigm Conflict in Conversion/Recruitment Research." *Journal for the Scientific Study of Religion* 24: 163–179.

Rizzuto, Ana-Maria. 1979. *The Birth of the Living God: A Psychoanalytic Study*. Chicago: University of Chicago Press.

Roberts, Carl W. 1989. "Imagining God: Who Is Created in Whose Image?" *Review of Religious Research* 30: 375–386.

Robinson, John P., and John A. Fleishman. 1988. "Ideological Identification: Trends and Interpretations of the Liberal-Conservative Balance." *Public Opinion Quarterly* 52: 132–145.

Roof, Wade Clark, and William McKinney. 1987. *American Mainline Religion: Its Changing Shape and Future*. New Brunswick, NJ: Rutgers University Press.

Roof, Wade Clark, and Jennifer L. Roof. 1984. "Review of the Polls: Images of God among Americans." *Journal for the Scientific Study of Religion* 23: 201–205.

"Rough Map of the Human Genome Completed." 2000. CNN, June 26. Retrieved April 27, 2008 (http://archives.cnn.com/2000/HEALTH/06/26/human.genome.05/index.html).

Rowatt, Wade, Paul Froese, Jordan LaBouff, and Megan Johnson. 2008. "The Religious Personality." In *American Piety Revisited*. Waco, TX: Baylor University Press.

Rowatt, Wade, and Lee A. Kirkpatrick. 2002. "Two Dimensions of Attachment to God and Their Relation to Affect, Religiosity, and Personality Constructs." *Journal for the Scientific Study of Religion* 41: 637–651.

Rushnell, SQuire. 2006. *When God Winks at You: How God Speaks Directly to You through the Power of Coincidence*. Nashville, TN: Thomas Nelson.

Sageman, Marc. 2004. *Understanding Terror Networks*. Philadelphia: University of Pennsylvania Press.

Sarfati, Jonathan. 1999. *Refuting Evolution: A Handbook for Students, Parents, and Teachers Countering the Latest Arguments for Evolution*. Green Forest, AR: Master.

Saroglou, Vassilis. 2002. "Religion and the Five Factors of Personality: A Meta-Analytic Review." *Personality and Individual Differences* 32: 15–25.

Schaefer, Charles A., and Richard L. Gorsuch. 1991. "Psychological Adjustment and Religiousness: The Multivariate Belief-Motivation Theory of Religiousness." *Journal for the Scientific Study of Religion* 30: 448–461.

Schaefer, Kurt. 2003. "Evangelicals, Welfare Reform, and Care for the Poor." In *A Public Faith*, ed. Michael Cromartie, 25–56. Lanham, MD: Rowman and Littlefield.

Schoenfeld, Eugene. 1987. "Images of God and Man: An Exploratory Study." *Review of Religious Research* 28: 224–235.

Shaw, Grew. 2003. "Poll Trends: Abortion." *Public Opinion Quarterly* 67: 415.

Sheahen, Laura. 2007. "God Is Not Threatened by Our Scientific Adventures." Beliefnet. Retrieved June 6, 2008 (http://www.beliefnet.com/story/198/story_19848_1.html).

Shearman, Sachiyo, and Timothy Levine. 2006. "Dogmatism Updated: A Scale Revision and Validation." *Communication Quarterly* 54: 275–291.

Sherkat, Darren, and Christopher Ellison. 1999. "Recent Developments and Current Controversies in the Sociology of Religion." *Annual Review of Sociology* 25: 363–394.

Shroeder, Gerald L. 1997. *The Science of God: The Convergence of Scientific and Biblical Wisdom.* New York: Free Press.

———. 2001. *The Hidden Face of God: Science Reveals the Ultimate Truth.* New York: Free Press.

Simmel, Georg. 1959. *Essays on Sociology, Philosophy, and Aesthetics.* New York: Harper TorchBooks.

Smith, Christian. 1996. *Disruptive Religion: The Force of Faith in Social Movement Activism.* New York: Routledge.

———. 1998. *American Evangelicalism: Embattled and Thriving.* Chicago: University of Chicago Press.

———. 2000. *Christian American? What Evangelicals Really Want.* Berkeley: University of California Press.

———. 2003. *Moral, Believing Animals.* New York: Oxford University Press.

Smith, Gary Scott. 2006. *Faith and the Presidency: From George Washington to George W. Bush.* New York: Oxford University Press.

Smith, Robert C., and Richard Seltzer. 1992. *Race, Class, and Culture: A Study in Afro-American Mass Opinion.* Albany: State University of New York Press.

Somers, Margaret. 1994. "The Narrative Constitution of Identity: A Relational and Network Approach." *Theory and Society* 23: 605–649.

Sorokin, Pitirim A. 1998. *On the Practice of Sociology.* Ed. Barry V. Johnston. Chicago: University of Chicago Press.

Spencer, Thomas. 2005. "Senator Says Storms Are Punishment from God." *Birmingham News*, September 28: 1A.

Spilka, Bernard, Philip Armatus, and June Nussbaum. 1964. "The Concept of God: A Factor-Analytic Approach." *Review of Religious Research* 6: 28–35.

Spinoza, Benedictus de. 1955 [1677]. *The Ethics.* Trans. R. H. M. Elwes. New York: Dover.

Stanley, Harold W., and Richard G. Niemi. 2006. "Partisanship, Party Coalitions, and Group Support, 1952–2004." *Presidential Studies Quarterly* 36(2): 172–188.

Stark, Rodney. 1999. "Secularization, R.I.P." *Sociology of Religion* 60: 249–273.

———. 2001a. *One True God : Historical Consequences of Monotheism.* Princeton, NJ: Princeton University Press.

———. 2001b. "Gods, Rituals, and the Moral Order." *Journal for the Scientific Study of Religion* 40(4): 619–636.

———. 2007. *Discovering God: The Origins of the Great Religions and the Evolution of Belief.* New York: HarperOne.

Stark, Rodney, and William Sims Bainbridge. 1985. *The Future of Religion: Secularization, Revival, and Cult Formation.* Berkeley: University of California Press.

Stark, Rodney, and Roger Finke. 2000. *Acts of Faith: Explaining the Human Side of Religion*. Berkeley: University of California Press.

Stark, Rodney, and Charles Y. Glock. 1969. "Prejudice and the Churches." In *Prejudice U.S.A.*, ed. Charles Y. Glock and Ellen Siegelmann. New York: Praeger.

Stark, Rodney, and Laurence R. Iannaccone. 1994. "A Supply-Side Reinterpretation of the 'Secularization' of Europe." *Journal for the Scientific Study of Religion* 33: 230–252.

Steele, David N., Curtis C. Thomas, and S. Lance Quinn. 2004. *The Five Points of Calvinism: Defined, Defended, Documented*. 2nd ed. Phillipsburg, NJ: P & R.

Steensland, B., J. Z. Park, M. D. Regnerus, L. D. Robinson, W. B. Wilcox, and R. D. Woodberry. 2000. "The Measure of American Religion: Toward Improving the State of the Art." *Social Forces* 79: 291–318.

Stenger, Victor J. 2007. *God the Failed Hypothesis: How Science Shows That God Does Not Exist*. Amherst, NY: Prometheus.

Stolberg, Sheryl Gay. 2007. "President Bush and Some Relatives of the Fallen Lean on Each Other." *New York Times*, November 9. Retrieved November 10, 2007 (http://www.nytimes.com/2007/11/10/us/10families.html).

Sullivan, Amy. 2008. *The Party Faithful: How and Why Democrats Are Closing the God Gap*. New York: Scribner.

Swatos, William H. 1988. "Picketing Satan Enfleshed at 7-Eleven: A Research Note." *Review of Religious Research* 30: 73–82.

Swatos, William, and Daniel Olson. 2000. *The Secularization Debate*. Lanham, MD: Rowman and Littlefield.

Talin, Kristoff. 1995. "Young People and Religious Fundamentalism in France." In *Fundamentalism and Youth in Europe*, ed. Luigi Tomasi. Milan: FrancoAngeli.

Tamayo, Alvaro, and Leandre Desjardins. 1976. "Belief Systems and Conceptual Images of Parents and God." *Journal of Psychology* 92: 131–140.

Taylor, Charles. 2007. *A Secular Age*. Cambridge, MA: Belknap Press of Harvard University Press.

Taylor, David. 1985. "The Lord's Battle: Paisleyism in Northern Ireland." In *Religious Movements: Genesis, Exodus and Numbers*, ed. Rodney Stark. New York: Paragon House.

Thomas, W. I., with Dorothy Swaine Thomas. 1928. *The Child in America*. New York: Knopf.

Tierney, John. 2007. "Are Scientists Playing God? It Depends on Your Religion." *New York Times*, November 20. Retrieved January 5, 2008 (http://www.nytimes.com/2007/11/20/science/20tier.html).

Tillich, Paul. 1957. *Dynamics of Faith*. New York: Harper & Row.

"Times Topics: Same-Sex Marriage, Civil Unions, and Domestic Partnerships."

2009. *New York Times*. Retrieved July 1, 2009 (http://topics.nytimes.com/top/reference/timestopics/subjects/s/same_sex_marriage/index.html).

"Town Is Warned of God's Wrath." 2005. *New York Times*, November 11, National Briefing Mid-Atlantic: Pennsylvania, A16.

Troeltsch, Ernst. 1931. *The Social Teaching of the Christian Churches*. New York: Macmillan.

Tucker, Robert C., ed. 1974. *The Marx-Engels Reader*. 2nd ed. New York: W. W. Norton.

United States Congress Joint Congressional Committee on Inaugural Ceremonies. 1989. *Inaugural Addresses of the Presidents of the United States*. Washington, DC: U.S. Government Printing Office.

Vergote, Antoine, and Catherine Aubert. 1972. "Parental Images and Representations of God." *Social Compass* 19: 431–444.

Vergote, Antoine, and Alvaro Tamayo. 1981. *The Parental Figures and the Representation of God: A Psychological and Cross-Cultural Study*. New York: Mouton.

Vergote, Antoine, Alvaro Tamayo, Luiz Pasquali, Michael Bonami, Marie-Rose Pattyn, and Anne Custers. 1969. "Concept of God and Parental Images." *Journal for the Scientific Study of Religion* 8: 79–87.

Wade, Terry, and Philip Pullella. 2007. "Pope Meets Drug Addicts in Brazil, Warns Traffickers." *Reuters*, May 12. Retrieved September 30, 2007 (http://www.reuters.com/article/latestCrisis/idUSN12236678).

Wald, Kenneth D. 1992. *Religion and Politics in the United States*. 2d ed. Washington DC: Congressional Quarterly Press.

Wallis, Jim. 2005. *God's Politics: A New Vision for Faith and Politics in America*. San Francisco: HarperCollins.

Walton, Hanes Jr., and Robert C. Smith. 2003. *American Politics and the African American Quest for Universal Freedom*. New York: Longman.

Warner, R. Stephen. 1988. *New Wine in Old Wineskins: Evangelicals and Liberals in a Small-Town Church*. Berkeley: University of California Press.

Weeks, Matthew, and Michael B. Lupfer. 2000. "Religious Attributions and Proximity of Influence: An Investigation of Direct Interventions and Distal Explanations." *Journal for the Scientific Study of Religion* 39: 348–362.

Wellman, James K. 2008. *Evangelical vs. Liberal: The Clash of Christian Cultures in the Pacific Northwest*. New York: Oxford University Press.

Whitcomb, John, and Henry Morris. 1960. *The Genesis Flood: The Biblical Record and Its Scientific Implications*. New York: P&R Publishing.

Whitehead, Andrew L., and Ashley Palmer-Boyes. 2009. "Man, the Glory of God and Woman, the Glory of Man: Gendered Images of God and Gender Role Ideology." Paper presented at the Society for the Scientific Study of Religion, annual meeting, October 23–25, 2009, Denver, CO.

Wilcox, Clyde, Sharon Linzey, and Ted G. Jelen. 1991. "Reluctant Warriors: Premillennialism and Politics in the Moral Majority." *Journal for the Scientific Study of Religion* 30: 245–258.

Williams, Rhys. 1997. *Cultural Wars in American Politics: Critical Reviews of a Popular Myth.* New York: Aldine de Gruyter.

Wills, Garry. 2006. "A Country Ruled by Faith." *New York Review of Books,* November 16. Retrieved January 20, 2008 (http://www.nybooks.com/articles/19590#fnr35).

Wilson, Edward O. 1998. *Consilience: The Unity of Knowledge.* New York: Knopf.

Wilson, John, and Thomas Janoski. 1995. "The Contribution of Religion to Volunteer Work." *Sociology of Religion* 56: 137–152.

Wilson, Keith M., and Jennifer L. Huff. 2001. "Scaling Satan." *Journal of Psychology* 135: 292–300.

Winchester, Simon. 2003. *Krakatoa: The Day the World Exploded, August 27, 1883.* New York: HarperCollins.

Wineburg, Robert J. 2001. *A Limited Partnership: The Politics of Religion, Welfare and Social Service.* New York: Columbia University Press.

Woodberry, Robert, and Christian Smith. 1998. "Fundamentalism et al.: Conservative Protestants in America." *Annual Review of Sociology* 24: 25–26.

Woodrum, Eric. 1988. "Determinants of Moral Attitudes." *Journal for the Scientific Study of Religion* 27: 553–573.

Woodrum, Eric, and Beth L. Davison. 1992. "Reexamination of Religious Influences on Abortion Attitudes." *Review of Religious Research* 33: 229–243.

Wuthnow, Robert. 1973. "Religious Commitment and Conservatism: In Search of an Elusive Relationship." In *Religion in Sociological Perspective,* ed. Charles Y. Glock. Belmont, CA: Wadsworth.

———. 1988. *The Restructuring of American Religion: Society and Faith since World War II.* Princeton, NJ: Princeton University Press.

———. 1994. *God and Mammon in America.* New York: Free Press.

———. 1996. "The Restructuring of American Religion: Further Evidence." *Sociological Inquiry* 66: 303–329.

Yancey, Philip. 1997. *Disappointment with God: Three Questions No One Asks Aloud.* Grand Rapids, MI: Zondervan.

———. 2000. *Reaching for the Invisible God: What Can We Expect to Find?* Grand Rapids, MI: Zondervan.

———. 2002. *Where Is God When It Hurts? A Comforting Healing Guide for Dealing with Hard Times.* Grand Rapids, MI: Zondervan.

———. 2005. *Finding God in Unexpected Places.* New York: Doubleday Religion.

Young, Matt, and Taner Edis. 2006. *Why Intelligent Design Fails: A Scientific Critique of New Creationism.* New Brunswick, NJ: Rutgers University Press.

Youtz, Herbert A. 1907. "Three Conceptions of God." *American Journal of Theology* 11: 428–453.

Zald, M. N. 1982. "Theological Crucibles: Social Movements in and of Religion." *Review of Religious Research* 23: 317–336.

Zelan, Joseph. 1968. "Religious Apostasy, Higher Education, and Occupational Choice." *Sociology of Education* 41(4): 370–379.

Zeleny, Jeff, and Michael Luo. 2008. "Obama Seeks Bigger Role for Religious Groups." July 2. *New York Times*. (http://www.nytimes.com/2008/07/02/us/politics/02obama.html?_r=1&ref=politics).

INDEX

Page numbers in bold indicate figures or tables.